The Good Americans

THE LOYALISTS IN THE AMERICAN REVOLUTION

The Good Americans

THE LOYALISTS IN THE AMERICAN REVOLUTION

by *Wallace Brown*

WILLIAM MORROW AND COMPANY, INC.

NEW YORK : 1969

Second Printing, October 1973

Published simultaneously in Canada by George J. McLeod Limited, Toronto.

Printed and bound in the United States of America by The Cornwall Press, Inc., Cornwall, N.Y.

Library of Congress Catalog Card Number 69-11500

For Carl Bridenbaugh

"I never had an idea of subduing the Americans; I meant to assist the good Americans subdue the bad."

—*General James Robertson*

Contents

Contents

Preface

❧ "... moderation is a crime in time of civil confusions."

Samuel Curwen, London, April 29, 1780

The American Revolution is important for innumerable reasons, not least the splitting of the British Empire. Had Britain and America remained united, even as loosely as Britain and Canada, world history during the last two centuries would have been much altered, possibly improved. Perhaps the greatest significance of the Revolution was the precedent it set. There had been other colonial uprisings, other popular revolutions, other denials of royal authority, other republics, but few of them were successful, and not one both combined these elements, and also was accepted and justified, even hailed, by much of the world. The great French Revolution was merely a later, more violent repeat performance, and in the years since the Declaration of Independence revolutionaries from Grattan to Gandhi, from Marx to Nkrumah, from Papineau to Ben Bella have been following the steps of the men of '76. But Yankee Doodle was not the only one "born on the Fourth of July." Hindsight and success have lent the stamp of respectable inevitability to the Revolutionaries, but there was a middle way between dependence and independence, the way of the American Loyalists. It is the story of these losers that this book seeks to tell.

A note on terms. Frequent mention in the text is made of "the claims commissioners" and "claimants." This refers to the British commission set up to hear the claims for compensation from Loyalists, that is, claimants, who had lost property and office by the Revolution. The surviving records of the commission are a prime source of information about the Loyalists, especially the rank and file.

Quotations from manuscripts are given verbatim, with the normal exceptions of expansion of abbreviations and ampersands, and the lower-casing of some capital letters. I have not used *sic* because its constant repetition would be tedious. Unusual spelling should normally be taken as evidence of eighteenth-century vagaries and not hasty proofreading.

I thank the Royal Society, Burlington House, London, for permission to quote from a letter in the Blagden Collection. The Society retains the copyright and all rights to this letter. Quotations from Crown-copyright records in the Public Record Office appear by permission of the Controller of Her Majesty's Stationery Office.

I have been so bold as to write this book entirely on my own. No part of it has benefitted from the criticism of colleagues and friends. Hence when I make the customary claim to sole responsibility for all errors of fact and interpretation, I really mean it. However, a few special notes of thanks are due. My prime debt is to the scholars whose work I have utilized so freely. Details may be found in my footnotes. A Canada Council Grant-in-Aid in 1964, although primarily used for a previous book, did help with the research on this one. The following rendered aid, directly or indirectly: Dr.

Frederick G. Banting, Dr. Charles Best, Charlotte Brown,
Dr. Morgan Cutts, and James Landis. Finally, this book is
directly the result of the long, friendly encouragement of
Frances Phillips.

W.B.

CHAPTER I

"The Minds and Hearts of the People"

◆§ "I told him [Sir Guy Carleton] the Colonies like a Boy his Cloaths had outgrown their first Government."

Chief Justice William Smith, June 29, 1786.[1]

In 1774, the imperial quarrel between the American colonies and Britain was deepening ominously. The patriotic, or, if you will, rebellious, citizens of Plymouth, Massachusetts, assembled with a carriage and twenty yoke of oxen in an attempt to raise the legendary Plymouth Rock from its bed and take it to the village green as the base for a "Liberty Pole." While the great stone was being lifted by means of several large screws, suddenly, without noise or warning, it split asunder, and the bottom piece dropped back onto the ground. The citizens were stunned by this setback to their efforts, and also, perhaps, by the unexpected swiftness of the event, which they interpreted as an omen foreshadowing their eventual separation from the home country. However, they proceeded as planned with the upper piece of stone, which was not to be rejoined to the lower until 1880. But the British Empire was permanently split.[2]

The true symbolism of the rock's separation should be seen not so much in the independence of America proclaimed two years later as in the internal division of Americans into Whigs and Loyalists that even in 1774 was splintering society and was soon to make the American Revolution in reality the first American Civil War. In fact it was more of a civil war than the better-known conflict of 1861-1865, which Southerners accurately call "The War between the States," involving as it did two distinct geographical areas. Loyalists and Whigs were concentrated individually in some places, but both were common everywhere, and many families were split over the Revolution. As a contemporary put it: "Nabour was against Nabour, Father against the Son and the Son against the Father, and he that would not thrust his one blaid through his brothers heart was cald an Infimous fillon." [3] Uncounted thousands of Americans robbed, persecuted, tortured, killed each other, and by the time the flames began to dim, about one hundred thousand Loyalists had become permanent exiles.

Before we can understand how this situation came about, it is necessary to take a brief look at the progress of the American colonies up to the eve of the Revolution.[4]

The American Revolution was the coming of age, expressed through necessary violence, of a colonial dependency, or, strictly speaking, of thirteen dependencies—a process that has only since become a commonplace. The Revolution has a complex history, but essentially a nation, rather to the surprise of most of its citizens, both the leaders and the led, had matured. As the radical Thomas Paine put it: "To know whether it be the interest of this continent to be independent, we need only ask this easy simple question: Is it the interest of a man to be a boy all his life?" [5]

British attempts to deny American maturity, whatever the particular failings of time and place, were doomed. British military success in the years following 1776 could only have been temporary, because the real solution of the American problem—dominion status—lay with future generations of politicians, who were influenced but hardly transformed by the result of the American Revolution. For example, after 1783 the British increased rather than relaxed their grip on Canada, and it was not until 1839, following two rebellions, one French, one English, that Lord Durham produced his famous Report recommending Canadian self-government; and even then he ran ahead of most British opinion.

The American Revolution, furthermore, was assured in the sense that a settled and powerful society, which not only occupied the over-1500-mile littoral from Maine to Florida and generally extended inland to the Allegheny Mountains 300 miles distant, but also was poised ready to sweep into the great Mississippi Valley beyond, could not remain in permanent subordination to a mother country separated by a lengthy, often stormy, Atlantic crossing.

A glance at selected aspects of America on the eve of the Revolution will demonstrate the rather advanced stage colonial society had reached.

If the combined colonies were much larger than the home country and geographically immensely more diverse, the population was much smaller: 2,500,000 (of whom 2,100,000 were white), compared with nearly 8,000,000 in England and Wales. But proportionately this is rather more than the population of Canada today compared with that of the United Kingdom, and in any terms two and a half million (the present population of New Zealand) is a substantial body of people. In 1775 the French Canadians numbered less than 100,000.

More important than the size of the colonial population was its amazingly rapid growth (it doubled every twenty-five years), which Benjamin Franklin described as early as 1751 in his pioneering Malthusian pamphlet *Concerning the In-*

crease of Mankind. This increase, only marginally the result
of immigration, signified a buoyant, thriving people, and
already men of vision on both sides of the Atlantic, such as
Franklin and Pitt, foresaw the need for an unlimited empire
on the North American continent.

In addition to scores of towns and villages, the colonies had
produced five major cities: Boston, Newport, New York,
Philadelphia, and Charleston. The largest, Philadelphia, with
a population of forty thousand, was probably bigger than
any other city in the British Empire except London. Not
only were the five leading cities sizable, they were old and
established. In 1775 New York was 150 years old; Boston,
145; Newport, 136; Charleston and Philadelphia, over 100.[6]
At the same time the Tidewater society of Virginia was about
170 years old and many farming and fishing villages in New
England dated back almost as far. The New World was not
nearly as new at the time of the Revolution as is sometimes
imagined. And it gives one further pause to recall that the
history before 1776 of the area that became the United States
is practically as long as the history since.

Colonial America, of course, had its crude frontier, but in
the longer-settled places a great deal of progress had been
made. Carl Bridenbaugh concludes that the colonial cities
"did more than match the provincial cities of Europe"[7] and
adduces striking achievements in fire fighting, provisions for
water supplies, street paving and lighting, and smallpox inoc-
ulation. Architectural distinction was evident in such
structures as Faneuil Hall and the Statehouse in Boston, the
Statehouse in Philadelphia, or the various beautiful buildings in Newport designed by Peter Harrison, the immigrant
Yorkshire architect. The smaller towns also had considerable
beauty, Salem, Massachusetts, being an outstanding example
in the North and Williamsburg, Virginia, in the South.
Throughout America a number of semiamateur, now half-

forgotten, joiner-architects had successfully adapted English models to a new environment.[8]

Moreover, an attractive civilized society was found beyond the colonial towns and cities. New England had produced a unique society of farmers, fishermen, and merchants living in simple, charming, often classically beautiful, villages centered on the green and the meetinghouse; in parts of the South, particularly Tidewater, Virginia and around Charleston, South Carolina, an aristocratic, mainly planter society could at its best boast the elegant estates of Washington's Mount Vernon or the Byrd family's Westover.

Nine tenths of the population lived in the countryside, where the availability of cheap land plus the generally favorable climate and soil created a prosperous, independent farming community. There was no real equivalent to the peasant class of Europe; starvation was almost unknown; and such home industries as spinning, weaving, and the making of home and farm implements kept the subsistence farmers, who were the majority, fairly self-sufficient. Out of such an environment in Pennsylvania German immigrants produced two masterpieces, the so-called Kentucky rifle and the Conestoga wagon (which became the covered wagon), twin tools in the conquest of the West.

Agriculture alone may make a country happy, but it rarely makes it rich. For this, trade and manufacture are necessary, and the colonies had both. Britain supplied many of the manufactured goods, but there were several important colonial industries, pre-eminently shipbuilding (a magnificent tradition in sailing ships maintained from the building of the first colonial ship in Massachusetts in 1631 until the present day), plus the production of naval stores (all along the coast, but especially in the middle colonies and New England), iron mining and smelting (widespread but centered in Pennsylvania), the distilling of West Indian molasses into

New England rum, and water-powered flour milling (particularly in New York, Pennsylvania, and Maryland). To these can be added many smaller local crafts (though very scarce in the South) such as printing, tanning, weaving, metalworking, glass-, brick-, shoe-, clock-, and potash-making, and the production of furniture and other household items.[9] The general extent of colonial progress is suggested by the facts that in 1776 one third of the British carrying trade was in colonial-made ships, and more pig iron—one seventh of the world's supply—was produced in America than in Great Britain; in silverware (for example, Paul Revere's in Boston) and cabinets (for example, Benjamin Randolph's in Philadelphia) the colonies could match Europe.

As for colonial trade, New England's exports included whale products, fish, barrel staves, and rum; the middle colonies, often called the bread colonies, had livestock, potash and surplus crops; the South, relying on slavery, produced the great staples: tobacco in Maryland, Virginia, and North Carolina, and rice and indigo in South Carolina and Georgia. The whole frontier back country was the home of the fur-bearing creatures whose pelts underlay a major international market.

Colonial trade and manufacturing were governed by various English laws embodying a policy usually dubbed the "Old Colonial System." It sought to implement a theory later designated as mercantilism, whereby the colonies were to be a source of raw materials and a market for the manufactures of the home country, which monopolized the colonial trade.

The Old Colonial System created certain problems in the colonies, including an adverse balance of trade, a shortage of specie, chronic indebtedness, and a certain restriction (more imagined than real) on enterprise, but on the whole it worked well. First, to a degree it fitted the requirements. America was what is now called an "underdeveloped country." Hence its natural role was primarily as an exporter of raw materials and an importer of manufactured goods. British goods, being the best and cheapest in the world at that time, would have been desired, Navigation Acts or not. Second, the colonists had the benefits of trade with the whole British Empire; hence the profitable traffic in supplies and slaves with the West Indies, and also the use of such skilled British middlemen as the tobacco dealers, and the benefit of coastal trading such as the food supplies sent by the middle to the Southern colonies. Third, the system was not completely doctrinaire. Thus New England fishermen were permitted to engage in the very profitable export of fish directly to Catholic southern Europe. Finally, where the law was particularly burdensome, it was either not enforced or evaded. The Molasses Act of 1733, which aimed at preventing the import of molasses from the non-English West Indies, was a dead letter, as were the Hat Act of 1732, which banned the export and limited the production of hats,[10] and the Iron Act of 1750, which sought to limit certain iron manufacturing. New England merchants genially smuggled molasses, New York and Rhode Island hatters happily made hats, and Pennsylvania ironmasters cheerfully manufactured iron goods.

The Old Colonial System created a quite spectacular prosperity in colonial America in the eighteenth century and was rarely complained of. The crisis came with the new British legislation and enforcement after 1763, when a constant colonial refrain was praise of the period before that date and a wish to return to it.

Most important is the fact that concomitant with the growth of colonial trade and industry was the rise of a rich class of planters, farmers, merchants, and manufacturers, an incipient aristocracy (in places even established) that, allied with the professionals—lawyers, doctors, clergy—and often with the various royal officials sent out from England, provided, in all areas, social and political leadership, often of a remarkable degree of sophistication and valor.

The cultural achievements of the colonies, though largely offshoots of European and more definitely British developments and generally no rival to those of the advanced Western nations, were creditable and augured well.

Colonial science had made a good start in the seventeenth century, especially in New England, where Puritan learning led to a possibly fatal embrace between Calvinism and science. John Winthrop, Jr., became the first American member of the Royal Society of London, founded in 1660. Early in the eighteenth century no less a one than Cotton Mather often contributed—mainly mathematical pieces—to the Society's *Transactions*. Elsewhere, in 1718, John Bartram established a botanical garden in Philadelphia; between 1739 and 1743 John Clayton brought out his *Flora Virginica,* which gained him a European reputation; and in 1755 Dr. John Mitchell published what became the standard map of America, and was, in fact, used for determining the boundary settlements in the 1783 peace treaty.

By the time of the Revolution the colonies possessed in Benjamin Franklin, through his work on electricity, a physicist of world stature; in David Rittenhouse (the inventor of a famous orrery) and Harvard's John Winthrop IV, leading astronomers; in William Bartram (son of John), whose American bird list drew praise from Linnaeus, an able biologist; in Cadwallader Colden and Benjamin Rush, outstanding physicians.[11]

Increase Mather had founded the short-lived Boston Philosophical Society in 1683, but real American success came in Philadelphia in 1768 when the combination of the Philosophical Society and the American Society created the American Philosophical Society, which gained European standing in 1771 with the first volume of its *Transactions,* containing an account of the American part in observing the rare transit of the planet Venus in 1769.

But perhaps America was already demonstrating a practical rather than theoretical ability, a Yankee ingenuity over pure science, the likelihood of producing a Ford rather than an Einstein. Perhaps Franklin's lightning rod was more typical than his electrical theory; perhaps David Bushnell's pioneer submarine of 1776 (actually used in the war), Oliver Evans' card-making machine of 1777, John Fitch's steamboat launched in 1787, or Eli Whitney's cotton gin of 1793 were most representative of the time and place.

Although the arrival in Newport in 1729 of the great English idealist philosopher Berkeley and the Scottish painter John Smibert had inaugurated an intellectual flowering in the pioneer seaside resort, and though Boston and New York had achieved much, the Revolutionary period was the golden age of Philadelphia, the focal point of the Enlightenment in America. The superb Franklin was in excellent company, which included David James Dove, the schoolteacher; William Smith, the provost of the Academy of Philadelphia; William Bartram, the colonial Audubon; Dr. Benjamin Rush, David Rittenhouse, Thomas Gilpin, scientist, inventor, and canal designer, respectively; and Charles Willson Peale, the artist. And this was merely the pinnacle of the first example in the Western world of a broadly based culture; the city's educational institutions and charitable foundations were perhaps a model for the age.[12]

If not creatively in the van of the European eighteenth-century cultural development loosely known as the Enlightenment, America was probably the country that embraced it most wholeheartedly, at least in practice; to many Americans and foreigners alike America seemed to offer proof of many dogmas of the *philosophes,* such as the ability of the human race to achieve, through reason, unlimited economic and spiritual progress, the efficacy of religious toleration, the existence of the "noble savage." It is rather symbolic that in Benjamin Franklin, the bourgeois Leonardo—scientist, inventor, oceanographer, statesman, and diplomat—many saw the epitome of the progress of the eighteenth century.

At a time when England had only two universities, Oxford and Cambridge, the latter of which was then sunk in desuetude, nine had been founded in America: Harvard and the College of William and Mary in the seventeenth century, Dartmouth, Brown, Yale, Columbia, Princeton, Rutgers, and the University of Pennsylvania in the eighteenth. The faculties of these colleges included some outstanding men; for example: Harvard boasted John Winthrop IV; Yale, President Ezra Stiles, a leading Newtonian, and President Thomas Clap, of varied scientific talents; Columbia (then called King's College), President Samuel Johnson, a follower of Bishop Berkeley; the Academy and College of Philadelphia (which became the University of Pennsylvania), Provost William Smith, editor of America's first magazine; Princeton, Jonathan Edwards, briefly president and the most important colonial theologian and philosopher, and John Witherspoon, president for a longer span and an advocate of the "common sense" philosophy; William and Mary, George Wythe, outstanding professor of law.

Schooling for children in the colonies was of a comparatively high level, especially in New England. The conclusion is that education at all levels was good and rather more widespread and democratic than in England. The result was a higher literacy rate.

The first printing press in America was built at Cambridge in 1639. The volume of books and pamphlets grew steadily, as did the audience for them. By 1765 a large reading public was served by twenty-five newspapers, a proportion of newspapers to population even greater than Great Britain's. Circulation of papers and other items was expedited by the colonial post office, which improved in 1753 when Franklin was made second-in-command, and by the construction of tolerable roads—by 1770 post riders could go from Portsmouth, New Hampshire, all the way to Savannah, Georgia. The first colonial magazine, the *American Magazine*, was founded in 1741. Almanacs, like *Poor Richard's*, were extremely popular. Libraries and booksellers were widespread throughout the colonies. In the early eighteenth century both Cotton Mather and William Byrd possessed private libraries of over forty thousand volumes, and the first public library was founded (by Franklin, naturally) in 1731 in Philadelphia.

America produced no Fielding or Richardson, in fact no novel at all until 1789, but the Revolutionary period was adorned by such poets as Joseph Stansbury, Jonathan Odell, Francis Hopkinson, Philip Freneau; such historical writers as Thomas Hutchinson, William Smith, and Cadwallader Colden; such a diarist as the New Jersey Quaker and humanitarian John Woolman; and more importantly by a wealth of political pamphleteers of astonishing range and ability, including John Dickinson, James Otis, Samuel Seabury, Richard Bland, and Daniel Leonard. The prose of Benjamin Franklin and Thomas Jefferson was worthy of comparison with the best in world literature.

Colonial painters were not of the first rank, but three native Americans achieved international success: John Singleton Copley, Benjamin West, and Charles Willson Peale, although it must be noted that Copley and West pursued their careers primarily in London. The only first-rate American fine art, now at last gaining proper recognition, is the forceful, primitive, melancholy art of the New England gravestones, which still arrest the discerning cemetery visitor, monuments to their anonymous colonial carvers.[13]

In short, it is not too much to say that, like Scotland, but with less spectacular results on the highest levels, colonial America enjoyed a cultural flowering in the eighteenth century; contemporaries compared Boston to Edinburgh, and it is clear that both Scotland and America had many similarities—social mobility, an active middle class, a sense of provincialism and even envy, and hence aggression, toward London.[14]

The future Loyalists had, of course, shared and sometimes played a leading part in all this economic and cultural progress, and some of the men mentioned in the foregoing paragraphs, for example, Copley, Colden, Smith, Stansbury, Odell, Seabury, and Leonard, were to remain loyal when the Revolution came. The Loyalists shared in the general maturation of America; they did not share in the desire for full independence.

Perhaps the acid test for any country is the quality of the leaders it can produce in an emergency, and the acid test for an aspiring colonial area its capacity for self-government. America easily, almost nonchalantly, passed both tests. Virginia could point to the ineffable Washington, a Revolutionary leader of genius, and to Thomas Jefferson and James Madison; New England, to John Adams and Samuel Adams, great statesman and great agitator, respectively; Pennsylvania, to Franklin, about whom nothing need be added. And these were not isolated figures. Behind them stood such able generals as Nathanael Greene, second only to Washington, Horatio Gates, George Rogers Clark, conqueror of the Illinois country, Ethan Allen, the great Deist, and even, for a time, Benedict Arnold; such state politicians as Stephen Hopkins in Rhode Island, William Livingston and John Jay in New York, Joseph Galloway, a Loyalist, and Robert Morris in Pennsylvania, Patrick Henry in Virginia, Christopher Gadsden in South Carolina; such rabble-rousers as William

Molineaux in Boston, Alexander McDougal in New York, and Charles Thompson in Philadelphia. Also active in the Revolution, but with reputations to be made in the future, were Alexander Hamilton, future Chief Justice John Marshall, and even the youthful Andrew Jackson.

So much for leaders. As for self-government, the colonial legislatures converted themselves to state governments with startling ease. Massachusetts, with its popularly elected constitutional convention writing a constitution then to be voted on by the people, set a precedent for the future democratic development of the Union. By 1780 all the former colonies had produced constitutions except Rhode Island and Connecticut, which found their colonial charters, minus the British connection, satisfactory, a fact that in itself is a noteworthy comment on the British colonial system. Together with the central government created by the Articles of Confederation the state legislatures maintained relatively free self-government and contrived to defeat in war the rest of the British Empire, at that time the strongest power on earth. Then, when the Articles of Confederation, in spite of great successes, notably the Land Ordinance of 1785 and the Northwest Ordinance of 1787, which together solved the key imperial problems of land distribution and rapid self-government, proved unsatisfactory, the representatives of the thirteen states produced in 1789 a written constitution remarkable for its longevity (apart from an aberration called the Civil War) and a uniquely successful implementation of federalism. An equal feat, despite the understandable persecution of the Loyalists during and after the war, was the comprehension of the idea and even the need for a loyal opposition, signified by the change of government in 1800, when the Adams Federalists were replaced by the Jeffersonian Republicans without bloodshed, arrests, or disgrace. The

American rebels had proved a fitness for independence un-
equaled in the history of colonialism.

The reason for this remarkable political success, it is fair
to add, is to be found in the colonial experience. Some form
of self-government dated from the election of an assembly in
Virginia in 1619, and at the local level the aristocratic Virginia parish system and the more democratic, more vivacious
New England town meeting began about the same time. By
1775 all areas save parts of the frontier had an effective local
government. All the colonies had in miniature a king, House
of Lords, and House of Commons in the generally royally
appointed governor and council and the popularly elected
lower house. Like literacy, the franchise was much more
widely spread than in Britain. The significance of this
colonial government is twofold. First, the colonists learned
the art of politics and government—forming parties, fighting
elections, passing laws, quarreling with the governor, or the
home country, or each other. Second, in practice each colony
became to a degree an independent country; in Tocqueville's
words, "the republic was already established in every town-
ship." [15] The lower houses consciously emulated the British
House of Commons, which they regarded as simply a coequal
institution, and amassed powers (particularly control of finance) and privileges. Distance and the tradition of going
their own way put the colonists in no particular awe of king
or parliament.[16]

The king, acting in his Privy Council, could veto the legislation of the colonial assemblies, but only 5½ per cent of all
eighteenth-century colonial acts were vetoed, and many of
those deserved it. The power and the privileges of the
colonial governments were never formally recognized by the
British Government, but prior at least to 1763 imperial
power was little exercised except in war and diplomacy.

Thus the future Whig firebrand, James Otis, was able to maintain that

> ... no constitution of civil government has yet appeared in the world so admirably adapted to the preservation of the great purpose of liberty and knowledge as that of Great Britain. Every person in America is of common right by Act of Parliament and the Laws of God entitled to all essential privileges of Britons, the true interests of Great Britain and her colonies are mutual, and what God in His Providence has united let no man dare attempt to pull asunder! [17]

Letting the colonies go their own way internally is often called "salutary neglect," the colonial manifestation of Sir Robert Walpole's maxim, "Let sleeping dogs lie." In effect salutary neglect, with some exceptions (notably the Stuart attempt between 1684 and 1689 to effect despotic rule through the institution of the Dominion of New England), had been the norm since the foundation of the colonies. England was distracted first by the quarrel and civil war between Parliament and the Stuarts, which racked English history from 1603 to 1689; then by the struggle, sometimes called the second Hundred Years' War, with France, as much European as colonial, which occupied a good deal of the period from 1689 to 1763, and, of course, continued until 1814 and the defeat of Napoleon. Finally the first two Georges took no initiative toward the colonies, which were, after all, mainly royal, existing by royal charters, while a Whiggish respect for contracts helped disincline Parliament from interference with those charters.

Nevertheless, since the Revolution of 1689 a fundamental imbalance had existed. Essentially the English Parliament was now sovereign, or well placed to become so, and the Revolutionary settlement legalized the fact. In America the colonial legislatures were in practice largely autonomous in internal matters, but they remained legally subordinate to the Crown, and to Parliament, insofar as Parliament really was sovereign. Thus the American Revolution was simply a confirmation of the 1689 situation in the face of an encroaching British Parliament.

Mellen Chamberlain, a perspicacious nineteenth-century historian, has left the best illustration of what he called "the ultimate philosophy of the American Revolution." In about 1842 he interviewed a ninety-one-year-old veteran of Lexington, Captain Levi Preston. The aged soldier said he had never felt any oppression, had never seen a stamp, never drunk any tea, never heard of Harrington, Sidney, or Locke. Why had Preston fought? "Young man, what we meant in going for those red-coats was this: we always had governed ourselves, and we always meant to. They didn't mean we should!" [18]

So far I have been stressing the positive side of early American history in support of an argument, to make a case. The colonies, of course, were not heaven on earth. They had problems, especially on the frontier, where genocide had long been practiced against the Indians, and there was the blot of slavery. Life as it was then for a majority of Americans would be considered intolerably hard by their descendants today, but then as now the average American was physically far better off than most of his fellow men elsewhere in the world.

The colonies had a remarkably advanced and mature civilization, but, it is fair to add, many things revealed them to be anything but united. There were serious sectional quarrels and even fighting sometimes, not just between large geographic sections such as New England and the middle colonies, or between the seaboard and the interior, but also between particular colonies, such as the bitter struggle in the 1770's between New York and New Hampshire over Vermont, and within a colony, such as the civil war known as the "Regulator Movement" in the 1760's in North Carolina. During the French and Indian War (1754-1763), which was the American phase of the Seven Years' War (1756-1763), the British had rejoiced, "Our bells are worn threadbare with ringing for victories . . . ," [19] while despairing of the unpatriotic behavior of colonial troops and legislatures, particularly their frequent disinclination to fight or pursue the war beyond their own immediate boundaries. An attempt at colonial union at Albany in 1754 had been a fiasco.[20]

A distinguished American historian once claimed that civil war was more likely in 1763 than rebellion against England, and a mere three generations after the end of the War for Independence, civil war did in fact come (not to forget that the Revolutionary war was also a civil war). It was the British Government's peculiar triumph that it succeeded in uniting to a very unexpected degree the disparate elements of the thirteen colonies in opposition to British policy.

Admittedly unity was not entirely a British achievement. Less noticed perhaps, but potent, were many other factors. These included intercolonial trade and business, marriage, migration, communications and the post office, religious affiliations (for example, the famed revival, the Great Awakening, which swept the whole country in the 1730's and 1740's), education, and cultural phenomena such as newspapers and books.

The squabbles of the colonists were more a sign of youthful exuberance than real weakness, and a common sharing of the American experience and traditions of self-government had produced a recognizable American character common to all colonies, what Crèvecoeur called the "new man."

It is easy to show that American life was nine parts English —English goods, language, institutions, books, thoughts, ideas, prejudices—but a tenth part was American, and just as a dash of blue paint to yellow gives green, so the colonial environment had produced Britons of a different hue, to whom the appellation "American" was already commonly applied, and with meaning.

The process of "Americanization" was termed by a great historian, Charles M. Andrews, the "silent revolution." [21] Early seventeenth-century American settlers found a medicinal herb that resembled, but was in fact different from, the dittany they knew at home. They called the new plant dittany and used it for medicine.[22] A lack of cardboard made the barrel the universal American container. Eighteenth-century builders copied Georgian houses but used native wood instead of English stone or brick, and a general labor shortage kept most colonial structures simple. In short, the American environment worked an inexorable, often subtle, change on colonial life, a change intensified by the long duration of the settlement.

America developed an embryo federalism, dictated by the size of the country, and lacked many of the institutions that set the tone in England. There was no single dominant capital city like London, no "Establishment" in the English sense—such things as the royal court, a national parliament and political factions, the officer corps, exclusive Oxford and Cambridge, the power of the established Church of England. In the colonies there were at least thirteen different political complexes, numerous colleges, and a wealth of religious sects locally controlled and rarely fully "established." Feudalism, or even a native hereditary aristocracy, with a few exceptions, had barely ever existed. Land, normally held in fee simple, was quite freely available, especially on the frontier. Religious toleration, the franchise, the middle class, a high standard of living, social mobility—all embraced or were available to a greater segment of the population than in the home country. The military was comparatively egalitarian. By Fidel Castro's definition of democracy as the people armed, colonial America, with its militia and minutemen, was democratic.

While Locke's theories had dimmed somewhat in English Whig orthodoxy since 1689, Americans embraced with a vengeance such doctrines as "natural" rights, government under law, delegation, contract, even the possibility, certainly the *right*, of revolution. Americans also kept alive the radical English dissenting tradition of such writers as Trenchard, Gordon, and the anonymous "Cato." [23] These views were disseminated throughout the colonies in the eighteenth century: in New England by the Congregational clergy and in Virginia and North Carolina by New Light Presbyterian clergy, who had made commonplace, decades before 1776, the rights asserted in the Declaration of Independence.[24]

Finally, a comment on the population. Many colonists were native-born, the products of several generations, and thus felt American rather than British, especially if they sprang from non-British stock. Of the immigrants many, especially the Scotch-Irish from northern Ireland, had left the British Isles, with no great love of the homeland, attempting to escape unfavorable conditions, and, of course, non-British immigrants, who were mainly Germans, were unlikely to feel close attachment to a foreign country. Eighteen of the signers of the Declaration of Independence were of non-English blood.

Thus in the sense that the American Revolution was simply a stage in the maturing of American society, it really began, as President John Adams put it, in 1620, having been "in the minds and hearts of the people from the beginning." (If Adams had not been a New Englander, he might more accurately have said 1607—the date of the first permanent settlement of Virginia.) But why the Revolution came when it did and the way it did must be explained by looking at the developments during the two decades preceding the outbreak of war in 1775. These events will be mentioned in the next chapter. Here it is only necessary to stress some important points.

Before 1763 what British control over the colonies there was had been either evaded or recognized as necessary and just, or if disputed had created only minor quarrels and resentment. With each advancing year of colonial growth, the time for any extension of British power became less and less propitious, and the years after 1763 were particularly unsuited to any attempts at increased control because the defeat of the French brought an air of intoxicating security to the colonies that dispelled feelings of reliance on British military forces. It is difficult to exaggerate the importance of the end of the endemic French threat, a danger that dated from the early 1630's when Massachusetts had been involved in the dispute over Acadia between two French rivals, de la Tour and d'Aulnay. The defeat of the French fulfilled the dreams of American imperialists and speculators, but the scramble for Western land (the chief area of endeavor, outside of trade, for ambitious colonists) rapidly led to collision with the British Government, which had wider considerations, such as the welfare of the French *habitants* and relations with the Indians. Thus British Western policy from the institution of the Proclamation Line of 1763 to the Quebec Act of 1774 was very unpopular.

Further, certain delusions of military grandeur had developed, stimulated by various American exploits. During King George's War of 1744-1748, following an English attempt on Cartagena that had failed, the Maine hero, Sir William Pepperrell, led a successful New England expedition against Louisbourg, the strong French fortress on Cape Breton Island. There was great dismay when Louisbourg was returned by the Treaty of Aix-la-Chapelle. A further lesson was drawn from General Edward Braddock's disaster near Fort Duquesne at the beginning of the French and Indian War in 1755, seemingly because of failure to take colonial advice, particularly that of young George Washington.

In 1763 anyone advocating American independence would have been dubbed an extreme eccentric. Yet a mere thirteen years later independence was declared. The reason was that for the British Government nothing failed so completely as success. And success went to the colonists' heads. The great victories of the French and Indian War gave rise on the part of the British to dissatisfaction with the colonists' behavior, the desire to make them pay a fairer share of the costs of imperial defense, and new problems concerning Canada and the West, leading to British attempts at reorganization, which resulted in chronic American opposition, an opposition aggravated by a postwar depression and stimulated by the new-found feeling of military independence.

Even if the new British policy had been implemented with exceptional skill, it would have been facing great odds. As it was, the early years of the reign of the far from brilliant George III were, for various rather complicated reasons, marked by an unusual instability and ministries headed by mediocrities, usually ill-informed mediocrities, whose policies managed to arouse some Americans (though certainly not always to action or even to the point of taking sides outright) in almost every quarter, of almost every degree of interest, and make them believe they were facing a religious, political, and military despotism such as Charles I had attempted to impose on Britain in the 1630's and 1640's (a parallel consciously drawn).[25] When eighteenth-century England required the very best leadership it could produce, it got some of the very worst.

The colonists had not been given to defining their position in the British Empire, but when the new British policy forced them to, they naturally demanded recognition of what they had already enjoyed—*de facto* self-government. When the British not only failed to do this but attempted to increase imperial control, a segment of the colonists were finally driven to declare complete independence, a free and equal status, for which the maturity and traditions of their society proved them ripe.

CHAPTER II

The Emergence of the Loyalists

ᭇ᷈ "Governments, like clocks, go from the motion men give them; and governments are made and moved by men, so by them they are ruined too."

William Penn [1]

Following the Peace of Paris of 1763 the British Government embarked on a policy of imperial reorganization that culminated in the outbreak of fighting at Lexington, April 19, 1775, and the Declaration of Independence, July 4, 1776. Here, briefly, are some of the most important British actions and colonial reactions.

It was Britain's need of cash rather than any deep-laid plot that provoked the American Revolution. George Grenville's ministry, rightly impressed not only with the cost of the late war, which had left great debts, but also with the continued expense of defending and administering an enlarged empire and the unfairly small proportion paid by the American colonies, set about reforming fiscal policies with the object of raising more revenue. Grenville was alarmed to find that the salaries of American customs officials were four times greater than the revenue the service brought in!

The Revenue or Sugar Act of 1764 lowered the duty on

imported non-British molasses from sixpence to threepence a gallon. This was not the popular measure one might expect because the new duty, unlike the old, was actually to be enforced, and to this end Grenville, in a general tightening-up policy, ordered absentee customs men to their posts, instructed the navy to be vigilant against smugglers, and widened the jurisdiction of the official, juryless vice-admiralty courts to try offenders. The new molasses tax threatened the New England rum industry and was made even more unpopular by another act of 1764 that forbade the colonies to make their widely used paper money legal tender. This was also regarded as an economic threat and reduced the money supply at the very time when the new tax increased the demand.

The problem of colonial defense was tackled by the ministry and inevitably became bound up with finance. A proclamation of 1763, as part of an imperial plan to control relations with the Indians, had already attempted to halt Western migration at the crest of the Alleghenies, and at the same time ten thousand soldiers were to be stationed in America, at considerable cost, to give security against both the Indians and any possible attempted French reconquest. These measures were immediately resented by such groups as Western frontiersmen and land speculators, and a Quartering Act that required the colonists to provide quarters and supplies for the English troops deepened a general suspicion. But it was the attempt to raise one third of the cost of this defense by a tax measure that brought some colonists to the brink of revolution.

The tax was imposed by the notorious Stamp Act of 1765, which required that stamps, bought from the government, be affixed to newspapers, playing cards, liquor licenses, and certain legal and other documents. The Stamp Act was one of the most inexpedient acts of Parliament in all history. It struck directly at a very influential segment of the population: lawyers, printers, tavernkeepers, and merchants; offenders were to be tried in vice-admiralty courts; and the act, like no previous piece of British legislation, was avowedly to raise a revenue. Thus the basic issue of the American Revolution, and the basic issue of political science—sovereignty— was involved. It was one thing for the British Government to exercise a general, somewhat vague, jurisdiction over the colonies, but if it could tax them at will, self-government was a mockery.

The result of the act was widespread riots, pamphleteering, and an almost unanimous defiance culminating in the Stamp Act Congress of October, 1765, in New York, where the representatives of nine colonies denied Parliament's right to tax them. Most effective of all, the colonists mistakenly believed, were the nonimportation agreements of colonial merchants, who would import no English goods until the act was repealed. This was done in March, 1766, by a new ministry under the Marquis of Rockingham. The old government had stepped down, but the previous three years had made the colonists ponder such things as the stationing of troops, evocative of the Petition of Right of 1628, Oliver Cromwell, and the Stuart dynasty of inglorious memory; the right of trial by jury, with memories too of the ill-fated Stuarts and even the Magna Carta; and most important, the whole problem of empire and sovereignty, focusing on the key question of the right of taxation, which in a way had been at the heart of the English civil war and the Glorious Revolution of 1688-1689.

In the colonial rejoicing over the repeal of the Stamp Act and the apparent triumph of the colonial argument that Parliament could not tax the colonies, the English Declaratory Act, which took a directly opposite position and maintained that Parliament could legislate "in all cases whatsoever," was rather lost sight of. The British Government had tacked, not changed course. But it was not long before a new ministry, headed by Pitt and Grafton, took up the old—and fatal—tack once again.

Charles Townshend, the chancellor of the exchequer, seeking further revenue from the colonies, introduced the Townshend Acts of June, 1767, which placed duties, designated for revenue, on several previously untaxed articles such as glass, paper, paint, and tea. Townshend's idea was to bypass colonial opposition to direct taxes, such as those embodied in the Stamp Act, by levying customs duties, which had long been collected (but not directly for revenue). That is, he planned what was then called an "external" tax instead of an "internal" tax.

Townshend also further tightened up imperial administration. He announced that the new revenues would be used to pay the salaries of colonial governors—a threat to the power of the assemblies, which had hitherto granted these stipends. A Board of Customs with headquarters in Boston was set up to enforce the Navigation Acts in general and to oversee the customs service. This Board, with the power to issue writs of assistance (general search warrants) in the pursuance of its duty, was intensely disliked as a foreign intrusion, and as time went by its zeal and corruption, what one historian has called "customs racketeering," [2] alienated a large part of the American merchant community.

Like the Stamp Act, the Townshend Acts met with widespread political opposition, popular denunciation, mob action, and a repetition of the nonimportation agreements. The climax of the disorder was the so-called "Boston Massacre" of March, 1770, when a mob goaded British troops, sent to support the new customs commissioners, into firing. The result was five American deaths.

Trouble and a new ministry under the neurotic procrastinator, Lord North (destined to remain in power for the next twelve years until the colonies were all but lost), resulted in the repeal of the Townshend duties, with the exception, for form's sake, of that on tea. Thus, as in the Stamp Act crisis, the Americans seemed to have won, and the next three years, 1770-1773, were calm and prosperous, with perhaps more quarreling among the colonies than with the home country.

But that calm appears to have been not altogether real, as is suggested by the burning by a mob in 1772 of the British naval vessel, the *Gaspée*, used to prevent smuggling, which had run aground at Providence, Rhode Island. Also, radicals, like Boston's Samuel Adams, the "pioneer in propaganda," were perfecting their organization, in particular the Committees of Correspondence, by which they communicated with each other throughout America, and which stood ready, a revolutionary machine, when the British made their next blunder.[3]

Like most British actions at the time, the Tea Act of April, 1773, was not inspired by malice, and initially it had more to do with the East India Company than with America. Because of its financial difficulties the company was allowed to sell tea, then the staple nonalcoholic colonial drink, directly to the colonies. By avoiding the English duty, the company hoped to sell lower-priced tea, but this meant dealing a severe blow to the colonial tea retailers and tea smugglers, whose profits would be threatened. Also the Townshend duty on tea would continue to be levied. The result was outrage; many of the merchant community and others of the well-to-do rejoined the radicals after the semidivorce of the previous three years, and the usual mob action took place, the most famous, or infamous, being the "Boston Tea Party" of December, 1773, when the radicals flung a large tea shipment into Boston Harbor.[4]

But this time there was no British retreat, as in 1766 and 1770. A series of "coercive" or "intolerable" acts clamped down on Boston. Most important, the port was closed, the Massachusetts government was altered to make it less independent (here indeed was the question of sovereignty), and certain trials involving royal officials were transferred outside New England to avoid local prejudice.

Events followed rapidly, leading to war and independence. Nonimportation was repeated, and on September 5, 1774, the First Continental Congress, composed of delegates from all the colonies except Georgia, met in Philadelphia to decide what action to take. The most decisive move was the adoption of the Continental Association, usually called simply the Association, which consisted of articles of agreement neither to import nor to consume English goods, and of a plan of enforcement: committees of safety were to be elected in each town, and Congressional and provincial committees, sometimes in practice simply the old Committees of Correspondence, were to coordinate matters. There was as yet no real demand for independence; what was wanted was redress of grievances as in the case of the Stamp Act and the Townshend Acts, but in contrast to earlier times a quasi-rebel government was set up.

The work of the committees in implementing the Association was very successful, and the Congress even began training troops. A clash was only a matter of time and came at Lexington, April 19, 1775, between Massachusetts minutemen and General Thomas Gage's British troops out of Boston. The Second Continental Congress met in Philadelphia the next month, embodied an army under George Washington, and, in spite of some attempt at peace, in fact took over the affairs of the country and waged war against Great Britain. When independence was finally declared in July of the next year, Forts Ticonderoga and Crown Point had been captured by Ethan Allen and Benedict Arnold, respectively (May, 1775); the Battle of Bunker Hill (June, 1775) had been fought; the British had evacuated Boston (March, 1776); and a British sea attack on Charleston, South Carolina, had been beaten off (June, 1776). The American Revolution was really over; all that remained were long years of bitter war, international and civil.

With this very brief background of events in mind, let us examine the evolution and attitude of those who became known as Loyalists or friends of government, as they called themselves, or Tories, as their opponents generally dubbed them.[5] One patriot even suggested that it would be more appropriate to call his own party the Loyalists, "while the advocates for the supremacy of the British Parliament should be called the friends of the USURPERS"; another referred to "renegado Americans (alias Tories)." [6] The problem of who were the Loyalists and how one defines them will be taken up later. For the purposes of this chapter let us simply assume that they were those colonists who sooner or later opposed independence and favored reconciliation with Great Britain. The expression "sooner or later" is used advisedly, because ending up a Loyalist almost never implied complete approval of British policy after 1763; usually just the opposite was the case. Also it should be emphasized at the outset that many colonists (possibly a majority), "Whig" and "Tory" alike, either had no strong views on the matter or if they did, preferred not to express them.

In 1763 there were no American Whigs or American Tories. These terms did not exist except in English politics. It is not clear as to just when "Tory" and "Loyalist" first were applied to loyal Americans. The *Oxford English Dictionary* gives 1774 as the first reference for "Tory" and 1781 for "Loyalist," but both were certainly current by about 1774. Connecticut's conservatives were dubbed Tories as early as 1768,[7] and usage may be found even earlier. Thomas Hutchinson wrote thus of the period around 1763:

> The terms, whigg and tory, had never been much used in America. The Massachusetts people, in general, were of the principles of the ancient whiggs; attached to the revolution [of 1688], and to the succession of the crown in the house of Hanover. A very few, who might have been called tories in England, took the name of Jacobites in America. All on a sudden, the officers of the crown, and such as were for keeping up their authority, were branded with the name of tories, always the term of reproach; their opposers assuming the name whiggs, because the common people, as far as they had been acquainted with the parties in England, all supposed the whiggs to have been in the right, and the tories in the wrong.[8]

"Tory" was certainly an "invidious appellation," as Samuel Curwen put it,[9] designed to suggest the despotic monarchism of British Toryism.

Connected with the foregoing is the fundamental but tricky question, When did the Loyalists *first* appear in the various colonies? One Whig satirist claimed the first Tory was Cain and that "the tory herd" was "Sprung from the ordure of 5000 years," [10] but more realistically the Stamp Act of March, 1765, was the measure that most obviously began the general division, if only in a very modest way. Several Loyalists were to date their Loyalism from this period, many becoming "obnoxious," as they put it, for their support of the British Government and their opposition to the mobs that assembled in most towns.[11]

In a few colonies the disturbances of the crisis had some effect on the future political Whig-Tory struggle. In Massachusetts the whole governing clique surrounding Governor Bernard and the future arch-Loyalist Thomas Hutchinson received an irreversible setback and was bitterly and brilliantly attacked by James Otis and others. Newport, Rhode

Island, was the scene of serious riots during which a group known as the Newport Junto, which somewhat foreshadowed the Loyalist party there, was broken up. In Connecticut the conservative Governor Thomas Fitch was permanently replaced by the radical Jonathan Trumbull, while in New York, Lieutenant Governor Cadwallader Colden jeopardized his political career by trying to enforce the act.

Martin Howard, Jr., a member of the Newport Junto, wrote the first Loyalist pamphlet, *A Letter from a Gentleman at Halifax, to His Friend in Rhode-Island,* in which he defended Parliament's supremacy and, although he deplored the Stamp Act, admitted the right to tax the colonies. Joseph Galloway took action against Philadelphia rioters and gave the British some support by his writings in the *Pennsylvania Journal.* A segment of the Anglican clergy, mainly in the North, made themselves distrusted by not clearly supporting the colonial position (they were committed to the British because they sought to establish a bishopric in America, a point to be discussed more fully later). And in all colonies suspicion fell on various royal officials. In general if the riots and lawlessness of the crisis were not finally to make Loyalists of all conservative Americans, they did give a good many of them a fright.

The Stamp Act crisis also produced the first Loyalist refugees or exiles, but this was only the merest shadow of what was to come after 1774. The exiles included Dr. Henry Flower, who left his native Philadelphia forever; George Mercer, the stamp collector in Virginia, who resigned and fled. Newport, if not America, saw the last of Thomas Moffat, Martin Howard, Jr., Augustus Johnston, and John Robinson, all prominent citizens and members of the Junto.

In a sense the Stamp Act crisis launched the Loyalists, but it was a very frail bark compared with the craft of ten or so years later. The crisis merely set apart a few ultras. Its effect in bringing to the fore such major patriot leaders as Samuel Adams and Patrick Henry was much more important. In fact Americans were more united in opposition to the Stamp Act than they ever were in support of independence. Most future Loyalists agreed, as one of them put it, that the "Republican Spirit . . . began to show itself at the time of the Stamp Act," but most also did not approve of British policy in 1765. Prominent examples are Joseph Galloway and Chief Justice William Allen in Pennsylvania, Chief Justice Thomas Jones and Chief Justice William Smith in New York, and Daniel Dulany in Maryland. Even Thomas Hutchinson, the patriots' great *bête noire*, was against the sugar tax and the stamp tax, though he did try to enforce them and did not deny Parliament's right to impose them. Privately, however, he went beyond either Daniel Dulany or John Dickinson in opposing the taxes.[12]

Finally, to complicate the picture further, it must be stressed that some future Whigs found themselves on the wrong foot, most notably Benjamin Franklin, who nominated his friend John Hughes as Stamp Collector in Philadelphia.[13]

The Stamp Act, then, though a beginning, was not the great precipitator of the Loyalists. The serious division between Whigs and Tories did not materialize until the final crisis following the Boston Tea Party of December 16, 1773. In a sense almost all Americans were Loyalists until late 1775, because until that time loyalty to George III was in general volubly asserted, his conspiring wicked advisers being blamed for British policy. Hence it is something of an anachronism to distinguish between Whigs and Tories before that date. In the meantime, although some future Loyalists doubtless viewed events with apprehension, their future leaders were, on the whole, either quietest or sometimes in the van of the opposition to Britain.

Many Loyalists were active in the illegal provincial congresses that met as war approached. Thus Isaac Ogden joined the New Jersey Congress, he said, specifically by Loyalist request, in order to oppose the radicals. Another Tory wryly testified that Ogden "always appeared to him to be one that first set the building on Fire and then ran away." [14]

John Joachim Zubly, a Swiss-born Presbyterian minister, destined to be one of Georgia's most outstanding Loyalists, wrote an anti-British pamphlet on the repeal of the Stamp Act, championed the dissenting churches against Anglican encroachments, in fact was a leading patriot, a delegate to the Second Continental Congress, before he balked at the idea of independence and remained loyal. Daniel Leonard, later, after his "conversion" by Hutchinson in 1774, famous as the Loyalist writer *Massachusettensis,* was a prominent patriot in the Bay Colony. In Maryland Daniel Dulany, well known as a Loyalist after 1773, was a celebrated Whig pamphleteer because of his *Considerations on the Propriety of Imposing Taxes in the British Colonies, for the Purpose of Raising a Revenue* . . . , published in 1768, which declared parliamentary taxes illegal in America and demolished the notion that the colonists could be or were in any way represented in Parliament. Finally, Joseph Galloway, perhaps the most eminent of all Loyalists, opposed parliamentary taxation, was a moderate but certainly Whig politician, and, of course, was a leading personality at the First Continental Congress.[15]

The main exception to this Whiggish Loyalist activity was a group of Anglican clerics, Samuel Seabury, Myles Cooper, Charles Inglis (all of New York), and Thomas Bradbury Chandler of New Jersey, who banded together to defend the monarchy and the Anglican Church. But even they were by no means reactionary, and their chief interest was the Church.

Few potential Loyalists approved of the Tea Act, but even

fewer approved of the tea dumping by the "Mohicans" into Boston Harbor. Many patriots were also aghast: the sacred right of property had been violated. The British Government, however, did not pause to garner any good will over the incident, and instantly made itself more unpopular than ever by the "Intolerable Acts," which restored Massachusetts to the role of injured innocent. Support for beleaguered Boston was very widespread and, like abstention from tea-drinking, became a test of patriotism. For example, the loyal Anglican cleric, Jonathan Boucher, became very unpopluar in his Maryland parish by refusing to preach in support of the Bostonians.

The First Continental Congress, which followed in September, 1774, contained a few future Loyalists, pre-eminently, as we have mentioned, Joseph Galloway, whose famous "plan" for a reformed American empire, a colonial union with internal autonomy subject to the over-all authority of Parliament, failed of adoption by only one vote. Chief Justice William Smith later told British officials that "he believe[d] that it was the Desire of all Members of that Congress except those from New England" to promote reconciliation.[16]

The Association decided on by the Congress in October, 1774, and dismay at the extremes to which matters were drifting, such as the adoption of the Suffolk Resolves, proved to be the first major factors in delineating the Loyalists on a nationwide basis. Local and provincial committees set up to enforce the Association were particularly zealous in pressing it upon those whose patriotism was suspect. Any who refused to support the agreement were blackballed and their names printed in the newspapers. This kind of activity provoked some Loyalist reaction. Samuel Seabury, the "Westchester Farmer," wrote effectively against the Association, and Timothy Ruggles, a prominent Massachusetts Tory, proposed a counterassociation, but like such other attempts elsewhere, it was not successful.

The testimony presented before the British claims commission, a body set up later to compensate the Loyalists,[17] is full of accounts of Loyalists who signed the Association either freely or under coercion. The Association was by no means the ultimate test of allegiance. Many future Loyalists were as ardent as those who remained Whigs in trying to get a redress of grievances; hence support of the Association was quite consistent with later loyalty when violence and outright rebellion became involved. However, James Simpson, the loyal attorney general of South Carolina, thought that "the signing of the Association was the most criminal of all obligations because productive of the most mischievous Consequences and had it been firmly resisted at first, a check would have been given to the Violent Proceeding." [18]

By early 1775 associations to oppose the British by force of arms had been set up in several colonies, and again committees went around gathering signatures for what were in truth "practically militia-rolls." [19]

The Battle of Lexington, April 19, 1775, meant that a state of virtual but undeclared war existed. The Second Continental Congress followed the next month, and only the action of moderate Whigs prevented an immediate declaration of independence. It was becoming harder and harder for many not to take sides.

On March 14, 1776, the Congress resolved that the Whig authorities "immediately cause all persons to be disarmed within their respective colonies who are notoriously disaffected to the cause of America, or who have not associated, and refuse to associate, to defend by arms, these United States." [20]

A typical example of the working of this resolve, one of many thousands, occurred in Northumberland County, Virginia. David Ball, David Ball, Jr., Thomas Waddy, Bartholomew Dameron, and George Ball were called before the county committee "as persons suspected of being inimical to the liberties of America"; they refused a patriot oath, whereupon it was resolved that their arms and ammunition be taken away for the use of the Congress.[21]

On June 24, 1776, the Congress declared that all colonists who adhered to or fought for Great Britain were guilty of treason and should be suitably punished by the colonial legislatures. Thus further stimulated, and soon even more so by the Declaration of Independence, the local committees, county and district, rooted out Tories, usually in a completely arbitrary manner, fining, imprisoning, banishing, releasing under bond, paroling, or disarming and confining them.

Finally, the great declaration of July, 1776, made the issue of Loyalism clear. Even before the actual Declaration of Independence the fact that events were manifestly tending in that direction had made Loyalists of some. The Reverend John J. Zubly, mentioned earlier, deserted the patriot cause at the Second Continental Congress because he feared the establishment of a republic, would be "little better than government of devils." [22] Similarly Robert Alexander, a Baltimore lawyer, a leading Maryland patriot, and a delegate to the Continental Congress, withdrew and became a Loyalist over the question of independence.[23] The British claims commissioners noted in their decision on a Loyalist who had been a colonel in the rebel militia: "However as he deserted the American Cause when they declared for Independence it is very possible that he might have done it upon Real Principle as many other good Men stopped at that period." [24] Sufficient American acceptance of the fateful step to overt independence was to a large degree the result of an astonishingly successful pamphlet, Common Sense, by the great English-born radical, Thomas Paine; but nevertheless many had misgivings, including John Dickinson, "the Penman of the Revolution," who was against it, and there is no reason to quarrel with the *Annual Register*'s claim that the Declaration was opposed not only by the Tories but by "many, who in all other matters had been among the most forward in opposing the claims of the crown and parliament"; in other words some of the erstwhile patriots became Loyalists.[25]

(With the Declaration of Independence the question of allegiance was finally posed for everyone. Approve it and you were a Whig or a patriot, deny it and you were a Loyalist or a Tory.) But a question can be posed without an answer being forthcoming. Many Americans, possibly a majority, had no desire to answer it; they preferred to sit tight, to avoid the war, the committees, the die-hards, to escape service in either army, to wait and see which side prevailed. One Loyalist voiced what was clearly a popular sentiment, declaring that he ("took no part at all but kept out of the Way as much as possible." [26])

The details of anti-Loyalist legislation during the war will be discussed in Chapter V. Here it is sufficient to mention that all the state governments required oaths of allegiance and renunciations of fealty to the king. Conversely, in areas where they gained control, the British administered oaths and gave certificates to erstwhile rebels who recanted. Here is the kind of certificate issued, in this case by the loyal mayor of New York, David Mathews:

I DO hereby Certify, That *David Brinkerhoff* has, in my Presence voluntarily taken an OATH, to bear Faith and true Allegiance to HIS MAJESTY KING George the Third,—and to defend to the utmost of his Power, His sacred Person, Crown and Government, against all Persons whatsoever. Given under my Hand at New-York, this *15* Day of *May* in the Seventeenth

Year of HIS MAJESTY'S reign, Anno. Dom. 1777. *D. Mathews* Mayor of the City of New-York.[27]

Normally, these oaths, from whichever side they came, were particularly pressed on those with known views, or on those who had been activisits in some way.

But one can take an oath and not mean it. As James Simpson testified, "A Temporary Submission to the authority of the usurped Government does not prove Approbation ... the Government of this Country had lost its energy, and the system adopted by the Americans was introduced with such sudden violence, it would have been fatal as well as ineffectual to have opposed it, many well disposed people were obliged to go down with the Stream." [28] One Georgian claimed that he had taken the oath at bayonet point, but the usual story was that it was the only way to save one's property.[29]

The claims commissioners did not consider that the taking of the oath prevented classification as a Loyalist, although they agreed with the claimant who "Thinks he is not so good a Subject as the man who took no Oath." [30]

The preceding pages have sketched in general terms the emergence of the Loyalists. The problem of the American Revolution, John Adams said, was to make thirteen clocks strike as one; the problem of the historian of the Revolution is to combine thirteen different stories—or more, because within each colony different areas often exhibit unique features. This book will concentrate only on the most important developments; no attempt will be made to be always comprehensive. However, to complete the account of how and when the Loyalists emerged, it is necessary to consider a few specific areas.

The colony of Massachusetts and the city of Boston certainly played the leading part in the outbreak of the Revolutionary War. Until about March, 1775, patriots elsewhere were in general simply reacting to events in Boston and the surrounding areas. Just as the Massachusetts Whigs manifested themselves the earliest and the most strongly, so did the opposing Loyalists. Even at the time of the Stamp Act, Massachusetts presents far more evidence of a considerable Loyalist commitment than any other colony, but even so the people involved were, as John Adams noted, a mere "handful"; [31] and during the years before the tea crisis, Massachusetts, unlike any other colony, shows clearly recognizable signs of a growing Whig-Tory split.

In June, 1768, Governor Bernard required the Massachusetts House of Representatives to rescind the resolution that had led to the Massachusetts circular letter rallying colonial opposition to the Townshend Acts. Ninety members opposed but seventeen supported the Governor and were known as "Rescinders," a clear badge of Toryism. The trial of Captain Preston, the officer involved in the "Boston Massacre" of March, 1770, singled out a few Tories by their aid to his defense.

The real crisis developed after the Tea Act, when in Boston alone the tea commissioners refused to resign, and the Tea Party began the immediate train of events that led to independence. While the Loyalists approved of neither the destruction of the tea nor, frequently, the coercive acts, they did remain basically committed to upholding royal authority in Massachusetts. Under the revised government decreed shortly after the Tea Party by the Intolerable Acts, Loyalists of the "better sort" accepted government positions as sheriffs or as members of the now royally appointed council or upper house (the thirty-six were known as "mandamus councillors"), actions which became an irrevocable commitment to Loyalism.

At the same time, in early 1774, Governor Hutchinson was replaced by General Thomas Gage, who arrived at the head of a detachment of troops to maintain order. This change in command has been termed the "occasion for the first associated action of the Tory party" in America.[32] The signing of, or opposition to, various Tory "addresses" of support for Hutchinson on his departure and Gage on his arrival marked off active colonials as either Tories or Whigs.

Meanwhile, in opposition the Whigs drew up a "Solemn League and Covenant" by which the signers pledged to end commerce with Britain until the Intolerable Acts were repealed, and after August 1, 1774, the signers would not trade with their fellow nonsigners. Gage forbade the signing of the covenant, while the Whigs printed nonsigners' names in the newspapers. In spite of Gage's troops, mob action forced the resignation of several mandamus councillors, and the patriots took over the control of the colony.

The only seat of British and Tory authority was Boston, fortified in late 1774, to which out-of-town Loyalists flocked to join their Boston brethren. Outside of this protected reserve, Whig committees sought out real or potential Tories, and enforced the Association. After Lexington the zeal of the committees understandably increased: some Loyalists were imprisoned, some had their property looted, others were confined to their quarters, some signed recantations, others fled to Boston or elsewhere. After Lexington Tory ardor also increased, and in besieged Boston a military organization was created: the Loyal American Associaters, one of several regiments, was formed, under the command of General Timothy Ruggles. And Gage's successor, Howe, organized city patrols and street-cleaning brigades on a civilian basis. Finally with the massing of the patriot forces, the British decided to evacuate. Dumfounded, most of the Loyalists within Boston, realizing they were too deeply compromised and fearing, with reason, the wrath of their Whiggish country-men, had to board one of the 170 ships that sailed with the retreating British for Nova Scotia on March 17, 1776.)

The events in Massachusetts from the Tea Party to the evacuation of Boston present a microcosm of the story of the American Tories: the early partial agreement with the pa-triot arguments, persecution and loss of property wherever British protection was lacking or withdrawn, deepening an-noyance with the British authorities (particularly Howe's lack of drive) and their failure to take Loyalist advice or use willing American allies, a waning confidence in British in-vincibility confirmed by the unexpected slaughter at the Battle of Bunker Hill, growing distress aggravated by the short rations and privations of the siege of Boston and the bitterness of civil war. (One sanguinary, native-born Tory lady exclaimed: "It would be a joy to ride through American blood to the hubs of my chariot wheels." [33]) Finally there was the ultimate blow, the disaster of exile to an unknown, in-hospitable land.

Colonies other than Massachusetts underwent the effects of the Tea Party, the Association, the Declaration of Independ-ence, and so on, but nowhere were the lines drawn so de-cisively or so dramatically. Nonetheless, in no colony did the Whigs experience serious difficulty in gaining control, and nowhere were Tory counterassociations or other organiza-tions successful. Everywhere the great majority of Loyalists parted company with the Whigs at a time that proved to be too late in the game. In New York, unique among all the colonies, moderates, Whigs, and future Loyalists kept control of the opposition to British policy; but the news of Lexing-ton gave the adamant Whigs effective power. Pennsylvania exhibited almost unanimous opposition to British policy from the Stamp Act onward, and only the question of out-right independence made the agonizing question of loyalty acute. In Virginia, as one Loyalist put it, "there were no Heats and Troubles . . . till the Blockade of Boston in the year 1775." [34] Lord Dunmore, the governor, in the second half of 1775 briefly rallied the Loyalists, only to be defeated in arms at Great Bridge in December. Similar action by Governor Martin of North Carolina at the beginning of 1776 also failed, with the patriot victory at Moore's Creek Bridge in February.

The final factor to mention in the precipitation of the Loyalists, and perhaps the most important, as in the case of Massachusetts, is the encouraging effect of a British military presence, which always created the opportunity for Loyalists or recanting patriots to stand up and be counted and sometimes be incorporated into military or civilian groups. Thus, there was the occupation of New York City throughout the war; of Philadelphia from September, 1777, to June, 1778; of Charleston from May, 1780, to December, 1782; of Savannah from December, 1778, to July, 1782.

The answer, then, to the question of when the Loyalists first appeared is that it was a long, drawn-out process varying with different individuals and different geographical locations. For a very few the Stamp Act was the occasion for an avowal of their loyal principles, but for the great majority the decision came in the years following the Boston Tea Party. It might be a resolve not to sign the Association in 1774; a refusal to take the oath in support of a new state government at any time following May, 1776; a decision, possibly only mental, not to accept the Declaration of Independence in July, 1776; a refusal to join the rebel army at any time after fighting began; or a move to seek the protection of the British occupying forces.

The decision could be precipitated by almost any public

issue or private happening from 1765 to 1783. It might be prompted by confrontation with a Whig committee, or a trivial argument with a patriot friend, or even by a friendly chat with a persuasive paroled British or Loyalist prisoner.

CHAPTER III

"The Welter of Conflicting Motives"

◆§ "It is the Cause of Truth against Falsehood of Loyalty against Rebellion of legal Government against Usurpation of Constitutional Freedom against Tyranny—in short—it is the Cause of human happiness, the happiness of Millions against Outrage and Oppression."

The Reverend Charles Inglis, September, 1777.[1]

The question of when and in what circumstances the Loyalists appeared is comparatively easy. Less so is the question of motivation. As the preamble to a Connecticut pardon act stated: "It is apprehended that very different motives and principles have influenced the conduct of the deluded few." [2] The reasons for the actions of some groups are more readily found than are those of others.

Royal (and proprietary) officials, from the colonial governor down to simple customs officers, were the most solidly loyal part of society, their loyalty being most ingrained. Isaac Hubbard, a royal official in Connecticut, remarked simply that "being a Servant of the Crown therefore he was in Duty bound to be loyal." On his way to join the British on the morning of the Battle of Lexington, Joshua Loring, a mandamus councillor and retired naval captain, assured a friend,

44

"I have always eaten the King's bread, and always intend to." The Whigs charged that simple greed motivated the office-holders, while the Tories retorted that their jealous Whig opponents sought their jobs and stipends. Both sides, of course, had their Tapers and Tadpoles, their Pooh-Bahs, but for many honor was strongly involved.[3]

This leads on to the subject of oaths. It was noted in the previous chapter that both sides pressed oaths upon each other wherever they could. Usually the recipient was taking such an oath for the first time. Officials, military officers, and Anglican clergymen were the only colonists who normally took a formal oath of allegiance to the king. Oaths were treated very seriously in the eighteenth century, and perjury, because of a belief in divine justice, was regarded as perhaps more heinous than it is today. Radicals usually argued, but not always successfully, that oaths to George III were no longer valid because of the king's despotic, unconstitutional behavior. In January, 1775, John Gallison, while protesting his devotion to the liberties of Massachusetts, told the town of Marblehead that he would not resign his military commission because he could not see how he "or any other officer is to Be absolved from an Oath." However, it must be stressed that the taking of an oath to the king was by no means a guarantee of loyalty. The Regulators, back-country farmers who had rebelled against the seaboard government in North and South Carolina around 1771, were not generally Tory, although many had taken oaths of allegiance when they were pardoned after the uprisings were crushed.[4]

Immigrants from Britain were more likely to be Loyalists than the native-born. Many arrived in the colonies during the Seven Years War as members of the armed forces, which inculcated loyalty. Normally, however, the more recent an immigrant the greater the chance of loyalty. He usually had not done as well as the longer-established immigrants, lacked their confidence, had stronger ties with the homeland, and generally felt more in need of a friend in the form of the British Government. Thus many Pennsylvania Loyalists were immigrants, the majority being comparatively recent arrivals. The great Loyalist strength in Georgia is certainly partly explained by the colony's high proportion (the highest of any colony) of immigrants. On the other hand, immigrants to America have traditionally included many who were glad to escape the homeland, and among recent arrivals who became outstanding Whigs we find Tom Paine; Generals Richard Montgomery, Horatio Gates, and Arthur St. Clair; and the great naval hero, Captain John Paul Jones.[5]

Germans were the main group of non-British immigrant Loyalists. They undoubtedly shared the immigrant's desire for protection, and many felt gratitude to the British Government, which had sometimes paid their passage and granted them title to land that they now feared to lose.[6] But ignorance of the English language compounded a general ignorance of the Revolutionary issues, and the majority of Germans remained neutral or Whig and were swept along by events in which they had little hand.

More Loyalists were born in Scotland than in any other country outside of America. The Scots, therefore, who gained as unsavory a reputation in America as they had by tradition in eighteenth-century England, require explanation. Some were merchants connected with British firms, a few were Indian traders, and others were demobilized soldiers, such as Allan Macdonald, husband of the almost mythical Flora Macdonald. Many were Highlanders, often recently arrived in the New World. It may seem strange that many of these Highlanders, who had fought the House of Hanover in the 1745 rebellion and remembered the defeat of 1715, should prove such staunch Loyalists. But they wanted to avoid being three-time losers (in vain, as it turned out), and, furthermore, they had been well treated and given land in America, taking oaths of allegiance in the process. Remaining clannish, the Highlanders followed their leaders, and their leaders were generally loyal.[7] Also the clan system was a ready-made form of political organization, and it was organization that most Loyalists fatally lacked.

Other Highlanders came from Argyllshire, where the Campbells, traditionally loyal to the English monarchy, held sway. Thus George Campbell recounted that his relatives had been loyal during the "Fifteen" and the "Forty-Five," in which latter affray he himself had served as a youthful combatant. In 1774 Campbell emigrated to Philadelphia. There an old friend, "whose Ancestors had been Dependents upon this Memorialist's Family, but who had emigrated in his Youth, and by his own Industry had accumulated a Fortune," tried to persuade Campbell to join the rebels, and he was offered command of a regiment. Campbell, however, said he preferred "his hereditary Loyalty to every consideration of Interest." [8]

William H. Nelson has suggested that the various Loyalist groups were usually "cultural minorities" in need of British help or protection, and fearful of an increase in the power of the majority. This theory is undoubtedly valuable. As Nelson points out; the Dutch and the Germans were Tory mainly where they had not been Anglicized, and New Rochelle, the only place where the French Calvinists still spoke French, seems to have been the one area of substantial Huguenot Loyalism. One can add such examples as Northern Anglicans; the small farmers of New York who had rebelled under Prendergast against their Whig landlords; the Highland Catholic tenants of Sir John Johnson; the Baptists of Ashfield, Massachusetts, who were struggling against the established Congregational Church, as were the Sandemanians in Massachusetts and Connecticut; the conferentie minority of the Dutch Reformed Church who feared the majority coetus group in the Hackensack Valley, New Jersey; the back-country farmers of the Carolinas who were restless under the dominating Whiggish seaboard; and Scottish merchants and creditors in the South who had little in common with their indebted American planter-customers.[9] Also the strength of Loyalism in Georgia is partly explained by Georgia's fear of Indian and Spanish neighbors and even her feeling of "minority" vis-à-vis the other more powerful and longer established twelve colonies.

Although their military significance will be discussed in the next chapter, the Indians and the Negroes should be noted here in the "cultural minority" context. The Indians made some attempt at neutrality,[10] but generally they were "loyal" (in the sense of favoring the British in the war) from motives of self-interest. Their supplies and trade came from the British Government, which they regarded as their protector; they were used to dealing with its representatives, like Sir John Johnson and Colonel John Butler, whose power they respected. Further, they had no enthusiasm for the westward-pushing, uncontrollable colonial settler and believed that the British rather than the Americans would be most likely to seek restraints over this movement.

In one of his sketches Crèvecoeur has a patriot address a Negro thus: "They say you are a good fellow, only a little Toryfied like most of your colour"; and a contemporary Tory testified that the Negroes were "strongly attached to the British." [11] There certainly was a widespread fear of Negroes among the Whigs, partly an extension of the perennial dread of slave revolt, and intensified by the mass desertion of slaves in response to a wholesale British offer of freedom that the patriots could never match. (Freedom was offered only to the deserting slaves of rebels, of course.)

But it is impossible to say what proportion of Negroes

were Whigs and what proportion Tories. With some notable
exceptions, the vast majority were too uneducated, unsophis-
ticated, or oppressed to take any personal part in the Revolution. As in the Civil War, many slaves must have remained
attached to benevolent masters from both sides. The Negro
who was active during the Revolution joined one side or the
other for reasons of personal advantage (such as, primarily,
freedom) rather than because of any political philosophy.
Few could have been politically aware. For example, William
Snow, a Negro tailor in Charleston, signed the Association,
he said, without knowing what it was.[12] And those who did
know the issues could not fail to be disillusioned by the
cynical attitude of both sides. In the case of one William
Prince, the claims commissioners judged that he was "a great
gainer by the troubles in America for being in a situation in
which he could loose nothing he has gained his Liberty and
comes in our Opinion with a very bad grace to plead sufferings. . . ."[13] Although unsympathetic, these words sum up
the position of the slave who became a "Loyalist" (or for that
matter, in different circumstances, a "Whig")—he had indeed
nothing to lose and everything to gain.[14]

Nelson has also suggested a geographical similarity among
many areas of Tory strength—they all "suffered or were
threatened with economic and political subjugation by
richer adjoining areas. The geographical concentration of the
Tories was in peripheral areas, regions already in decline or
not yet risen to importance." Thus, as in the case of "cultural
minorities," imperial help was sought: such loyal frontiersmen as trappers feared advancing civilization; the maritime
Loyalists of the three old counties around Philadelphia
feared the political power of the West and cherished economic links with Britain; in Rhode Island, Newport was
facing stiff competition from Providence, which rivalry became translated into a Loyalist-Whig clash.[15]

As we have already seen from our consideration of royal officials and of minority groups, and as we shall see further in those groups representing economic interests, the old legal phrase, *cui bono,* was very much involved in the decision to side with Britain. Probably more lawyers were Whig than Tory, but an inclination to the latter position was aided by the good fees and salaries paid to those employed by the British authorities. Thus the "giants of the law" were usually loyal; struggling lawyers who were outside the "Establishment," American Robespierres, were likely to be radical.[16]

John Adams attributed Loyalism almost entirely to British threats and the promise of "advancement, honour, glory, wealth and power." [17] Clearly *cui bono* should also be applied to merchants and others whose livelihood depended on trade with the British. Many such merchants, especially recent immigrants or members of British houses, were indeed loyal, naturally inclined to economic and political conservatism.[18] It is probable that those who benefitted from British bounties (cash subsidies for certain products) were often Loyalist.[19] Conversely, many merchants who saw better economic prospects through independence were Whigs. Thus in New York City, a recent scholar has concluded, the Whig merchants were all engaged in illicit trade.[20] Good examples of loyal traders include many merchants of Newport, New York, and, par excellence, Scotsmen throughout the South, particularly in Virginia, where they were almost unanimously loyal, and also a doubly suspect minority as "foreign" creditors with intimate transatlantic trading relationships.[21] David Ramsay, the Whig historian, argued that the South Carolina Loyalists were certain selfish merchants and planters who knew they would be hurt by the end of British trading ties, and a recent historian has noted that most of the artisans who were Tories (a minority of the whole) in Charleston were dependent on British trade.[22]

Trade with the British armed forces in the years before 1775 made many merchants, especially in New York, Loyalists during the years that followed.[23] With the outbreak of fighting and the increase in war operations, engaging in trade with, or services for, the British army became a stronger temptation, and a perennial problem for the Whigs, who passed laws, offered rewards, even excuted offenders.[24] Rebel attempts at price-fixing plus an "aversion to rag-money" and a desire for "solid coin" (specie) resulted in the British forces being much better supplied than the American.[25] John Granger, who ran a livery stable in Pennsylvania, bluntly admitted that the arrival of the British army put him "in the way of making a Fortune."[26] All manner of people were involved in this illict (from the American point of view) trade, from innkeepers, peddlers, printers, and artisans to the richest merchants; from bakers, drovers, and yeoman farmers to the great planters.[27] Dr. Benjamin Church, the celebrated Tory spy and double agent in Boston, apparently sought cash; cash to support a mistress and build a luxurious house.[28]

Dedicated Loyalists were scornful of those who merely sided with the British "for sake of making money."[29] There was a hint of Loyalist dissatisfaction with those who crossed over into British lines and then did nothing except receive charity, thus giving foundation to Whig charges that Tories simply wanted to escape Whig taxation and army service.[30] Of course the individual elements in the various mixtures of greed and principle can never be separated out. Any civil war exhibits a full gamut of motives, from the basest to the noblest. Some of those who traded with the British were convinced Loyalists, some were neutrals, some were Whigs. Some, in the last two categories, were swept willy-nilly into the Loyalist camp because their actions were too well known and they had become compromised.

But the Whig side was often economically more atractive. Arthur M. Schlesinger, Sr., has suggested that although the merchants did not usually favor independence, "the line of least resistance" was to accept it, especially if their wealth was not removable and their business and customers could not be transferred to the British lines. Also, although many lawyers were Loyalists, many others, like certain merchants, were sham Whigs. William Franklin reported that Isaac Ogden, a New Jersey lawyer who was a member of the provincial congress, went in, despite what Ogden himself said, "as many of his Profession did, with a view of promoting his popularity and preventing others from running away with his business." [31]

However, loyalty was not always a simple matter of self-interest. It is true that, quite apart from the consideration of their oaths, royal and proprietary officials often were loyal because they would lose their jobs by rebellion. But many officeholders were able people who could have had (although some never guessed it) attractive appointments with the Whig regimes. Many, indeed, found themselves in dilemmas like that of Robert E. Lee, who was proffered command of the Union forces at the start of the Civil War. For example, Achilles Preston of Connecticut was a loyal lieutenant colonel who refused a higher rank in rebel service and thus "sacrificed at the Shrine of Loyalty." [32] Similarly, among the merchants, principles sometimes counted for more than the purse, a conclusion reinforced by the number of merchant-partners who chose opposite sides (assuming that the economic advantage, wherever it lay, was clear).[33]

A majority of Loyalists were farmers of some kind, yet this group contributed proportionately less than others. Thus the loyal farmer was much more the odd man out than anyone else. This reinforces a basic conclusion that motives for loyalty were essentially personal. But a few words can be said about some groups of farmer-Loyalists, particularly those in North and South Carolina and New York, which areas, especially the last two, produced well over half of the loyal farmers, although even there they were decidedly a minority group.

In North Carolina many of the farmers were Scottish immigrants, whose loyalty has already been explained. South Carolina's loyal farmers were a mixed group, but more were immigrants (Scotch-Irish, Germans, Scots, in descending order of importance) than native-born. David Ramsay drew attention to this upcountry Loyalism. He ascribed it to Regulator influence; a fear (on the part of the immigrants) of losing land titles; an acceptance of Governor Campbell's argument that the whole dispute was over "a trifling tax on tea," which the upcountry farmers did not use anyway; and finally the apathy and remoteness of the farmers, who were contented and undisturbed by "distant evils" in Massachusetts and the British Parliament. Ramsay makes sense, except that most ex-Regulators were Whigs. More relevant than the Regulators is the fact that Camden and Ninety-Six, the two chief British inland military strongholds, were also the chief centers of Tory power, apart from Charleston.

If New York and South Carolina produced more than half of the loyal farmers, New York by itself counted for the greater part of that number. This seems to stem partly from the antirent riots of 1766, which were harshly suppressed by the landlords, aided by such New York City magistrates as John Morin Scott, who later became a Revolutionary leader. The farmers noted that whereas the Stamp Act rioters were mildly treated, their own leaders were condemned to death. Thus the royal pardon given to the rebel Prendergast revealed the king to the tenants as "a shield against rapacious landlords." Many farmers, as a recent historian has put it, "when the Revolution came, turned against it wherever the landlords were for it." This attitude was implied by Abraham Yates, Jr., in a 1787 Independence Day oration, when he said, "It is admitted that there are poor as well as rich Tories . . . yet we know by experience that there would not have been a Tory in fifty in our late struggles if they had not been disaffected by the rich." Some Tory tenants hoped for land reform if the king defeated their landlords, and William Smith claimed that the Quaker Hill area, where the tenants made their last stand in 1766, was forty to one against independence.[34]

Most of the great New York landlords were in fact Loyalists, including Sir John Johnson, Guy Johnson, Oliver DeLancey, Frederick Phillipse, Philip Skene, Roger Morris, John Watts, Beverley Robinson, John Harris Cruger, and the following extensive landholding families: the Floyds, the Jessups, the Purdys, the Rapaljes, the Waltons, the Joneses, the Bayards, the Cuylers, the Baches, the Van Cortlandts, and the DePuysters.

These great proprietors were some of the richest men and families in the colonies. For compensation, Sir John Johnson claimed £103,162; Oliver DeLancey, £108,957; Beverley Robinson, £79,980; and Roger Morris, £68,384. Most, but not all, were natives of America. Many, like Guy Johnson, Indian superintendent, or Judge Thomas Jones, were royal officials; several served on the royal council; all were part of the New York aristocratic governing clique, which was tied together by marriage and kinship. Both Beverley Robinson and Roger Morris, for example, married daughters of Frederick Phillipse. Much of their land came from royal grants. Phillipse mentioned to the claims commissioners that his manor had been granted in 1693 by William and Mary. The Johnson family fortune had been built up by royal favor. Politics, religion (the proprietors were normally Anglican), social position, and self-interest all conspired to keep most of the great landlords royal.

It is not surprising, therefore, that most farmer Loyalists were not tenants of Whig landlords involved in the antirent riots. The majority were actually following their landlords rather than opposing them. Beverley Robinson told the commissioners that the regiment he raised and commanded during the Revolutionary War was made up mainly of his own tenants. But the most imposing examples are the numerous Loyalists who resided on land belonging to the Johnson family.

Sir William Johnson died on the eve of the Revolution, but his son, Sir John, and his nephew, Guy, ably maintained the family's interests and took most of their tenants with them to the British side. As early as May, 1776, Sir John fled to Canada with 175 followers. A substantial segment of these tenants were Scottish Highland Catholics who had arrived as recently as 1773 and were naturally dependent upon, and owed gratitude to, their landlord. There is a claim for compensation from their Irish priest, the Reverend John Mc-Kenna, who told the claims commissioners that he went to New York in 1773 with three hundred Highlanders from Fort William, not one of whom joined the rebels; all instead followed him to Canada, where they formed the Royal Highland Emigrants and the Royal Yorkers, with McKenna as chaplain.

It must be noted, however, that not all tenants of Loyalist landlords followed their leaders. William Houghton, who had four tenant families settled on his land at the head of Lake George, Albany County, told the claims commissioners that all chose the rebel side.

Farmers are usually conservative people, and the mass of New York farmers was no exception. Most were probably content with their lot, and had little interest in the political issues of the Revolution, and no taste for rebellion. Further, the New York countryside was never alerted in the way the Massachusetts hinterland was. Rural New York had an almost feudal air; there was no vigorous local government, no town meeting, no Samuel Adams in New York City to bestir and organize the country-dwellers.[35]

Finally two more occupational groups, doctors and teachers, must be briefly considered. The reason that doctors lead all categories of professional men in supplying Loyalists may be the expensive medical training, often in Europe, that caused doctors to be drawn from that richer section of the population most likely to produce Loyalists. The reason for the comparatively few loyal teachers is not clear, but it may be that teachers are inherently more radical than doctors. They were certainly paid less.

The only set of religious beliefs obviously connected with Loyalism was that of the Anglican Church. There are doctrinal and social reasons for this. With the sixteenth-century Reformation, the English monarch had become head of the Church in place of the Pope. Allegiance to the Church, now the Anglican and not the Catholic Church, was allegiance to the king. The Anglican Prayer Book kept loyal thoughts to the fore with regular royal prayers, and often a colonial parson's refusal to drop them led to his dismissal.[36] The whole tone of the eighteenth-century Anglican Church, seen in sermons and pamphlets, was one of zealous loyalty, of "the Christian Duty of Peaceableness"; and in those days religion and politics were much more basically intertwined than today.[37] Loyal clerics could refuse the Sacrament to rebel members of their congregations, which may have brought some recalcitrants around.[38]

Outside of the South, mere membership in the Anglican Church put one under Whig suspicion, and some Anglicans were rather forced into Loyalism. Fear on the part of the

Whigs, of course, was not unreasonable. In the years following 1763 the Anglican Church had been in the van of the pro-British forces—almost the sole American support for the Stamp Act was Anglican—and the demand for an American bishop had angered countless non-Anglicans, and even some Anglican laymen. Also, Anglican proselytizing zeal and success had not made that church popular in the North.[39]

Socially the church had most attraction for the fashionable, wealthy, urban part of society, from which Loyalists were likely to emerge. In New England Anglicans were a minority, conscious of the need for British protection against the hostile Congregational majority. The Anglican ministers were often British-born, and the American-born ones were often Anglophiles. All Anglican clerics had to be ordained in Britain, where they took their oaths of allegiance. The Reverend Thomas Barton, a close friend and relative of the great patriot scientist Rittenhouse, was himself very Whiggishly inclined but would not break his oath. "This," he lamented, "was . . . [my] only crime (if a crime it be)," and for it he was banished "from all that are most dear to me." [40] Many clergy, chiefly in the Northern colonies, were missionaries sent out by the British Society for the Propagation of the Gospel, and thus depended upon the homeland for their stipends.

Everywhere Anglicans, lay and clerical, were divided, but in New England they were most likely to be loyal, in the middle colonies they were more evenly divided, and in the South Anglican Loyalists were a minority. In short the Loyalism of Anglicans was in inverse proportion to their numbers. Fatally, the church lacked any real continental organization, and the Anglican system in the South, where it was almost a kind of Congregationalism, differed greatly from that in the rest of the country. Also it should be remembered that more Anglicans than members of any other denomination signed the Declaration of Independence.[41]

Samuel Shoemaker, when asked what people thought of the war in 1776, replied that "all the Loyalists and most of the rebels thought that Great Britain would prevail." [42] Such sentiments were commonplace, and a belief in British invincibility certainly impelled many Americans to become Loyalists.[43] In 1775 Jerathmeel Bowers of Massachusetts expected five thousand British regulars to dispose of the rebellion with ease, an event to be followed by the execution of its leaders.[44] In 1777 a Whig ascribed Loyalist success in Somerset and Worcester counties, Maryland, to rumors of British military success, thanks to which the Tories "threw off all restraint," having "taken it for granted that the whole contest was over." [45] A Virginia Loyalist was not the only one to admit that he only joined the British when he "thought they would prevail." [46] The Reverend Jacob Duché of Pennsylvania, somewhat in anticipation of the recent "better red than dead" controversy, wrote to Washington in October, 1777, forecasting American defeat:

> Perhaps it may be said, that it is "better to die than be Slaves." This indeed is a splendid maxim in theory. . . . But where there is the least Probability of an happy Accomodation, surely Wisdom and Humanity call for some Sacrifices to be made, to prevent inevitable Destruction.[47]

John Singleton Copley was one of the few Loyalists perceptive enough to forecast an American victory right from the start, but he thought it would be a victory bought at such cost that he called his family to Europe for safety.[48]

Even though so many people honestly believed the British would win, the Loyalists, a minority everywhere, often needed a British military presence, as already mentioned, to flush them from their nests—hence the obvious connection between the British occupation and Loyalist strength in Georgia, South Carolina, New Jersey, New York, and elsewhere. New York had more Loyalists than any other colony— partly a reflection of the long occupation of New York City and the fact that one third of the military engagements of the war took place in this colony. Also the occupation stimulated Loyalism in the adjoining parts of Connecticut and New Jersey. The capture of Philadelphia clearly had a bearing on Loyalism in Pennsylvania, in nearby Delaware, and in southern New Jersey. The British forces at Newport, Rhode Island, and the fort at Penobscot, Massachusetts, should also be remembered in the present context.[49]

Of course, many colonists behaved in the manner of the Vicar of Bray; "we are at present all Whigs until the arrival of the King's troops," wrote one Tory disarmingly in 1775.[50] The historian Jared Sparks told an amusing story: In June, 1775, the provincial congress of New York was alarmed to learn that George Washington, rebel commander in chief, and William Tryon, royal commander in chief, were expected in New York City on the same day. The congress dispatched a force prepared to welcome "either the General, or Governor Tryon, whichever should first arrive, and wait on both sides as well as circumstances would allow." [51]

Military occupation, then, was an essential prop for Loyalism, and there can be no reason to dispute the *Annual Register*'s conclusion that "without the great and continual assistance of the royal army, the well-affected inhabitants, in no part of America, were in a condition to make head against the rebels." [52]

Conversely the lack of a British stronghold inhibited Loyalism. Thus Loyalism in New Hampshire, Connecticut, Delaware, Maryland, and North Carolina suffered from the lack of British occupation of an important town.

The presence of strong Whig neighbors also stunted Loyalism. The prime example was Georgia, which would probably have kept out of the Revolution, as Sir James Wright
remarked, if only the Savannah River, the boundary with
South Carolina, had not been so narrow.[53]

The British occupation was, in truth, a mixed blessing for
the Loyalists. For one thing, British defeats had as great an
effect in lowering morale as their successes had in raising it,
and the former proved much more decisive and permanent.
Since 1763 British forces had been regarded as the most formidable in the world, but as the list of defeats at the hands
of the American rebels grew, Loyalist confidence became increasingly difficult to sustain. As one Tory succinctly put it,
"I am much disappointed with these Conquerors of the
World." [54] The recurrent story was the arrival of the British,
rejoicing and the organizing of the Tories, and then withdrawal (sometimes virtually betrayal of the Loyalists) by the
British either voluntarily or after defeat, with the result that
the compromised citizens were obliged to depart with the
army or remain to face the music. Thus Tom Paine's forecast of 1776 was fulfilled: "Many a disguised tory has lately
shown his head, that shall penitentially solemnize with curses
the day on which Howe arrived upon the Delaware." [55]

In North Carolina, February 27, 1776, fifteen hundred
Loyalists rallied to the royal standard and in a battle that
lasted three short minutes were routed. The *Annual Register*
commented accurately on the Loyalists' defeat: "But now,
their force and spirits were so entirely broken, their leadership sent to different prisons, and the rest stripped of their
arms, and watched with all the eyes of distrust, that no future
effort could reasonably be expected of them." [56] Loyalism
was indeed never again a serious threat to the state, but had
the crucial three minutes dictated a different turn of fortune, Tory strength would have been a far different matter.

In Virginia, in 1775, the victory of Dunmore, the royal governor, at Kemp's Landing encouraged Loyalists. But in December the Governor was defeated at Great Bridge, which loss, combined with the failure of John Connolly's expedition in the spring of 1776 to rally the west, greatly dampened loyal enthusiasm. Cornwallis's presence in 1780 gave a tremendous boost to Loyalism, soon crushed by the surrender at Yorktown. Finally the abandonment of Savannah and Charleston marked the end of all active Loyalism in the South.

In the middle colonies the *coup de grâce* was the evacuation of Philadelphia in June, 1778. John Potts wrote that, as a result, the Loyalists "abandoned themselves to a lethargy very nearly bordering on despair." [57]

The story was the same in the North. Gage's departure from Boston in 1776 signaled the end of Loyalism as any kind of real force in Massachusetts. Commenting on the disaster at Saratoga in 1777, a Loyalist wrote, "No sooner was the Fate of General Burgoyne's Army known than every Friend to Government was obliged to take refuge in the Woods." [58]

Samuel Curwen, writing in 1780, summed the whole thing up in this rather gloomy, but realistic, picture:

We have beaten the rebel army, and expelled that army out of Carolina with half their number, have rivetted the inhabitants to our interests; they are become loyalists and have sworn allegiance, and that they will always do whilst you can command their estates and persons. This reminds one of the lines in Hudibras:

'Tis he that breaks an oath who makes it;
Not he who for convenience takes it.

That the Americans practise this rule is true, but how far they believe it to be just, I won't say. For proof I refer you to

Rhode Island, Philadelphia, and those parts of Long Island and the Jerseys, relinquished; there are besides many other instances; while under British power they are loyal, that power removed, they as naturally return to their former condition as any elastic body returns to its natural form when the force is removed.[59]

Even the presence of the British forces without any defeat was often detrimental to the Loyalist cause. The overwhelming impression one gets from the Loyalists' testimony is that their strength would have been considerably greater had the British Government and its army shown more interest and finesse in dealing with their real or potential allies, or at least avoided harassing them (for details on British harassment of the Loyalists, see Chapter IV, below). It is very clear that the British Government was generally woefully negligent in rallying and making use of the Loyalists. A petition of March, 1785, from several leading Loyalists put it nicely when it stated that three men had remained loyal "as much from inclination as encouragement." [60]

If Loyalist attitudes were in part determined by the presence or absence of British troops, and by their victory or defeat, Loyalist beliefs were also often molded by British education. Frequent examples (though a definite minority of the whole) are found of Americans educated in England who became Loyalists. One of the Dulanys of Maryland, talking of his loyalty, mentioned his English education and the fact that he had been "bred from infancy in an affectionate regard for Great Britain, in veneration for her constitution and Laws." Another Dulany stated categorically that he "inherited" his loyalty from his father and grandfather. Many examples of this kind, such as the case of Sir John Johnson, could be added. But contact with England through education and family has not always resulted in leaders devoted to the preservation of colonial status, as the recent history of India and British Africa shows. The four South Carolina signers of the Declaration of Independence had been educated in England.[61]

If we had been able to ask the Tories why they were loyal, most would probably have replied simply that they were opposed to the "temper of the times." And why were they opposed? Because they were conservative, because they were satisfied with things as they were, or at least feared revolution more than they feared British encroachments.

Crèvecoeur put it quite simply: "I am conscious that I was happy before this unfortunate Revolution. I feel that I am no longer so; therefore I regret the change"; and he mentioned the "respect I feel for the ancient connection, and the fear of innovations, with the consequences of which I am not well acquainted." [62]

Fear of change could take a thousand forms, but uppermost in the minds of most well-to-do Loyalists was the dread of social change, foreshadowed by the rise of mobs after the Stamp Act crisis. In 1774 John Singleton Copley was gravely shaken by the arrival at his house of a mob searching for a friend of his. The experience made him doubly resolved to leave for Europe, and not only to gain artistic experience.[63]

In 1780 Samuel Curwen complained that "those who five years ago were the 'meaner people' are now by strange revolution, become almost the only men of power, riches and influence. . . . The Cabots of Beverly, who you know, had but five years ago a very moderate share of property, are now said to be by far the most wealthy in New England." One Loyalist declared, "If I must be devoured, let me be devoured by the jaws of a lion, and not gnawed to death by rats and vermin," a thought echoed by a Georgian lady's assertion that with the Revolution "everywhere the scum rose to the top."[64] Many Loyalists believed an American republic would inevitably decline into an anarchy and end up a despotism,

becoming a satellite of a foreign power or else perhaps begging for re-entry into the British Empire.

There is a distinct aristocratic veneer to Loyalism. Dr.
Benjamin Rush stressed the Loyalist love of luxury and roy-
alty, and the general attachment to "the pomp and hierarchy
of the Church of England." [65] As New York filled up with
Loyalist refugees, there was a complaint from the Loyalists
themselves that far too many refused to serve "as common
soldiers." [66] Men like Peter Oliver and Crèvecoeur were certainly aristocrats. The latter suspected "a certain impatience
of government, by some people called liberty"; he argued
that the colonists were prosperous under a free government,
and the trouble was that the people "from their childhood,
were bred to censure with the utmost impunity the conduct
of their governors." [67] Reasoning along these lines, a few
Loyalists planned to establish a nobility in America after the
revolt was crushed.[68]

In 1776 Paine declared, "Every Tory is a coward . . . fear
is the foundation of Toryism." Three years later the *Connecticut Courant* had a Loyalist confess that "interest and
cowardice sway us all." [69] Thomas McKean, the Pennsylvania
patriot, dubbed the Loyalists "the timid." [70]

Evidence to support this typical Whig opinion can be
found in the statements of the British and often of Tories
themselves. Ambrose Serle, who as secretary to Lord Howe in
New York became disillusioned with the Loyalists, quoted
his master in December, 1776, as observing "to me this morning, that almost all the People of Parts and Spirit were in the
Rebellion." A few days later Serle himself complained of the
Loyalists: "Alas, they all prate and profess much; but when
You call upon them, they will *do* nothing." Lord Cornwallis
designated the Loyalists as "timid," and while praising their
fortitude condemned their "indecision." [71] On occasion even
Rivington's *Gazette* echoed these sentiments.[72]

It is certainly true that far more men of "parts" were Whig than Tory. And it is easy to illustrate Loyalist timidity in either individuals or groups. For example, there is Lord William Campbell, governor of South Carolina, who "uniformly recommended the royalists to remain quiet" until the British forces arrived—meanwhile, of course, the Whigs took over; [73] or Edmund Trowbridge, Harvard class of 1728 and judge of the Massachusetts Supreme Court, who, as the Revolutionary quarrel deepened, took down and destroyed his full-length portrait of Governor Thomas Hutchinson and remained, in spite of his Loyalism, quiet and unmolested until his death in 1793.[74] There are many Loyalists who fled their homes at the first hint of danger, many who changed sides as the fortunes of war fluctuated, many whose behavior was quietist, or highly equivocal, as they attempted to keep a foot in both camps. As for groups, the South Carolina Loyalists are exceptionally open to the charge of timidity and equivocation—"tergiversations," as a Whig paper put it.[75]

But timidity was not always, perhaps not even usually, the rule. Some Loyalists were never daunted, such as Philip Skene of Skenesborough, New York, who, even when jailed at Hartford, Connecticut, would "still harangue the people from the prison windows," as Governor Franklin related.[76] Every colony produced bold Loyalists. Even South Carolina could boast William "Bloody Bill" Cunningham, the personification of audacious, partisan warfare.

It took great courage to express a violently unpopular minority view, to undergo social ostracism, economic ruin, imprisonment, and to face sometimes even physical torture and death, all of which many met with great fortitude. Many Loyalists stuck to their position even when it was clear that they were, admittedly contrary to all their expectations, on the losing side. Scores of Loyalists (we have already mentioned the case of Achilles Preston) refused tempting offers of positions with the rebels. Further, many were Loyalists in spite of the lack of British encouragement, discussed above, and even in the face of British harassment.[77]

The American-born Tories (and some of the foreign-born) were every bit as American as their Whig brethren. They feared social change and any increase in the power of the democratic element in society, but one looks in vain for Loyalists who were opposed to liberty or the rights of Englishmen. Chief Justice Thomas Knox Gordon, a successful Irish immigrant to South Carolina, was not a hypocrite when he protested that "no Man wishes better to the Liberties of the Colonies." [78]

William Franklin, cursed with an open mind, no equipment for a patriot, was quite Whiggish in his attitude toward Britain, had a genuine if aristocratic regard for the well-being of New Jersey, and admitted that real American grievances existed. But he believed even more strongly in legitimacy and the British Empire, would not countenance riots or revolt, and despised members of the ruling class who did. He could not see why legal opposition was not enough. Addressing the New Jersey legislature in 1775 concerning the respective merits of peaceful redress or riotous agitation, he said: "You have now pointed out to you, Gentlemen, two Roads—one evidently leading to Peace, Happiness, and a Restoration of the Public Tranquility—the other inevitably conducting you to Anarchy, Misery, and all the Horrors of a Civil War." Franklin died in 1813, a forgotten exile in London, distrusted by both sides because he understood both sides.[79]

The great majority of Loyalists did not even favor the "new" English legislation after the Seven Years' War. The quarrel was over the *mode* of opposition; the Loyalists would not admit violence, and believed the future of their country would be ruined by revolution and independence. It was not a case of colonial rights or "passive obedience," but rather one of whether the colonies' future well-being could be best assured within the Empire or without. The Loyalists had a fundamental trust in Britain, the Whigs a fundamental distrust.[80]

At the end of the war a letter to Sir Guy Carleton from the Associated Loyalists bound for Port Roseway, Nova Scotia, invoked their devotion to the king and "that constitution, under which we had been particularly blest." Jacob Rundell of Cortlandt's Manor, New York, wrote that in joining the British he fled "from Usurpation to the best of Constitutions." The Reverend Charles Inglis considered the British constitution "the best political fabric that ever existed." [81] Beverley Robinson, Sr., of New York was loyal, he said, "not only to recover my Estate, but [to] have the happiness of contributing in restoring my Country to a Just mild and happy Constitution." Statements like these are common. And one did not need to have been particularly familiar with the subtleties of the British constitution (written and unwritten) to feel this way. Anthony Mosengeil, a German copper-mining expert resident in New Jersey, asserted that he joined the Loyalists, "being accustomed to regular and established Governments." An Alsatian Loyalist characterized the Americans as "deluded" and labeled their ways "Licentiousness," compared with the "true Liberty" of Britain.[82]

No one who studies the Loyalists for any length of time can doubt that there flourished, especially among the educated, a genuine, often touching zeal for British constitutional ways. Also, these Loyalists, in support of their position, pointed to the amazing growth and prosperity of the colonies within the Empire and to the great freedom already enjoyed—how much more could a reasonable man want? they asked—and many argued that, if anything, the power of the masses should be diminished.

Admiration for the British constitution was often closely allied with a belief in monarchism or even king-worship— usually worship from afar. But exiled Samuel Shoemaker of Philadelphia came away from an interview at Windsor Castle, conducted partly in German, enthralled by George III. Perhaps the meeting merely served to confirm long-held views.

> I cannot say, but I wished some of my violent Countrymen could have such an opportunity as I have had. I think they would be convinced that George the third has not one grain of Tyrany in his Composition, and that he *is* not, he *cannot* be that bloody minded man they have so repeatedly and so illiberally called him. It is impossible; a man of his fine feelings, so good a husband, so kind a Father *cannot be a Tyrant.*[83]

Constitutionalism is the reason why so many "thinking" Loyalists did not take a stand, indeed, often were Whigs, until independence was the issue.[84] Another pill, almost as difficult to swallow as independence, was that great *volteface,* the alliance between the rebels and the ancient enemy, the French, concluded in February, 1778. Rivington had a field day of sarcasm in his *Gazette.* Charles Inglis forecast the result would be to place Americans "under the despotic rule of our inveterate popish enemies, the inveterate enemies of our Religion our Country and Liberties." [85]

The towns contributed proportionately (but not in absolute numbers) more heavily to the Loyalist ranks than did the countryside. Appreciation of the ancient constitution and the dangers of the French denotes some sophistication. It was in the towns that sophistication was most likely to be found. Further, the towns were sites of the royal administrations, places of immigration and British occupation, homes of traders, professional men, and the wealthy in general.

By its policies in the years following 1763 the British Government can validly be regarded as the aggressor, the innovator, even the real revolutionary, because it upset the American *status quo*. Whig strength and Loyalist weakness is partially explained by the fact that several colonies were in practice almost *de facto* self-governing republics with few serious internal divisions, or at least none likely to create a dangerous Tory party.

As early as 1704 it was remarked that in Rhode Island "they did all things as if they were out of the dominions of the crown," and the same could be said of Connecticut.[86] Rhode Island's colonial charter served as the state constitution until 1843; Connecticut's, until 1818. Pennsylvania, with its vigorous tradition of religious and political freedom and its strong unicameral legislature independent of the proprietory governor, was a semiautonomous republic. Virginia and South Carolina were dominated by powerful planter-aristocrats who commanded wide popular support and thus, especially in the "Old Dominion," (Virginia), presented remarkably tenacious opposition to British encroachments. New Hampshire was another quite homogeneous colony and, uniquely, was never invaded by the British, which inhibited the growth of Loyalism. All these colonies, as they became states, were easily able to slough off the minority Tories without serious social disruption: New Hampshire ejected Governor Wentworth and his clique, many members of which were his relatives; Rhode Island lost a group headed by certain Newport merchants; Connecticut lost a few dissatisfied inhabitants of Fairfield County; Pennsylvania was more seriously weakened by the defection of talented and powerful, but not numerous, Loyalists from

Philadelphia and the surrounding area; Virginia, the most
unitedly Whig colony, simply ejected a number of foreign-
born merchants; South Carolina, with a few exceptions, lost
a large, but rather innocuous, immigrant group of farmers,
traders, and royal officials.

Serious political division often produced a Loyalist movement, and, of the above, Rhode Island's and Pennsylvania's
Loyalists were partly the products of colonial divisions.

Newport's Loyalist tradition stems from a rather shadowy
body called the Newport Junto, mainly immigrant Anglicans
and officeholders, such as Martin Howard, Jr., Dr. Thomas
Moffat, and George Rome, who deprecated the opposition to
the Sugar and Stamp Acts in 1764 and 1765, and generally
supported royal power against popular power. Howard and
Moffat fled during the Stamp Act riots, but the Junto's influence lingered on (to an extent with Governor Wanton's family, although the Governor himself was a moderate Whig),
but never at the heart of Rhode Island politics, which re-
volved around the rivalry between Samuel Ward and Stephen
Hopkins, both Whigs.

It should be added that Newport's position as the center
of Rhode Island Loyalism, as with most Loyalist areas, was
the result of a combination of factors. To the influence of the
Junto should be added the fact that Newport was the site of
the royal administration, had a good deal of trade within
the British Empire, was vulnerable to sea attack, and was
indeed occupied by the British. Further, Newport's behavior,
as we have mentioned, may have been influenced by fear of
its great rival, Providence, less vulnerable to sea attack and a
Whig stronghold.[87]

As described in the previous chapter, Massachusetts is the
great example of an area where the cleavage between actual
or potential Whigs and Loyalists developed early. During the
Stamp Act crisis the whole executive clique, in particular

Governor Bernard and Thomas Hutchinson, received an irreversible blow to its prestige.

From 1765 on, the chief political problems of the day—such as "rescinding," the Captain Preston trial, the nonimportation movement, the tea question, support of Hutchinson and Gage—served to divide Massachusetts society still further into Whigs and Tories. Moreover, the Revolutionary contest became intertwined with the perennial struggle between the "ins" (Hutchinson, the Olivers, and so on) and the "outs" (the two Adamses, Otis, and the rest of their faction).

The situation in New York was similar to that in Massachusetts, with the Tories again found among the "ins." As Van Tyne has put it, as the imperial quarrel deepened, polarization took place; the Loyalists "merged into the old Episcopal or DeLancey party, and all the opposition became identified with the Presbyterians or the Livingston party." The Tory party was partly a clan: the DeLanceys, DePuysters, Waltons, and Crugers were related "by blood or marriage to more than half of the aristocracy of the Hudson Valley." [88] The DeLanceys and Livingstons had been in constant opposition in the decades preceding the Revolution, and Van Tyne even maintains that the former were "forced" into the Loyalist side because their enemies were Whigs. The mixture of principle and expediency in politics is always difficult to measure, but one faction tends automatically to oppose what its rival favors. Flick notes that by 1770 the two parties were quite well defined, and that after that date every question became a party issue. However, apart from the ultra-Tories led by Governor Cadwallader Colden, the quarrel was still over the *mode*, not the question, of opposition. Both groups opposed the Stamp Act, and only Colden, typically, attempted to enforce it. The moderates continued to support most anti-British measures up to and including those proposed by the First Continental Congress, but at the Second Continental Congress only one of the five New York delegates supported independence.[89]

The Loyalists had great political strength in New York. On the eve of the Revolution, the twelve-man New York council was unanimously loyal. Only in New York did the Loyalists succeed in keeping control of the legislature, and indeed of the whole early revolutionary machinery, in particular the well-known Committee of Fifty-One and the election of delegates to the First Continental Congress (the assembly refused to elect any to the Second). This control was the result of the DeLancey party's machinations, but in the long run it proved of no avail. After Lexington the Whigs simply superseded the assembly with an extralegal convention, a provincial congress, although at first even it did not favor the Declaration of Independence.[90]

So far we have advanced rather broad analyses of the reasons for Loyalism among various groups, and we must not lose sight of the highly individual, personal nature of the decision to take the Loyalist side. This nature is suggested in many ways. Woodbury Langdon of New Hampshire remarked in connection with his rebel brother that "such a differance of sentiment between the nearest relations is far from being an uncommon circumstance in this unhappy civil war." [91] Certainly there are scores of examples of families that were divided over the issues of the Revolution. The most famous errant son is probably Benjamin Franklin's illegitimate Loyalist offspring, William. But in general the younger generation in divided families tended to be Whig. Sometimes even marriages were split. Elizabeth Henry of the Ninety-Six district of South Carolina was turned out by her Whig husband, and she later continued her royal ways by carrying intelligence for the British.[92]

Most leading Whigs had some loyal relatives, and most leading Loyalists had some rebel kinsmen. But humble examples are also easily found. A Negro Loyalist, Benjamin Whitecuff of New York, declared that his father took the opposite side.[93]

In a play published in 1857 a Whig daughter justifies her remaining home while her loyal father joins Sir William Howe with the words: "Your loyalty will secure you with the tories, and my whiggism will protect us with the other faction." [94] Several Tories, sometimes rightly, sometimes wrongly, were accused at the time of such opportunism. The Dulany family of Maryland were so charged, which led to a bloody duel in London's Hyde Park between Lloyd Dulany and the Reverend Bennet Allen, a Maryland clergyman.[95]

The many examples of members of the same business or firm (we have already mentioned merchant-partners in this regard) who presumably shared the same economic interests yet split on Revolutionary politics are another indication of individualism of motivation. However, here again there was sometimes suspicion of a deliberate decision to keep a foot in each camp.[96]

The best way to illustrate the personal nature of Loyalism is to look at a few individuals.

The Reverend Mather Byles, American-born and one of the few loyal Congregational clergymen, deserves brief mention. It seems that Byles lived in unprecedented intimacy (for one of his religion) with the royal officials of Massachusetts, and thus socially found himself a Loyalist. Further, the cultivated punster and poet in him was uncongenial even to the early Revolutionary developments. It is reported that in March, 1770, as Byles, with his friend Dr. Nathaniel Emmons, was watching the three-thousand-strong funeral procession of Crispus Attucks, a victim of the "Boston Massacre," Emmons dubbed the dead man "that half Indian, half negro,

and altogether rowdy, who should have been strangled long
before he was born." Byles retorted, "They call me a brain-
less Tory; but tell me, my young friend, which is better—to
be ruled by one tyrant three thousand miles away, or by three
thousand tyrants not a mile away?" [97] Byles was deprived in
1776 of the church position he had held for over forty years,
and died in 1788 in poverty and disgrace.[98]

The Reverend Jacob Duché, a native Philadelphian and
Anglican, was a Loyalist whose motives are worth consider-
ing in detail. At first he appeared to be a zealous, uncompli-
cated Whig. He attended the First Continental Congress in
1774 and conducted official prayers. On July 7, 1775, he
preached before a battalion of Philadelphia troops, deliver-
ing a sermon (later dedicated to George Washington) en-
titled *The Duty of Standing Fast in Our Spiritual and Tem-
poral Liberties*. On July 20, 1775, in a sermon before the
Congress he spoke of defending the American "hedges of Liberty" against British encroachment. Following the Declaration of Independence he accepted the position of chaplain to
the Congress, and his first prayer asked God to "defeat the
malicious designs of our cruel adversaries."

And so he continued, an esteemed Whig cleric, until the
bombshell of October 8, 1777, when he wrote to Washington
urging him to give up the struggle.

All shared Washington's astonishment and the incredulity
of Duché's brother-in-law, Francis Hopkinson, a signer of the
Declaration of Independence, who told Duché that he found
"it impossible to reconcile the matter, and style of this letter
with your general conduct, or with the virtues of your
heart. . . ." It should be noted that Duché's wife, her relatives, and Duché's father were all "violent" Whigs.[99] This,
said Samuel Shoemaker, "induced him to be Chaplain of
Congress." [100]

The fascinating question is why Duché had turned about.

Or had he been dissembling all along? Duché himself tried to argue at the end of the war that "he was always a Patriot and so continues," [101] that he had not expected the men of the Congress "to persist in their Independence." [102] His letter to Washington explained that he had accepted the chaplaincy of Congress hastily, "without consulting my friends," his motive being that "I thought the churches in danger, and hoped, by this means, to have been instrumental in preventing those ills I had so much reason to apprehend. . . ."

Perhaps his next words better explain his state of mind. The Congress had blundered and was confused; the "most respectable characters" had withdrawn and been "succeeded by a great majority of illiberal and violent men." In Pennsylvania the leaders "were so obscure, that their very names were never in my ears before, and others have only been distinguished for the weakness of their understandings, and the violence of their tempers." As for the New Englanders, "can you find one that, as a gentleman, you could wish to associate with? . . . Bankrupts, attorneys, and men of desperate fortunes. . . ."

Fear, one feels, rather than apprehension for his church, was the motivating force for Jacob Duché. October, 1777, when he resigned, was a bad time for the American cause. Writing to Washington after the war, Duché explained his "continual apprehensions for you and all my friends without the British lines. I looked upon all as gone; or that nothing could save you, but rescinding the Declaration of Independency." Hopkinson ascribed his brother-in-law's actions "to the timidity of your temper, the weakness of your nerves. . . ."

Hopkinson added to his list of factors "the undue influence of those about you," and Duché's letter to Washington hints at as much:

I wished to follow my countrymen as far only as virtue, and the righteousness of their cause would permit me. I was, however, prevailed on, among the rest of my clerical brethren of this city, to gratify the pressing desires of my fellow citizens by preaching a sermon to the second city battalion. . . . Further than this I intended not to proceed. . . .

But, of course, he did; he drifted on, weak, not really knowing where he stood, or possibly too aware of the subtleties of the situation, always noted for his gentle character, which perhaps accounts for his lack of steadfastness.

At the end of 1777 Duché fled to England, where he enjoyed a successful career, but when the war ended, he tried to get permission to return to the United States, and he wrote to Washington accordingly. In 1790 Duché did finally return to what was his true home and spent his remaining nine years in Philadelphia.[103]

Pennsylvania is one of the colonies that shows most signs of social conflict during the Revolution. Fear of this influenced some of the conservative well-to-do Loyalists. James Allen's diary shows this fear at work, apparently as the decisive factor in edging him from the Whig into the Tory camp. In May, 1772, he wrote, "I am at present much engaged in prosecutions for breaches of the laws of Trade and have libelled four or five Vessels and Cargoes for Captain Talbot of the Lively Man of War. I am doing as a Lawyer what I would not do as a politician; being fully persuaded of [the] oppressive nature of those laws."

Three years later, in July, 1775: "The Eyes of Europe are upon us; if we fall, Liberty no longer continues an inhabitant of this Globe: for England is running fast to slavery. The King is as despotic as any prince in Europe; the only difference is the mode; and a venal parliament are as bad as a standing army."

By October, 1775, he was cautiously drilling with the

American militia. "My Inducement principally to join them is; that a man is suspected who does not; and I chuse to have a Musket on my shoulders, to be on a par with them, and I believe discreet people mixing with them, may Keep them in Order." The same day he complained that "the most insignificant now lord it with impunity and without discretion over the most respectable characters."

Five months later, in March, 1776: "The plot thickens; peace is scarcely thought of—Independency predominant. Thinking people uneasy, irresolute and inactive. The Mobility triumphant. . . . I love the Cause of liberty; but cannot heartily join in the prosecution of measures totally foreign to the original plan of Resistance. The madness of the multitude is but one degree better than submission to the Tea-Act." Next month: "A Convention chosen by the people, will consist of the most fiery Independants; they will have the whole Executive and legislative authority in their hands. . . . I am determined to oppose them vehemently in Assembly, for if they prevail there; all may bid adieu to our old happy constitution and peace."

In 1777 a contemporary wit put the point nicely, writing of William Allen, Jr., who had been a lieutenant colonel in the American army, "which station he resigned—not because he was totally unfit for it, but because the Continental Congress presumed to declare the American States Free and Independent without first asking the consent, and obtaining the approbation of himself and wise family."

Henry Van Schaack was a crown officer whose loyalty was not ingrained. In fact this American-born official and merchant consistently opposed British policy after 1763, and only the question of independence drove him into Tory neutralism. Henry Cruger Van Schaack (a nephew) argued that his uncle's "great difficulty, and it was that which mainly deterred him from participating in the revolution (as declared by him to a friend in after life), was the oaths he had taken as a public officer." [104]

Peter Van Schaack, the lawyer brother of Henry, argued in an extremely subtle and learned fashion against the Declaration of Independence and armed rebellion, and attempted to remain neutral. Drawing largely on Locke, he wrote that his principles were "founded on the immutable laws of nature, and the sacred rights of man-kind," but he sympathized with much of the Whig cause, and supported nonimportation, nonconsumption, and the Continental Association. His neutralism separated him from what his son termed his "particular friends, John Jay, Egbert Benson, Theodore Sedgwick, and Gouverneur Morris," all of whom took the Whig side. Carl Becker has examined the subtle process that sent the two friends, John Jay and Peter Van Schaack, with similar backgrounds and views, into opposite camps. In short, Jay submitted to a *fait accompli;* Van Schaack followed his conscience.

William Smith, chief justice of New York and later of Quebec, is a good example of an intellectual Loyalist. However, in the beginning, he was aptly designated "an eighteenth-century Whig"; as a Yale-educated Presbyterian whose mother was a Livingston, he opposed the ruling (Anglican) DeLancey faction, and he was popular for his opposition to the stamp tax (for which he became known as "Patriotic Billy"), and indeed to all Parliamentary taxation and the Intolerable Acts, including the Quebec Act. However, he could not approve of independence, and maintained until the end his devotion to the British constitution, writing in 1788: "Every ecomium I ever read in its favour is short of my idea of its perfections . . . of all modes of government I pronounce it to be the best." [105]

Smith, incurring the deep suspicion of both sides, developed into a sensitive, "legalistic Tory," committed to the unity of the Empire (he approved of schemes along the lines of the Albany Plan, an attempt inspired by Benjamin Franklin, in 1754, to federate the colonies primarily for the purpose of coordinating Indian affairs) and the supremacy of Parliament. At the same time he denied Parliament's right to tax, shared most Whigs' views, and regarded the British as responsible for the Revolution. But armed revolt was an even greater crime than any wrongs inflicted by the British, and at length he was forced to choose the Tory side.[106]

Individual case histories could be amassed almost ad infinitum. The ferocious Colonel David Fanning of North Carolina appears to have favored the Whigs until robbed by a party of patriots.[107] John Adams wrote that Jonathan Sewall, a great friend and fellow lawyer, was seduced by Governor Hutchinson into the Loyalist camp.[108] This may be true, especially insofar as Sewall accepted several royal offices from 1767 onward. But it may be noted that at that time the event which alienated him from his Whig friends and acquaintances (James Otis in particular) was the refusal of the Massachusetts General Court to grant a petition concerning a badly managed estate that Sewall had inherited from an uncle.[109]

For evidence of Loyalist motivation I have drawn on what the Loyalists themselves said and on what other people have said about them, and I have made inferences from what I know about the period in general. The examples we have discussed have all lent themselves to some guesses at what may have prompted various people to choose the Loyalist side, but the question of motivation is one of the most vexing in all historiography, and we must beware of monolithic explanations. As the great English historian, R. H. Tawney, once wrote, "Only a charlatan will dogmatize on the welter of conflicting motives which find their agonizing issue in the choice of allegiance in a Civil War," [110] and we must admit that the revolution was in good part a civil war.

In general terms, we can say that most Loyalists had, or thought they had, something material or spiritual to lose from the break with Britain. This fear was the great unifying factor. Officials had their jobs to lose, lawyers their fees, merchants their trade, landowners their proprietorships, Anglicans their dream of a bishop, king-worshippers and aristocrats their idol, Anglophiles their membership in the Empire, some Regulators and Massachusetts Baptists their hope of royal help, Negroes their freedom, Indians the British alliance against the frontiersmen. Conservatives and the better-off in general had most to lose in a revolutionary upheaval; the timid became Loyalists in areas occupied by British troops; some officeholders, and perhaps the Highlanders, were loath to break their oaths of allegiance.[111]

But we must not claim that these explanations are exhaustive. Such matters as psychological pressures—say, alienation from one's Whiggish social circle for some personal, perhaps irrational, reason—usually remain hidden, even from the people involved, and hence far more so from a later writer. The Reverend Jonathan Boucher believed that personal considerations were paramount with the Whigs—"private grudges gave rise to public measures"—and this could equally be applied to the Loyalists. Unfortunately, Boucher added, these matters "lie beyond the reach of ordinary historians." [112]

And the remarks of these two Loyalists will illustrate the further difficulties—even impossibilities—inherent in the task of trying to ferret out motivations. Dr. Redmond Burke of North Carolina admitted that, although a genuine Loyalist, he joined the rebel army to extend "his professionary knowledge." Mathew Lymburner of Massachusetts was one of possibly a great many who "affected to be neutral in political disputes . . . but in private was a Loyalist." [113]

So far I have been generally assuming that the Tories made a fairly rational decision to remain loyal. But probably comparatively few took a reasoned position. Most colonists, like most people anywhere, followed their leaders. And most of the American leadership was Whig. This helps to explain why Loyalism barely existed in Virginia (thanks also, as we shall see, to the ill-advised efforts of the Loyalist colonial governor) and was strong in South Carolina, why it was stronger in New York than in Massachusetts.

Governors whose ability strengthened Loyalism in their respective colonies would certainly include James Wright of Georgia. However, ability and popularity were not always enough to bring a colony to the Loyalist side. In New Hampshire John Wentworth, despite great gifts, was unable to rally much of a Loyalist party; in Maryland John Eden was popular but a very lukewarm Loyalist (a trait shared by Lieutenant Governor John Penn of Pennsylvania). On the other hand strong action by able governors could sometimes do the Loyalist cause more harm than good. The two prime examples are Thomas Hutchinson, who came to be detested in Massachusetts, and Lord Dunmore, whose arming of Negroes and almost terroristic tactics alienated most of Virginia. In the vital early stages of the Revolution the two leading Loyalists in America were undoubtedly Hutchinson and Joseph Galloway, politicians who shared a fear of anarchic democracy and a desire for British support. Unfortunately for their cause, they did not share even a common acquaintanceship, far less a coordinated policy. Loyalist leadership remained confused and fragmentary. One looks in vain for that genius in organizing ability that characterized, in different ways, such Whigs as Samuel Adams or George Washington.[114]

Of all the Loyalists' endeavors their contribution to the British war effort was the most significant. It is to the war that we must now turn.

CHAPTER IV

"The Late Ill-Mannaged War"

&§ "Howe is as much deceived by you [Loyalists] as the American
cause is injured by you. He expects you will all take up arms,
and flock to his standard, with muskets on your shoulders. Your
opinions are of no use to him, unless you support him per-
sonally, for 'tis soldiers, and not tories that he wants."

Thomas Paine.[1]

It is not my intention to retell in any detail the story of the
war for American independence, which lasted from the Battle
of Lexington in April, 1775, until the signing of the peace
treaty at Paris in September, 1783. But a brief reminder of
some of the main events should serve as a useful background
against which to set the war role of the Loyalists, which is the
main subject of this chapter.

After the evacuation of Boston in March, 1776, the eventual failure of a patriot assault under General Richard Montgomery and Colonel Benedict Arnold on Canada in the
winter of 1775-1776, Governor Josiah Martin's defeat at
Moore's Creek Bridge, North Carolina, in February, 1776,
and the repulse of a British sea attack on Charleston, South
Carolina, in June, 1776, the primary scene of military operations shifted to New York, where General William Howe,

aided by his brother, the admiral, landed a large British army in the fall of 1776. Washington was unable to halt the British advance and was forced to make his famous retreat across New Jersey and take up a position at Trenton in December, 1776, while Howe remained on the other side of the freezing Delaware River. Two brilliant American victories by Washington at Trenton (December 25-26) and at Princeton (January 3, 1777) checked the British until the spring.

The British plan for 1777 was for General Howe to move against Philadelphia and there to meet an army under General John Burgoyne, which would have advanced from Montreal via Lake Champlain. Thus, having cut off New England and subdued the rebel headquarters of Philadelphia, the combined armies were to move south and complete the subjugation of the colonies. A nice plan, and Howe very tardily did reach Philadelphia in September, 1777, and he defeated Washington at Germantown. But in October, Burgoyne was surrounded by General Horatio Gates and Benedict Arnold at Saratoga in upstate New York and surrendered.

While Howe spent a rather convivial time in Philadelphia and Washington wintered rather less convivially at Valley Forge, the American victory at Saratoga convinced the French that the rebellion could succeed and helped clinch the alliance of February, 1778, which gave the Americans what almost certainly proved to be crucial French economic and military aid and recognition.

In the spring of 1778 Howe was replaced by Sir Henry Clinton, who because of the French threat was ordered to evacuate Philadelphia and march the army back across New Jersey to New York. New York, though ringed by patriot forces, remained the great British stronghold until the peace treaty, but major fighting had in fact ended in the North, and the British came to see their greatest hope in the South.

About two years of comparative stalemate followed (apart

from small actions and guerrilla warfare); the Americans failed to take Newport, which had been easily occupied by the British in December, 1777; and the British captured Savannah in December, 1778.

Then in May, 1780, Clinton and Charles, Lord Cornwallis, the second-in-command, occupied Charleston, South Carolina, with a large army, the idea being to sweep northward, restoring America to allegiance in the process. Cornwallis's victory over General Horatio Gates at Camden, South Carolina, in August, 1780, augured well, but in October Major Patrick Ferguson was badly defeated by back-country patriots at Kings Mountain, and in January, 1781, the British again suffered a reverse at the Battle of Cowpens, a reverse for which a brilliant but too costly victory over the Americans at Guilford Court House, North Carolina, in March did not fully compensate. Meanwhile General Horatio Greene and others to Cornwallis's rear were restoring the back country of Georgia and South Carolina to patriot control.

However, winter, 1780-1781, was in some ways the nadir for the rebel Americans. Cornwallis would be sure to carry on northward when spring came; the patriot army was tired and weak; and morale had not been raised by Benedict Arnold's defection. The French were decidedly pessimistic and were prepared to abandon their upstart allies.

But spring indeed was not far behind, and it proved to be a patriot spring. Cornwallis continued his expected advance through Virginia but unexpectedly, because of temporary French control of the sea by de Grasse, became hemmed in on the Yorktown peninsula, and finally on October 19, 1781, he was obliged to surrender. That proved to be the end of major fighting, although the peace was not signed for another two years.

Outside of actual military service there was much opportunity for the Loyalists to serve the British. In occupied areas they could forage or dig as sappers, make gunpowder and cartridges, serve under a paymaster or barrack master or with such civil departments of the army as the commissary, ordnance, or hospital, or join the various companies that helped police such occupied towns as Boston, Philadelphia, New York, Charleston, and Savannah. The prime example was Philadelphia, where Joseph Galloway, holding the office of Superintendent of the Port, vigorously organized the Loyalists into everything from spies to various volunteer patrols. In New York City there was similar activity, and productions at the Theatre Royal were frequently canceled because the Loyalist performers were out on duty.[2] In 1779 the British permitted Loyalists to commission privateers, and many were fitted out. Quite a number of seafaring Loyalists with their intimate local knowledge were invaluable to the British war fleets and landing parties as sea, lake, and river pilots. Several Loyalists were particularly useful in guiding British ships through the chevaux de frise (submerged obstacles) that guarded many American harbors. Thus they aided the British naval war; and on land many served as guides.

In unoccupied, or Whig, areas, Loyalists were used as what has since become known as a fifth column. They could spread frightening rumors, proselytize their neighbors, disseminate royal proclamations and offers of pardon that encouraged desertion, or even actively recruit. They helped escaping British prisoners and sometimes raided the mails.[3] Many Loyalists, by forwarding dispatches and the like, facilitated British communications. There was certainly an organized message service between New York and Canada.[4]

Some other less mundane, possibly more glamorous, service must be mentioned. Spying for both sides was comparatively easy in the sense that there was no language or nationality problem. An American, or indeed anyone who could possibly pass for an immigrant (and that included just about everyone), could not readily be distinguished as a Loyalist or a patriot. Naturally, both sides set up an espionage or intelligence system, and a recent student of the subject concludes that both sides were served about equally well,[5] but in the Revolution, as in most conflicts, espionage was largely irrelevant to the outcome.

The Loyalists were obvious spy material, and no less a person than Count Rumford spied for General Gage. Innumerable refugees quoted their supplying of alleged intelligence as proof of loyalty, but of course intelligence has to be sifted and acted upon intelligently, a well-nigh impossible task.

There was the usual spying ritual. At Worcester, Massachusetts, the identifying gambit was to ask what was for breakfast, to which the fitting (or was it equivocal?) reply was, "Tea or anything else." There were the usual celebrated turncoats (who chose "freedom," as the phrase went a few years ago), most notably Benedict Arnold, whose name rightly has become a synonym for treachery; the usual "double agents," for example, Dr. Benjamin Church of Boston, who communicated information to the British while a member of Paul Revere's Whig spy ring; even the inevitable woman, Mrs. Ann Bates, an ex-Philadelphia schoolteacher who has been boldly dubbed by John Bakeless "the most successful female spy in history" for her ability to gather military information, which she did disguised as a peddler; also the usual wild, dramatic plots, in particular a scheme to kidnap George Washington in New York; the tragic-romantic execution of an attractive figure, most notably Major André, Arnold's unfortunate go-between; and more soberingly the usual executions of obscure, humdrum, often pathetic spies. Here is a typical news item from a colonial newspaper:

Chatham, November 9. Last Monday morning was taken at Rahway, concealed in a barn, Thomas Long, alias Bunkeye, a noted villain for his cruelties to many of our prisoners, and who has been active in carrying off several of the inhabitants.

He was found without arms, therefore could be considered in no other light but as a spy, for which he was tried, found guilty, and received sentence of death, which was duly executed on Thursday last.[6]

Perhaps the most distinguished Tory spy of all was James Moody, a native of New Jersey, who left a "narrative" of his "exertions" for the British and so convinced the British claims commissioners that he received generous recompense for his loyalty. Moody was a swashbuckling Scarlet Pimpernel whose activities, though they included a great deal of espionage work, bold rescues, and daring kidnapping, encompassed the whole gamut of Loyalist war activity—engagements as a lieutenant in Cortlandt Skinner's New Jersey Regiment, guerrilla and plundering raids, robbing the rebel mails. His young brother was executed at Philadelphia in 1781 after having tried to break into the Statehouse, and Moody himself, having been hounded and taken prisoner after capturing, with a mere seven men, eighteen important New Jersey rebels, only avoided execution by escape.[7]

But few spies lived the romantic life of Moody. The pedestrian side of espionage is suggested by James Van Emburgh of New Jersey, who was an agent for two years; "then finding that laying out of Nights proved hurtful to his Constitution," he joined the quartermaster's department.[8]

Interference with the money supply (clipping the edges of coins, forging, and so on) is an ancient criminal activity, but the British were the first in history to use counterfeiting as an economic weapon, an idea possibly suggested by Dr. Benjamin Church, the Massachusetts spy, and his brother-in-law, John Fleming, a printer.[9]

The Loyalists were considerably involved in the manufacture and dissemination of counterfeit continental money, an activity in which the British placed some confidence and which the patriots treated very seriously. A future governor of New Hampshire wrote of one notable passer of counterfeit money in that state: "Damn him . . . I hope to see him hanged. He has done more damage than ten thousand men could have done." [10] In Rhode Island, apparently for being involved with a counterfeiting operation, Mrs. Charles Slocum was pilloried and branded on both cheeks, and her ears were cut off, a ferocious punishment even for a man by the standards of the day.[11] Rewards were given for the capture of counterfeiters—in July, 1777, John McKinley, the president of Delaware, offered such a reward, in the amount of three hundred dollars,[12] and judging from the space devoted to counterfeiting in the patriot newspapers, it was a real problem. For example, in July, 1777, the state newspapers were asked to print a detailed description of forged eight-dollar bills.[13]

The counterfeiting problem was increased by the fact that the forging of money required less skill than it does now, owing to the more primitive printing techniques employed in the production of legitimate bills; the greatest difficulty for the counterfeiter was obtaining the right paper, but even that could be purchased quite legally.[14]

The full extent of the Loyalist involvement in counterfeiting is not known, and perhaps never will be. Many areas await research. However, several claimants mentioned counterfeiting to the claims commissioners. Two outstanding examples are Isaac Clemens, a New York silversmith, who said he had counterfeited £2,000,000 in paper money, adding rather plaintively that he had gotten no payment except the "pleasure of having distressed and confused the rebels" (perhaps he was expected to provide his own payment!), and George Smith, an engraver and jeweler from Jamaica, New York, who was employed "to engrave Plates to imitate Paper Money of the Americans." [15]

New Hampshire had a considerable counterfeiting operation,[16] and in Worcester County, Massachusetts, there were thirty-nine wartime convictions involving counterfeiting. The reason for all this activity here was that Jonathan Bush of Shrewsbury, Massachusetts, kept a hotel that was a distributing center. The hotel was on a Tory route to New York and remained the counterfeiters' headquarters throughout the war.[17] As early as January, 1776, forging had begun on a British ship in New York Harbor, and by April, 1777, the Loyalist Hugh Gaine's *Gazette* was carrying the following advertisement:

> Persons going into other Colonies may be supplied with any Number of counterfeit Congress-Notes, for the Price of the Paper per Ream. They are so neatly and exactly executed that there is no Risque in getting them off, it being almost impossible to discover, that they are not genuine. This has been proved by Bills to a very large Amount, which have already been successfully circulated.
>
> Enquire for Q.E.D. at the Coffee-House, from 11 p.m. to 4 a.m. during the present month.[18]

Thomas Anburey later noted that several persons who had availed themselves of this offered counterfeit money had bought plantations with it in Virginia.[19]

The British and the Loyalists (aided by simple criminal counterfeiters who continued pre-Revolutionary activity) won the battle of the currencies. Inflation reached the ludicrous proportions recently made familiar by most European currencies in the wake of the Second World War—Washington complained to John Jay that "a wagon-load of money will scarcely purchase a wagon-load of provisions." [20] British gold was preferred to the Continental paper currency even by the patriots, many of whom traded with the British, and "Not worth a Continental" became a stock phrase for worthlessness. Counterfeiting was an irritant, but without it the American paper money would still have depreciated and the Congress's serious financial problems would have remained.

As the *Annual Register* for 1779 expressed it: "Money is justly considered as the great sinew of war; and its want necessarily cramped all the military operations of the Americans." [21] If everything had turned on American governmental economic strength, the British would have crushed the Revolution easily.

A brief word must be added concerning ladies and the war. Women, both Whig and Tory, had opportunities to collect money (for example, a loyal New York group financed the appropriately named privateer, *The Fair American*), weave, spin, and "make do" on the home front, which sometimes meant harvesting crops and supervising the family property while husbands were absent. Women embroidered flags, nursed the wounded, buried the dead. Loyalists (and even some patriotic addicts) gathered to drink tea, known to Whigs since the Boston Tea Party as a "noxious weed." The younger Peter Oliver noted in Boston a "Club composed of 8 ladies. They meet over a tea table once or twice a week, in opposition to the Rebells. They keep up their spirits strangely." [22]

By generally supporting the menfolk, women could contribute much to male morale. But some lady Loyalists possibly went too far. Several were attracted to British officers, and a few became their mistresses. Tom Paine even charged that New York prostitutes were unanimously loyal.[23] He may have been right, for the British had more hard cash than the Americans. In Boston native-born Mrs. Dorcas Griffiths, notoriously known as a "Common prostitute," deserted John Hancock for a British marine officer and finally, in London. gained a Loyalist pension.[24]

In 1778 a Frenchman inquired about "the artifices and subterfuges, with which the Tories kept alive each others hopes." [25] Today, historians are acutely aware of the power of the written and spoken word in any conflict: propaganda, if you like. The American Revolution was the first rebellion in modern history where the battle of words was of particular importance, because for the first time a large literate population, well and traditionally served by newspapers, pamphlets, and orators, was involved. It is appropriate, therefore, before discussing the military war, to glance at the propaganda war.

Newspapers were the most important medium in the battle of words, a medium dominated from the start by the Whigs. The Stamp Act, which threatened the very existence of newspapers, first galvanized their owners into sustained opposition to British policy. From then on many of the famous Whig pamphlets first appeared in the newspapers; for example, John Dickinson's influential *Letters from a Farmer in Pennsylvania* . . . began as twelve articles in the *Pennsylvania Chronicle* (1767-1768), which then, as normally happened, were widely reprinted in other journals.

A few newspapers were inclined to the British viewpoint, but not one was *consistently* friendly before the military occupation at the beginning of the Revolution. As the crisis deepened, even sympathetic printers (as the owner-printer-editors were known) came under increasing pressure to banish any Tory, or even neutral, opinion from their columns. At the early date of 1770 John Mein's distinctly Tory *Boston Gazette* folded from lack of patronage. Loyal editors faced violence as well as boycott. As the claims commissioners said later, the printer's trade was "more dangerous . . . than the sword." [26] By 1774 only Boston and New York had anything like a Loyalist press, and by the end of 1775 only that in New York remained.

With the war the concept of a free press disappeared (each side, with justification, accused partisans of the other side of being "public liars" [27]), and most of the forty or so American newspapers became outright Whig organs. Isaiah Thomas, probably the greatest American journalist of the age, had steered his *Massachusetts Spy* from comparative neutrality to staunch Whiggery by the time of Lexington. The best Northern newspaper, Benjamin Ede and John Gill's *Boston Gazette,* was always a patriotic vehicle for Samuel Adams and his chums, while the best Southern paper, the *South Carolina Gazette,* was also perennially Whig.

British military protection made it possible to set up a number of Tory printers, and as many as fifteen papers finally appeared at some time in this way. The greatest Loyalist journalist (and the only important printer of Tory pamphlets from all over America) was James Rivington. An immigrant Londoner, he was forced by Whig violence to close his New York *Gazetteer* in 1775, but after the arrival of the British it was reborn in 1777 as the *Royal Gazette,* and throughout the war this was *the* great Loyalist newspaper for all the colonies, partly because New York was the Loyalist capital. The city even boasted two more loyal publications, one of which was Hugh Gaine's *New York Mercury.* Gaine, after a brief Whiggish spell in 1776, printed the paper under British aegis from 1776 until 1783. Similarly, in Philadelphia James Humphreys, a pioneer book publisher, resurrected his *Pennsylvania Ledger* (closed by the Whigs at the end of 1776) from December, 1777, to May, 1778, after which he fled with the departing British troops. Other papers (of rather less importance) nurtured by British occupation include the *News-Letter* (run for a while by Margaret Draper after her husband's death), which appeared in Boston at the beginning of the hostilities, and the *Royal Gazette* and the *Royal Georgia Gazette,* published in Charleston and Savannah toward the close.[28]

Starting in 1765 with Martin Howard, Jr., of Newport's

A Letter from a Gentleman at Halifax . . . , Loyalist views were represented by several able pamphleteers, most of them Northern Anglicans. The Reverend Samuel Seabury was possibly the best, as shown by his *Letters of a Westchester Farmer* (1774-1775), a clever protest against the Association that stressed the hurt to the farmers and argued that real freedom lay in maintaining the British connection. Seabury was abetted by his fellow clerics, Myles Cooper and Charles Inglis (author of a good reply to *Common Sense*), in New York, and by Thomas Bradbury Chandler in New Jersey, all powerful writers, who together mounted the earliest, most sustained, and only coordinated Loyalist counterattack against the Whigs (a fight partly the result of the Northern Anglican desire for an American bishopric, the demand for which was growing stronger even without the Revolutionary crisis).

Massachusetts produced two worthy non-Anglican propagandists, Jonathan Sewall and Daniel Leonard, both vigorous proponents of Loyalism in the *Massachusetts Gazette,* the latter crossing swords as *Massachusettensis* with John Adams as *Novanglus* in a famous written debate on the main Anglo-American issues of 1774-1775. Joseph Galloway, a dissenter from Philadelphia, was, after 1775, a most prominent Tory and the most tireless pamphleteer and Loyalist spokesman throughout the Revolutionary period and beyond.

The South notably lacked Tory propagandists, though James Chalmers of Maryland may be mentioned for his *Plain Truth,* a reply to Paine's *Common Sense.*[29] Also, 1774 had seen the publication of *A Letter from a Virginian,* a critique of the First Continental Congress, conceivably written by the Reverend Jonathan Boucher.

There is no doubt that the Loyalists were largely outclassed as writers, just as they were outfought as soldiers. Two Loyalists alone (both Anglicans) excelled in their respective fields: the Reverend Jonathan Odell of New Jersey was prob-

ably the best satirist of the period; Joseph Stansbury of Penn-
sylvania was probably the best poet. But in general the
Loyalists could not match the Whigs, who could boast such
prose writers, to name only a few, as John and Samuel Adams,
Josiah Quincy, Joseph Warren, William Livingston, John
Dickinson, John Witherspoon, and, the greatest of all, Tom
Paine; and such poets as Philip Freneau and Francis Hop-
kinson.

It was not just because the Whigs had more and better
talent, controlled many of the printers, and stamped out
criticism—or because the British had earlier failed to impose
controls on the Whig press—that the Loyalists lost the war of
words. As always in a national crisis, a sense of patriotism
prevented many citizens from even listening to the other
side. On December 29, 1774, Rivington's *Gazette*, during its
more neutral phase, had a patriot called "Ickabod" recount
that he accidentally read a portion of a Tory pamphlet, "but
as soon as ever I found what side of the question they
espoused, I threw it down determined never to read another
line of it."

But even when Loyalist arguments got a hearing, they
lacked the appeal of those of the Whigs. In the end the Whigs
were able to present independence, religious and civil liberties as easily grasped, exciting concepts sanctioned by God,
law, tradition, and clear self-interest. Brilliant use was made
of atrocity stories, from the so-called "Boston Massacre" of
1770 to accounts of the notorious wartime prison ships. Hate
was cleverly focused, pre-eminently by Paine, on the person
of George III.

In contrast, Loyalist arguments centered on vague or dull,
complicated, legalistic schemes (which, in truth, were sometimes too sophisticated for popular consumption), like Galloway's plan for reform within the Empire; the Loyalist picture
of a beneficent king and mother country became increasingly

unconvincing with growing British military occupation. It is not surprising that several leading Loyalists, such as Seabury, Sewall, and Leonard, faded as writers after 1775. And, of course, events made a radical stand in the sixties quite conservative ten years later. Also it may be noted that a few excellent Loyalist authors did not publish until after the troubles were over. Thus the account of the Revolution by the Anglican divine from Maryland, Jonathan Boucher, did not appear until 1797, and his *Reminiscences* was delayed until 1925; Crèvecoeur's *Letters of an American Farmer* came out in 1782, but his more specifically Loyalist *Sketches* was also delayed until 1925.

The Loyalists were weakened by the fact that they didn't have to defend Loyalism per se before 1775 or 1776, because until then most Whigs were "loyal." Also, future Tory printers—Rivington, Gaine, and the others—sincerely tried to let all shades of opinion have a voice. (Rivington printed not only Seabury, but also Alexander Hamilton; not only *Massachusettensis*, but also *Novanglus*.) This is not surprising, because most Loyalists agreed with the Whigs that in the ten years before independence the British had committed serious infringements on American liberties, and both sides continued to draw from the common stock of Locke, Harrington, Sydney, Blackstone, Montesquieu, *et al*. Thus many able Loyalist writers only really displayed their talents in these early years, but on the Whig side—for example, John J. Zubly in Georgia and Daniel Dulany, author in 1765 of a famous pamphlet opposing British taxation in Maryland. Perhaps a sign of the weak foundations of Loyalism was that as war hopes dimmed in 1781, even such an apparent stalwart as Rivington secretly became one of Washington's spies.[30]

As the war continued, much Tory writing, with its aristocratic hauteur, lacked popular appeal. There were constant sneering references to the vulgar origins of the patriot leaders ("General Convict," "Colonel Shoeblack") and repeated, ironically self-defeating forecasts of the imminent collapse of the rebellion, to be caused by depreciating Continental currency, natural republican anarchy and incompetence, or victory for the manifestly superior British forces. The doctrinally inconsistent French alliance of 1778 gave the Loyalists, especially Rivington, a field day, and Tory denunciations of the move may have increased patriot unease at the embrace of the ancient Catholic enemy. But actually, all the Loyalists could do after July 4, 1776, was make witticisms, score debating points. Only by military victory could their views have prevailed.

The American Whig historian of the time, David Ramsay, sagely wrote that "in establishing American independence, the pen and the press had merit equal to that of the sword." [31] The decade and a half before the Declaration of Independence does indeed bear witness to the crucial role of Whig writers, but when it comes to actual victories, the pen is never mightier than the sword. The Loyalist propagandists during the war could not have changed its outcome even if they had been greatly superior to their Whig adversaries; as it happened, they were distinctly inferior.

Finally, it must be added that the propaganda battle was not confined to the printed word.[32] There were sermons; lay orations; the deliberations and the motions of the legislatures, courts, private clubs, and revolutionary committees; word-of-mouth rumors; rousing songs, slogans, and catch phrases. In such oral propaganda the Whigs again usually outclassed the Loyalists. There were some powerful Anglican preachers, but on the whole they were no match for the "Black Regiment" of Dissenters. The Tories produced no popular orator like James Otis, no brilliant agitator like Samuel Adams; at best they could show an able debater like Thomas Hutchinson or a witty cleric like Mather Byles, but such men could not sway the masses (nor did they intend to). The Whigs retained control of all the legislatures except New York's and of most of the apparatus of government everywhere, so the best the Loyalists could do was in some places to gather signatures for petitions or make feeble attempts at forming their own committees and associations. Taverns, those places of gossip, toasts, and song, remained predominantly Whig. As for popular demonstrations, where ideas were expressed not in words but in visual symbols (effigies, Liberty trees, poles, flags), or in terms of actions (as on fast days) or the remembrance of events (as on anniversaries), the Loyalists, by their very nature, did not try to compete.[33]

Spying, counterfeiting, forging, privateering, policing, and pamphleteering are, however, somewhat on the periphery. And while it is true that, by their auxiliary and nonmilitary functions, the Loyalists did free British soldiers for the front, and, conversely, tied up patriot troops by occasioning a fear of insurrection in areas of Tory strength, it remains for us to investigate just how many fighting men the Loyalists actually contributed. Quantitative estimates vary considerably. During the course of the whole war the number of Loyalists who fought on a regular basis for the king, at every rank from drummer boy to field officer, has been put at between 30,000 and 50,000. Many others served in the militia or with irregular guerrilla bands. In 1780 perhaps 8,000 Loyalists were in the regular army, at a time when Washington's forces numbered only about 9,000. Some Loyalists took part in almost every important engagement of the war.[34] A recent scholar maintains that during the war over 15,000 served in the Provincial Line (that is, local American regiments raised as part of the British army), that from December, 1780, until the end of the war the provincial corps maintained a strength of 10,000, and that probably a further 10,000 served in the militia and other units.[35]

In the course of the war at least 312 companies in fifty separate provincial corps were commissioned,[36] and several Loyalist regiments and individual Loyalist commanders fought with distinction. Those worth particular mention include the following: General Cortlandt Skinner, whose New Jersey Volunteers was the largest of the Loyalist regiments; General Oliver DeLancey, the senior Loyalist officer in the British army in America, who raised 1,500 men in a Refugee Corps that played a decided part in the Southern campaign and pillaged the New York area; Benedict Arnold, a man who showed the best of his undoubtedly great ability on the rebel side, but who led a successful British expedition in 1780 into the James Valley, Virginia, burning Richmond, and the next year as a diversion attacked New London, Connecticut, in an essentially unimportant though vicious raid in which the defenders at Fort Griswold were massacred and the town put to the torch; Colonel John Graves Simcoe, who commanded the Queen's Rangers of New York with distinction at the Battle of the Brandywine, September, 1777, and in various exploits in New Jersey and Virginia, during the course of which the Rangers killed or took prisoner twice their own number in patriot soldiers; and Colonel John Hamilton, raiser of 1,400 North Carolina Volunteers (who saw action in South Carolina and Georgia as well as their home state), a leader to whom, as Charles Stedman, a contemporary historian of the Revolution, wrote, "the British nation owed more, perhaps . . . than to any other individual Loyalist in the British service." [37] There is no doubt that the best Loyalist troops were the equal of any the patriots produced.

The above mainly represent regular fighting units, but the Loyalists were more effective in local or guerrilla fighting. New York produced a small galaxy in this field that included

Sir John Johnson, the famous Indian agent and commander of the Loyal Greens (made up mostly of Scottish immigrants); Colonel John Butler and his Tory Rangers; and their Indian ally, the religious Mohawk chieftain, Joseph Brant, who kept most of the Six Nations loyal, with the exception of the Oneidas and Tuscaroras. These men and their followers were a constant threat to the entire New York frontier and Canadian border area, and out of Niagara, under a British colonel, Barry St. Leger, inflicted heavy patriot losses in an ambush at Oriskany in upstate New York, August, 1777. The next year two outlying areas, the Wyoming Valley in Pennsylvania and the Cherry Valley in New York, were ravaged by Butler, aided by Brant in the latter case. Butler, because of the excesses of the Indians, has traditionally been hated in the United States, and D. W. Griffith made him the "heavy" in his last great epic film, *America*. However, a recent scholar concludes that Butler's black reputation is "almost wholly unsubstantiated." [38]

In Georgia the leader of the Creek Indians, Lachlan McGillivray, with his son Alexander, of later fame, helped keep his tribe fairly loyal. John Stuart, the Southern Indian superintendent, raised the Cherokees against the Carolina back country, but unfortunately they massacred Loyalists and rebels alike.

The Indians were never going to turn the tide of war, but they added an element of extra bitterness to the fighting because of the many "atrocities" they committed. There was some hypocrisy in American complaints about the Indians, because the patriots were glad to use them when they could. The Tories treated the Indians gingerly. Several claimants admitted having fought with the patriots against "friendly" Indians on the borders of the Carolinas, an act they considered entirely different from fighting against the regular British forces.

Generally the South outdid even New York in the violence of its partisan warfare, and it produced several fierce warriors, predecessors in a way of better-known nineteenth-century figures such as Jesse James. For example, in South Carolina William Cunningham was known and feared as "Bloody Bill" for his exploits in the back country, and in Georgia Thomas Browne had a deserved reputation as a "sanguinary" officer.[39] But North Carolina supplied perhaps the most ferocious Loyalist soldier of all in Colonel David Fanning, a native American who "commanded a number of free-booters . . . much feared by the Rebels," as one Tory put it in understatement. His exploits included a raid in September, 1781, on Hillsboro in which he captured Governor Thomas Burke and his council. Fanning fought until the bitter end, ceasing only when he got news of Cornwallis's surrender at Yorktown.[40]

Several British officers led Loyalist, or predominantly Loyalist, troops effectively. Young Lord Francis Rawdon, styled "the ugliest man in England," [41] commanded the Volunteers of Ireland—largely made up of Irish Loyalists, including deserters from the patriot army—who had some success in the Southern campaign, especially at the battle of Camden in August, 1780.

Pre-eminent among British leaders of the Loyalists were Major Patrick Ferguson and Colonel Banastre Tarleton, who also made their reputations in the Southern campaign. Ferguson's bold, successful career in the South Carolina back country was cut short when his American Riflemen were defeated and he himself was killed at King's Mountain in October, 1780; while Tarleton, who, like Ferguson, had been a great success at the siege of Charleston, led his famous Tory legion of cavalry victoriously and bloodily across South Carolina, notably in the massacre of Colonel Abraham Buford's force at Waxhaws, May, 1780, at the battle of Camden in

August, and in the defeat, a couple of days later, of General Thomas Sumter. But like Ferguson's Riflemen, Tarleton's forces finally met a decisive setback when at Cowpens, January, 1781, they were overwhelmed in a brilliant action by the patriot heroes, Daniel Morgan's riflemen. Unlike Ferguson, Tarleton escaped with his life, and he was later heard of in Virginia, where he made an audacious attempt to capture Jefferson at Monticello.

The Loyalists were important in a good deal of the major fighting, especially in the South, normally alongside the British and the Hessians, and occasionally, as at Kings Mountain, by themselves (though their commander, Ferguson, was British). The activity in which Loyalists were predominant was partisan fighting or small raids, such as Governor Dunmore's against the Virginia coast in 1776; Governor William Tryon's against Danbury, Connecticut, in 1777, and against Fairfield and New Haven in 1779; Butler's against Cherry Valley in 1778; and Arnold's against New London, Connecticut, in 1781.

In a way the symbolic Tory activity was the kidnapping raid—semimilitary, cloak-and-daggerish, sometimes ludicrous, peripheral to the main action, more likely to irk than really hurt the enemy. Fanning's capture of Governor Burke has already been mentioned. Other examples include the seizure and imprisonment in November, 1776, of Richard Stockton, a signer of the Declaration of Independence, by a Tory band in Monmouth County, New Jersey; [42] and Joseph Galloway's plan to capture the governor of New Jersey, William Livingston, and his council at Trenton, and later his plot to capture the entire Congress! [43] The most famous plot of all, occurring in the summer of 1776, involved Governor Tryon and Mayor David Mathews and aimed at kidnapping Washington in New York City—Mathews "tampered," as he put it, with the general's guards, but a careless letter gave the show away. [44]

A fairly minor factor in the war, but one that must be mentioned, is the approximately half million Negroes, mostly slaves, who lived in America and whom neither side could ignore. The British, with least to lose, took the initiative in recruiting Negroes. In 1779 Sir Henry Clinton proclaimed freedom for all rebels' slaves who deserted to the British, an offer originally made in 1775 in Virginia by Lord Dunmore.[45] As the war progressed, the Whigs were forced to follow suit. Some Negroes took part in most of the important Revolutionary battles, and in a few outstanding exploits, but the Negro was not decisive for either side. The arming of fugitive slaves by the British caused great concern among the Americans and may have made Whigs of some. For both sides Negroes were less important as troops than as auxiliaries—to spy, act as guides, serve as builders, drive wagons, and generally help behind the lines (here Negro women often served as nurses). Many Loyalists put their slaves on board privateers, and several skilled Negroes were valuable as pilots.

The most important aspect of the Loyalist military involvement, in whatever form, was that it turned the war into a civil war. Contemporaries were agreed on the unfortunate results of this. A writer in Rivington's *Gazette* began with the observation that "civil wars are the most cruel and bloody, and attended with circumstances of peculiar horror" and devoted a long article to the theme, while in London the *Annual Register* pronounced with reference to America that "civil wars are unhappily distinguished from all others, by a degree of rancour in their prosecution, which does not exist in the hostilities of distinct nations, and absolute strangers."[46]

The horrors of civil war can be well illustrated by a detailed account of the engagement on October 7, 1780, at Kings Mountain, South Carolina, where all the combatants except the Loyalist commander, Ferguson, were Americans.

At noon about nine hundred tough patriot backwoodsmen,

armed with deadly Deckhard rifles, reached Kings Mountain, where Major Patrick "Bull Dog" Ferguson, an intrepid Scottish Highlander, had deployed his force of about 1,100 Loyalists. One month earlier the "Bull Dog" had marched out from Ninety-Six, then proceeded up the Broad River toward Charlotte, North Carolina, where he was supposed to rendezvous with General Cornwallis. But the local hill-folk gathered, ominiously massing themselves against him, and he had to abandon this objective, retreat, and seek the apparent safety of the steep, 60-foot-high stony spur of the Kings Mountain range of the Blue Ridge, which provided a formidable 500-yard-long natural fortress from where "he defied God Almighty and all the rebels out of hell to overcome him."

The patriots, skilled in Indian fighting, dismounted and surrounded the narrow spur. At about three o'clock in the afternoon they began the battle with a war whoop as they made their way up the declivity, using trees and scrub for cover. Many removed their hats and tied handkerchiefs around their heads as protection against the mass of branches.

Colonel Cleveland, one of the patriot commanders, is supposed to have exhorted his men thus: "My brave fellows, we have beat the Tories, and we can beat them. They are all cowards. If they had the spirit of men, they would join with their fellow-citizens in supporting the independence of their country."

Atop the hill, Major Ferguson relied on bayonet charges to repel the patriots, but with only temporary success.

The crack-shot backwoodsmen, one of their leaders crying, "Damn the Tories," finally gained the summit, and a bloody, disorganized, hand-to-hand melee ensued with the Loyalists soon getting the worst of it. Ferguson desperately cut down two unauthorized white flags and had two horses shot from under him, before he was shot dead in a final suicidal charge. He must have realized that he could expect little mercy because of his earlier provocative behavior, especially the plundering and ravaging of western South Carolina.

When the weary, beaten Loyalists, now led by Abraham DePuyster (of the old and distinguished New York family), raised a white flag and asked for quarter, they received the vengeful, chilling reply, "Tarleton's quarter!"—that is, no quarter, in acknowledgment of Tarleton's massacre of patriots at the battle of Waxhaws, North Carolina, earlier in the year.

The patriot commanders, Colonels Shelby, Campbell, Sevier, McDowell, and Cleveland, were powerless to stop the killing for some time, as old scores, the baneful legacy of civil war, were paid off. Finally discipline was restored, and Colonel Campbell ordered "three huzzas for Liberty." One hundred fifty-seven Loyalists lay dead, 163 seriously wounded, and 698 were taken prisoner, while the patriots had lost a mere 28 men plus 62 wounded. Ferguson had disastrously misjudged the use of the hilltop. As one of the patriot attackers, James Collins, later wrote: "Their great elevation above us had proved their ruin; they overshot us altogether, scarce touching a man except those on horseback, while every rifle from below seemed to have the desired effect." Collins continued: "Next morning, which was Sunday, the scene became really distressing. The wives and children of the poor Tories came in, in great numbers. Their husbands, fathers and brothers lay dead in heaps, while others lay wounded or dying, a melancholy sight indeed!"

But the killing was not at an end. A week after the battle, while the patriots and their captives were encamped at Rutherfordton, Colonel William Campbell was informed that there were many parole-breakers, criminals, and murderers among the Loyalist prisoners. A demand went up for justice and for revenge for previous executions of patriot prisoners by such as Tarleton. A drumhead court convicted forty of the prisoners, condemned twelve to death, and in the evening, by torchlight, actually hanged nine of them, three at a time, from an oak tree.

Meanwhile, at Kings Mountain, the dead had been buried

. . . but it was badly done. They were thrown into convenient piles and covered with old logs, the bark of old trees, and rocks, yet not so as to secure them from becoming prey to the beasts of the forests, or the vultures of the air. And the wolves became so plenty, that it was dangerous for anyone to be out at night, for several miles around. The hogs in the neighborhood gathered into the place to devour the flesh of man, inasmuch as numbers chose to live on little meat rather than eat their hogs, though they were fat.[47]

Bitter clashes between Whigs and Tories can be found in every colony. Occasionally these were set battles between regular troops, as at Kings Mountain, but more often they took the form of guerrilla fights. These fights were more than normally bitter when postbattle trials and executions were added, as they often were, especially by the patriots. If the British had held to the tenable view that all patriots were traitors, mass extermination of prisoners would have followed. This did not happen, but as a correspondent in Rivington's *Gazette* complained, patriots who made predatory raids on Tory areas called themselves heroes and if captured were treated as prisoners of war, while the Loyalists were denounced as traitors and murderers and stood to get executed if taken.[48] This was no hyperbole. At about the same time a Whig paper reported that in New Jersey a band of plundering Tories were "way layed by a party of armed men who put the whole to death on the spot."[49]

Cornwallis's sweep through the South, 1780-1781, was marked by as bitter civil war as one could find in the whole conflict, but it was in New York City that the Loyalists became best organized and even took the law into their own hands. In April, 1780, Clinton authorized a "Board of Directors of the Associated Loyalists" (or Refugees, as they were also known), presided over by William Franklin, to look after the Loyalists' interests and coordinate their activity.[50] This activity included political and social matters, and apart from British support (loyal members were given arms, money, and small sailing craft), the Board raised funds through a public lottery.[51]

The Board was best known, however, for "annoying the coasts of the revolted Provinces and distressing their Trade either in co-operation with your Majesty's Land and Sea Forces, or by making diversion in their favour when they were carrying on operations in other Parts,"[52] and for its direction of plundering raids into the surrounding rebel-held country, particularly New Jersey, which became a scene of "waste and havoc." The raids were often well planned and successful because the participants were, sometimes literally, fighting in their own back yards. The *Annual Register* described the situation rather well, noting that much mischief was done "without producing any effect, or at least any good one, with respect to the main objects, and great purposes of the war." In other words, the enemy was stung into greater effort without being seriously injured.[53]

The climax of the Board's harassing activity was the unauthorized retaliatory execution of Huddy. The "Huddy Affair" illustrates many facets of the tragedy of executions on both sides. On April 12, 1782, at Gravelly Point, New Jersey, a patriot captain, Joshua Huddy, a brave and able member of an old New Jersey family, was about to be hanged. The reason was that two weeks earlier a Loyalist, Philip White, also from an old New Jersey family, had been killed. White had gone ashore from his schooner, the *Wasp,* at Long Branch, Monmouth County, presumably to view his property, which he had been forced to forfeit. Attempting to return to his ship, White had been captured at the water's edge, and later when he tried to escape into a bog, he was cut down by a Whig sword stroke.

To the Loyalists this was murder, one of many such killings in the hate-filled area of guerrilla warfare surrounding the Loyalist stronghold of New York City. Accordingly, the Board of Associated Loyalists got Clinton's permission to take Joshua Huddy from a prison ship anchored off Sandy Hook in order to exchange him for a Loyalist prisoner. But Clinton was deceived by the Board. Captain Richard Lippincott, another native of New Jersey and commander of the sixteen-man Loyalist party that had taken custody of Huddy, had different orders. Lippincott transported the unfortunate Huddy, selected because of his reputation as a zealous Whig, to Gravelly Point on the Jersey shore and there instructed him to make his last will and testament. This done, Huddy was made to stand on a barrel, a rope was flung over the limb of a tree, his neck inserted into the noose at the end of the rope, and without trial or further formality he was hanged.

A placard pinned to the body read:

> We, the refugees, having long with grief beheld the cruel murders of our brethren and finding nothing but such measures daily carried into execution, we therefore determine not to suffer without taking vengeance for the numerous cruelties; and thus begin, and I say, may those lose their liberty who do not follow on, and having made use of Captain Huddy as the first object to present to your view; and we further determine to hang man for man while there is a refugee existing. *Up goes Huddy for Philip White.*[54]

After the war Clinton regretted the Board's action.[55] Apart from the appalling prospect of endless murder that it opened up, Huddy's death became part of an international *cause célèbre* when Washington countered by selecting by lot a British prisoner, Captain Charles Asgill, to be executed in return, a fate the captain finally escaped through diplomacy and a pardon.

The rebels won the war, or, to put it more accurately, the British lost it. The American victories in the field were important, of course, but not decisive. On the whole the British got the best of the fighting; they were able to capture and occupy leading towns with comparative ease, yet to their mystification the rebellion continued. The reason was that Washington and his army were defeated but never destroyed. The colonies had no "capital" in the European sense. Charleston, Norfolk, or Philadelphia could be controlled, yet the surrounding countryside remained rebel territory. As the British lamented: "The capture of an American town, doth not imply the conquest of the vicinage. We took New-York. Did that secure the *province* in our interest?" [56] The Loyalists were in the majority in a very few places, hence the success of sheer military power was inconsequential.[57]

The British faced other, rather secondary difficulties: the lack of a unified command both within the army (Cornwallis's being hemmed in at Yorktown stemmed partly from this) and between the army and the navy, a situation exacerbated by frequent interservice quarrels; the logistic problem of supplying a large, but not large enough, army over such great land and sea distances (a problem that a recent scholar has suggested was actually solved rather well); [58] the mediocrity of the naval and military commanders, such as Admiral Arbuthnot and General Clinton, who was kept in command too long, against his own will. Further, there was the incompetence of George III and of Lord North's ministry, which included poor civilian heads of both the army and the navy— Lord George Germain and the Earl of Sandwich, respectively.

The American war for independence may be viewed as a war between the patriots and the British, as a civil war of another kind between Americans, and as an international (heavily European) war, involving not only France but several other countries, including Spain, Holland, and even Russia. It is upon the first two facets that we must concentrate in discussing the Loyalists, but to explain why Britain lost, it is necessary to mention the third. French intervention plus an anti-British European naval coalition threatened the Channel, the West Indies, India, and elsewhere, and prevented the British from concentrating fully on the American theater. This was seen quite clearly in Loyalist circles during the first year of the French alliance, as when John Potts wrote to Joseph Galloway, "It is very evident that unless Government can disengage itself from an European war and employ a greater force and more vigor in the prosecution of this, the game is certainly up, and America lost." [59]

But, as we said, the Americans did not really beat the British; the British simply gave up. The defeat at Yorktown, though severe, was not decisive: only 7,000 men were lost; 30,000 remained, and more could be had; Halifax, New York, Charleston, and Savannah were still occupied; de Grasse's control of the sea was only temporary; acute financial and military problems remained for Washington and the Congress. Why then did the British give in? Their country "had lost its nerve"; the country gentlemen in Parliament had lost all confidence in the ministry and would no longer support the war.[60]

What part did the Loyalists play in the over-all strategy and war plans of the British? It is no exaggeration to say that they were the linchpin, at least by 1779. At the very beginning of the rebellion the British tried most unsuccessfully to use the Loyalists, but once the British regulars had gotten themselves ready, the Loyalists were subordinated [61] and British military hopes were placed in the action of their own troops, who were to smash Washington's army and capture strategic points such as Philadelphia, the apparent "capital" of the rebellious colonies. But even in this first stage the existence of the Loyalists helped determine British plans. For example, the Southern expedition of 1776, which degenerated into an abortive sea attack on Charleston, and Burgoyne's attempted advance in 1777 from Canada down through New England were both predicated on mass Loyalist support, confidently predicted by two well-known Tories in the North, Colonel Philip Skene and Governor Tryon, and by the governers of Virginia and the Carolinas in the South.[62]

After Burgoyne's surrender at Saratoga, the lack of results from the occupation of Philadelphia and New York, and Washington's patent refusal to be drawn into a decisive battle, a new British policy emerged, contained in a memorandum of Germain's: "The great point to be wished for, is that the inhabitants of some considerable colony were so far reclaimed to their duty, that the revival of the British constitution, and the free operation of the laws, might without prejudice be permitted among them." Or, as General James Robertson later put it, "I never had an idea of subduing the Americans; I meant to assist the good Americans subdue the bad." [63]

Clinton was to defeat the Continental army, or at least eject it from specific areas, which was to be followed by policing by Loyalist militia and a restoration of civil government.[64] This policy depended on the Loyalists' (or at least the Loyalists and the apathetic) being in a majority, an article of faith for most Tories, and one shared by the British Government and some of the military commanders. Germain was convinced; General Robertson agreed that "it is on this foundation we should build our hopes"; and even the French minister, Gérard, was impressed with Loyalist strength.[65]

British strategic thinking, therefore, resulted in the campaign of 1780-1781 into the South, where it seemed the

Loyalists were most numerous, and where they were certainly mainly untested. Also, it was expected that the area's dependence on Britain for the export of its agricultural staples, its thinly spread population, the threats of the pro-British Cherokees on the frontier, and the large numbers of slaves who could be wooed to the British side would aid matters.[66] At first the plan seemed to be succeeding well. The assurances by the former attorney general of South Carolina that there were great numbers of Loyalists in that area were confirmed by the British capture of Charleston, May, 1780, and soon Cornwallis's victories, particularly at Camden, apparently restored the entire colony to the Crown. Frederick Mackenzie, a British officer, confided in his diary, "I do not see how the Rebellion can possibly exist much longer." [67] But the vision proved ephemeral. Patriot commanders Nathanael Greene, Thomas Sumter (the "Gamecock"), Francis Marion (the "Swamp Fox"), and others launched successful counterattacks. The North Carolina Loyalists did not rally as expected, and although the British more than held their own in the set battles, the Southern back country was given over to violent civil war and the Whigs grew to unexpected strength as too many Tories proved to be merely fair-weather friends.[68] Mackenzie bemoaned the fact (and this may have something of a painful ring to modern American ears) that, with Greene's success, the so-called Loyalists had switched sides and, to add insult to injury, "were supplied with arms which they now use against us." [69]

Paul H. Smith, the expert on the use of the Loyalists by the British during the war, concludes that the matter was badly handled. The British were never fully clear as to what the Loyalists' role should be, and accordingly the Tories were "alternately ignored and courted. . . . Plans to use them were in the main *ad hoc* responses to constantly changing conditions." Piers Mackesy shows that this is something of an exaggeration, but there is certainly much truth in Smith's conclusions. Smith also notes British overestimation of Loyalist strength, which led to a second error, the failure to send enough reinforcements to America. Finally, the Southern campaign after 1778, which was predicated on Loyalist strength there, "forced Britain to divide her armies at the very moment the French threat was most serious." [70]

Another recent scholar, Howard H. Peckham, concludes quite simply that the British placed "a naive and fantastic reliance on the Loyalists," [71] but if a population, oppressed by Whig despots, were in fact merely awaiting British liberation, which is what the Loyalists and the British commanders persuaded themselves of, then the British strategy was eminently sensible and likely to succeed. The British never pretended to be trying to conquer America, they were merely liberating the population from Whig oppression—therefore their strategy was based on error, but an error unavoidable so long as the British commanders and the Loyalists wished to take this view of the situation.

Loyalists were forever arguing that a majority of the people in some area would rise and rally to British rule if only they got better support from the army.[72] But either the alleged minority Whigs—actually a much larger group, and from whose number were to come many of the "ralliers"—were made of much sterner stuff than their Loyalist brethren or, more likely, the Loyalists were whistling in the dark, living in a dreamworld. This attitude led to serious Loyalist underestimation of Whig strength [73]—which helped the rebels perfect their organization while the Tories stood by motionless. The evidence of campaign after campaign—Gage in Massachusetts, Burgoyne in the Hudson Valley, Howe in New Jersey and Philadelphia, Clinton and Cornwallis in the South—failed to shake this basic belief.

The Loyalists' criticism of the British for not making

vigorous use of them and not supporting them properly was often valid, especially in the case of Howe and Clinton, but it must be remembered that the British faced a fatal dilemma. A full commitment to the Loyalists would have meant pushing civil war to extremes, obliterating the American patriots, giving the Loyalists their revenge. This was impossible because the British objective was never to utterly crush the Americans, it was to defeat the rebel army and conciliate the population. Hence Howe's orders were not simply to win battles but to find a peaceful settlement, and the same motive was behind the arrival of the Carlisle Peace Commission in 1778. The more the Loyalists were aided, the less conciliation was likely to be achieved.

From the king down, the British commanders never considered the Americans as enemies in the way, say, that the French were considered enemies. There was no systematic ravaging of the countryside, no equivalent of Sherman's march to the sea, a policy that might conceivably have ended the rebellion. Even the full severities justified by the rules of war, such as putting to the sword garrisons that had refused to surrender, were not always exacted during the various campaigns. In spite of the many horrors and atrocities of the war, the British army's behavior was mild compared with the conduct in contemporary European wars, but the Americans, not having experienced anything like a Drogheda or the ravaging of Bavaria by Marlborough, could not have been expected to realize it.

The British army was inhibited not only by policy but also by the widespread sympathy at home for the American rebels. Ever since the Stamp Act there had been strong criticism of the Government by opposition politicians who, not always with complete justification, had become linked with the American cause. The war was not a popular one in Britain, especially among the lower classes. Recruiting was diffi-

cult; even some officers refused to serve. General Richard
Montgomery, leader of the American attack on Quebec in
1775, was a former British officer, and there were others as
well in the patriot army. The Loyalists, blaming everyone
but themselves for their plight, complained frequently and
bitterly about British support of the rebels.[74]

It is clear, then, that the Loyalists were crucial to British
strategy and crucial in the failure of that strategy. The question now arises as to the ways in which the British misused
their American allies.

The Loyalists, in common with many British critics at the
time and since, were baffled by the British generals' apparent
reluctance to press advantages. John Weatherhead, a New
York Loyalist, testified concerning Howe's action at the battle of Brooklyn, August, 1776: "It cannot be denied that if
the Ardour of the Troops had not been restrained but that
they had been permitted to pursue the freighten'd Fugitives
within their own Lines the Rebellion could not have existed
two hours longer." [75] An exaggeration, but Howe's backward-
ness was a grave error.

Although Clinton suffered great unpopularity, the Loyalist *bête noire* was undoubtedly Howe. "I cursed, but *Howe*
I cursed, guess you," groaned Jonathan Sewall.[76] Howe's "de-
bauchery," mainly a too apparent preference for the pleasures
of the bed and gaming table over those of the battlefield, was
notorious and confirmed the Tories' low opinion of the
faint-hearted and hesitant general.[77]

But by 1778 Howe had resigned, and the great defect in
Germain's plan to reclaim the South with the aid of the
"natives" was the attitude of Clinton, who was not very
sanguine concerning the Loyalists and was reluctant to use
them or give them civil power.[78] And this was quite apart
from Clinton's considerable defects of personality and judgment.[79]

The Loyalists, and subsequent historians, allowed one main exception to the general disillusionment with the British commanders. A letter from an officer at Ninety-Six, South Carolina, described Cornwallis as follows:

He treats a Loyalist like his friend, embarked on the same cause, and if the meanest of them has business with him, he attends them himself and makes them eat and drink with him; by such treatment as this, he . . . owes in a great measure his success in this province, and such behaviour, with the speedy establishment of a civil government, will keep it in subjection.[80]

Cornwallis's attitude to the Loyalists may have been good, and he was the only British commander with the decisiveness likely to win the war, but most scholars would agree that the headstrong general must bear a good deal of the responsibility for the Yorktown disaster.[81]

It was the constant cry of the Loyalists that British failure to accept Loyalist schemes was causing American victory. After the peace treaty, Colonel Simcoe wrote pithily of "the late ill-mannaged War." [82] It certainly was ill-managed, but how far adoption of Loyalist schemes would have helped it is difficult to say.

Lord Dunmore, the governor of Virginia, brashly assured the British after the war that he had put forward various plans "for putting an end to the Rebellion which he is certain would have been successful had they been attended to." [83] John Patterson of Pennsylvania told the claims commissioners that his plan for the certain raising of Washington's siege of Boston was ignored.[84] Thomas Robinson, one of Delaware's leading citizens, claimed that in June, 1776, he had collected 1,500 followers to restore law and order to the colony but had had to disperse them when Sir Andrew Hamilton, commander of H.M.S. *Roebuck,* was unable to supply them with arms.[85] Jonathan Boucher attributed the loss of parts of North Carolina to "Want of Support," and accordingly, he said, the Loyalists there "like many others, I imagine . . . soon fell off." [86] Loyalist complaints of this sort could be cited ad infinitum.

But if the truth be known, the Loyalists were, by and large, passive and paralyzed unless firmly led by the British. It was said of a town meeting, called in Boston to debate the question of repayment for the destroyed tea, that "the battle went to the patriots by default." [87] Most Loyalists did not bother themselves during the elections to the Continental Congresses. The constant refrain was that the British should have organized, the British should have recruited, the British should have intervened. . . . The tone is caught in William Rankin's cry, after the war, that the Pennsylvania Loyalists' "unabated zeal in the Royal Cause was never called into Action and they were obliged to Submit." [88]

As the war dragged on, many Loyalists even came to believe that it was being deliberately prolonged to serve the interests of British war profiteers. Also some Loyalists must have wondered why, if it was British policy to eject the Whigs and restore loyal civil rule, this was never done in New York City in spite of the long years of occupation.[89]

Even if British strategy had been based on more accurate assumptions than it was, the handling of the Loyalists would still be open to serious question.

Colonial recruits had been used by Britain in earlier American wars in the eighteenth century, but the British had not— and the situation continued that way—solved the problem of integrating provincial and regular troops. At first expecting a short war, and remembering past experiences and the time it took to train provincials, the British neglected Loyalist soldiers. Even as the war progressed and British strategy leaned more heavily on Loyalist support, military policy in regard to this group left much to be desired. For years, in spite of the prejudice against it, the British encouraged enlistment in the army rather than in the more popular militia. There was simply a pious hope that Loyalists would be recruited (many were, of course, but mainly through Loyalist initiative), and otherwise there was no seriously thought-out plan. Typically, and perhaps this sums up the Revolution, the British treated provincial troops as second-class citizens. For example, provincial officers were not given permanent rank, were not granted half pay on retirement or gratuities if wounded, and they ranked below regulars; no provision was made for hospital care and orderly rooms. Reform did come in late 1778 and early 1779, and Rivington's *Gazette* contained many advertisements for "aspiring heroes" to enlist, but a good deal of damage had already been done.[90]

The British soldiers' natural prejudice against colonial soldiers—what the *Annual Register* called a "sovereign contempt" for Americans, "both as men and soldiers"[91]—was reinforced by memories of the poor provincial showing during the French and Indian War, and although this attiude was modified as the war progressed (mainly by *patriot* exploits, from Bunker Hill onward), the Loyalists in arms had justifiable complaints about their shabby treatment.

British errors of military and political judgment are one thing, but definite harassment of the Loyalists is less excusable. For a start, there was the attitude of the British officers toward Tories, which, as was regularly bemoaned, was characteristically supercilious. It was reported by a Whig source that the British "called the friends to liberty only rebels; but the Tories they called d——d traitors and scoundrels."[92] Colonel Robert Gray, a South Carolina Loyalist, recalled that "almost every British officer regarded with contempt and indifference the establishment of a militia among a people differing so much in customs and manners from themselves." [93]

There runs through Loyalist testimony a baleful chorus of the injuries done loyal Americans by the British army. Among the claims for compensation submitted to the British Government after the war were many for losses caused by the "depredations" of the British rather than by the rebels.[94] The troops had to requistion supplies and shelter and could not always inquire if their victims were Loyalists. The *Pennsylvania Gazette* published a letter concerning Newark, New Jersey, where "as to plundering, Whig and Tory were treated with a pretty equal hand," and where a well-known local figure, Captain Nutting, "who had always been a remarkable Tory, and who met the British troops in the Broad Street, with huzzas of joy . . . had his house robbed of almost everything, his very shoes taken off his feet, and they threatened to hang him." [95] A regular complaint from Loyalist merchants was that their ships were taken as prizes by the British just as if they belonged to the rebels.[96]

Much as we have discussed the benefits, for some, of British occupation, we should note, too, that the very presence of a body of infantry troops or sailors, even friendly, inevitably created friction and "incidents." Early in 1775 aggrieved inhabitants of Roxbury, Massachusetts, deplored ice-skating by British soldiers on the Lord's day.[97] The naval commander at New York was obliged to place a curfew on sailors' shore leave because "it has been represented to me, that innumerable Riots and Disturbances have happened in the Streets of this City, to the great annoyance and apprehension of the Inhabitants, by Seamen belonging to his Majesty's Ships. . . ." [98]

In December, 1781, the Loyalists of New York even found it necessary to ask Clinton to remove the British officer directly responsible for the issuing of rations and relief. A petition signed by 354 persons complained of the daily "Ill Usage" and "Inhumanity" of Colonel Roger Morris, Superintendent of Refugees, who, it was added, was "by no means unfriendly to their [the rebels'] Cause." [99] There was a pervasive Tory belief, partly justified, in the general corruption of the British army in the realm of supplies, compensation, pay, and so on.

One Loyalist recalled that "unfortunately the Royal and American Army by turns encamped" on his farm, "threw down and burnt and destroyed the inclosures wasted the stock and cut down the Timber thereon," while another decried a similar situation: "What the one left the other gleaned—it was the Man's misfortune, and was no uncommon thing." [100]

If the Loyalists suffered from the British and the American troops, it was agreed that they (and all Americans, for that matter) suffered even more from 30,000 hired German mercenaries, 17,000 of whom were from Hesse-Cassel—hence the general name Hessians.[101] The Hessians were wilder than the British, but national rivalries were also involved. In 1778 General James Robertson found it necessary to advertise in New York, appealing to the city to treat Hessians "with the civility due to strangers," at the same time offering twenty pounds reward for some sailors who had knifed and robbed three Germans, and announcing that General Schmidt was "taking every step to prevent or punish any insult or injury" caused by his troops.[102]

Daniel Coxe related the following incident:

But the British Army in the meantime very unexpectantly advancing from Brunswick to Trenton in pursuit of Washingtons Army over the Delaware, and taking post there, his [Coxe's] Houses Offices and Estate were seized up as Quarters for Hessian Troops under the Command of Col. Rhode, and not withstanding his well known public and loyal character and every remonstrance of his friends and Servants to the Contrary, his Rooms, Closets, Stores and Cellars were all broke open ransacked and pillaged and every species of Furniture, China, Glass, Liquors etc. plundered destroyed or taken away, his Servants compelled to fly for safety and Shelter elsewhere, and most wanton Desolation committed on his Property and Estate....[103]

The combined effect of British and Hessian depredations was driving even the Quakers to arms, alleged one contemporary.[104] A New Jersey Loyalist wrote to a friend that British depredations were making "many persons rebels," while a Long Islander added, "The army has done more essential injury to the King's Cause than the utmost efforts of his enemies," refrains that could be repeated from letters and utterances of the day countless times.[105]

Matthew Robinson of Rhode Island reported damage to his property from the Whigs, the Hessians, the British, and the French,[106] the full gamut, except for the Indians. The *Annual Register* for 1777 commented on the Indians—"The friends of the royal cause, as well as its enemies, were equally victims to their indiscriminate rage"—and cited the murder by Indians, attached to St. Leger in New England, of a Miss McCrea, whose father was a Loyalist and who was betrothed to a British officer. "By this means, the advantages expected from the terror excited by these savage auxiliaries were not only counteracted, but this terror rather, it may be thought, produced a directly contrary effect." [107]

Subjected to slights, insults (both real and imagined), and plundering, the Loyalists understandably lost heart. Hardluck stories were rife. The Reverend Joshua Wingate Weeks reported that a Carolinian merchant, rather than submit to the rebels, had sold all his belongings, purchased indigo with the proceeds, and embarked for Rotterdam, but fourteen days out the British captured the ship and ordered it to New York. Weeks continued:

> To defend his cause would cost him a great deal, to lose it was loosing his all—and in either case he was ruined. . . . if a good and peaceable subject dwells among them, he is a rebel—if he sells and quits them he is ruined: And in this embarrassed situation has every friend of Government been lost from the beginning of the rebellion to the present hour. So that now very few have any inducement to own themselves friendly to English laws and liberties.[108]

Isaac Ogden, approving a proposal to execute patriot hostages in return for murdered Tory prisoners, wrote to Galloway that it would evince "a certain *spirit* that has long been wanting" and persuade the Loyalists that "some attention is paid to them." [109] Loyalist petitions to the British frequently alluded rather sarcastically to British neglect. For example, in 1779 a petition to General John Vaughan signed by Cadwallader Colden and other principal New York Loyalists suggested that Vaughan "cannot be ignorant of the causes which formerly depress'd the spirit of loyalty and prevented it from being so usefully extended as it otherwise might have been." [110]

Loyalist discontent received almost continual augmentation from British defeats, evacuations, and failures to support uprisings.[111] An English officer remarked that the Loyalists could not be expected to "declare their sentiments until they find us so strong in any one place as to protect them after having joined," and he went on to note the disastrous results of abandoning them "to the fury of their bitterest Enemies." [112] The same officer also wisely observed that the error of expecting great Loyalist support had led to dissipation: too many expeditions to too many places, "by which means we have not been in sufficient strength in any one," and thus rebel opposition had been stimulated without being crushed.[113]

The Loyalists' suspicions of British good faith received final bitter confirmation with the Yorktown surrender when it was learned, "intelligence as surprising as vexatious," according to one Loyalist,[114] that the proposed Article Ten of the surrender terms protecting Loyalists from punishment for having joined the British army was dropped, "having the Effect," as Clinton later eagerly testified, "throughout the Continent on the minds of the Loyalists that they considered themselves as given up by the Army." [115] The effect of Article Ten "requires no comment," added Germain; the Loyalists had "received many promises but no support." [116] Most of the Loyalists who had been at the battle were evacuated in the one British ship that was allowed to leave Yorktown, but their disillusionment remained complete.

The Loyalists' military failure was due largely to their own mental attitude. They had an erroneous belief in British invincibility. And as we have said, many of their leaders, originally opposed to British treatment of the colonies, waited until very late in the game to declare themselves Loyalists and thus faced great difficulties when they tried to stem a movement they themselves had done so much to advance. Although there were Tory Associations, the raising of armed bands, and some intercolonial communication, the Whig organization, from local committees to the Continental Congress, was too well established and too experienced, and in every important area the Tories, whatever their numbers, were effectively and early disarmed and suppressed, often with astonishing ease, by the unaided Whigs. There was not a single province where the Whigs were ousted except by British military power.

The Whigs had the advantage of knowing clearly what they were fighting for—namely, independence and power—

and what they stood to lose—everything, including their lives. This gave a desperate quality to the rebels' actions. In contrast, the naturally conservative Loyalists were loath to do anything precipitate, and their goals were muddled and hazy. The often subtle concepts behind their opposition to independence, and also their desire for reform within the Empire, did not make for easy slogans. Moderate parties are always at a disadvantage in a revolutionary situation, and the Loyalists were further hindered by being trapped as middlemen. British support actually worked against their organization, as they could hardly be expected to take the initiative; whereas the Whigs, starting from scratch, ignoring legalities, had an enormous advantage. Thus, in the matter of raising troops, the Loyalists had to await British action, while the Whigs were free and anxious to arm quickly. In the early part of the Revolution the Loyalists, like the French nobility at the same stage of the French Revolution, made the mistake of failing to lead.

One gets the constant impression that too many Loyalists, in contrast to the patriots, were afraid of getting their hands dirty. The fact that the Tories drew heavily from the snobbish, well-to-do sections of society partly accounts for this, and as Colonel Haldimand wrote: "The true spirit of a refugee Loyalist driven from his country by persecution is to carry arms, but there is no end to it if every man that comes in is to be considered and paid for as an officer." [117]

Thus the Loyalists had a fatal dependence on the British. The contrast between Whig and Tory attitudes is well illustrated by the Loyalist commentator, the Reverend Joshua Wingate Weeks, who, after bemoaning at great length British neglect, turned to the patriots thus:

The Congress use every art in the world to bring over the disaffected to espouse their cause. They hang the turbulent, imprison the dangerous, fine the wealthy. They allure the ambitious with the hopes of preferment and distribute estates to those who have lost their property for the sake of joining them. And by such means as these, they have strengthened their cause amazingly. Whereas on the part of the King nothing has ever been done of this kind.[118]

In spite of the brave service of Loyalist regiments and individuals, the general effect of the Loyalists on the war was negative. Partly because they were necessarily subordinated to the British officers, the Loyalists produced no military figures who could remotely compare with the best men the patriots had. Such men as Fanning and Butler certainly had ability, but they were never likely to alter the course of the war. Ironically, the better the Loyalists fought and the more severely they harried the enemy, the more they stiffened, by hatred, the morale of the patriots.

In British strategy the reliance on the chimera of a Loyalist majority eager to flock to the British standard led directly to the disaster at Yorktown, which in turn led to a political collapse in Britain that brought peace and Whig victory.

Why the Americans succeeded is a complex question; whether the British *could* have won, given different policies, commanders, and so on, is even more complex. Answers must remain hypotheses, fundamentally unprovable. One thing should be stressed: victory lends a retrospective inevitability to the history of a war.[119]

It appears that at best the British could have destroyed Washington's army and occupied the country more harshly and decisively. Thus military victory could have been gained. And had the Loyalists and the apathetic existed in sufficient numbers, the Whigs could have been proscribed and banished, imprisoned, or executed, and loyal civil rule re-established. But this is merely a fantasy: the number of Loyalists was overestimated, the British would have been resented much more fiercely than in 1765 or 1775 or 1776, the expense and the troops required to hold down a hostile area as large as America would have been more than Britain could bear in the long run (it would have been as impossible as the North's attempt to hold the South in subjection after the Civil War), and an endemic partisan movement would have worked a steady and fatal attrition on the British forces. British "victory" would have been a disaster for both countries. Relations would have been poisoned, the American republic would have been born under the most inauspicious circumstances, and the remarkable history of the early national period could only have suffered.

CHAPTER V

"Damn the Tories": Persecution

⚜ "The Cry was for Liberty—Lord, what a Fuss!
But pray, how much liberty left they for us?"

Anonymous, Loyalist Rhapsodies.[1]

What might be called official or semiofficial action (it was hardly legal until July 4, 1776) against the Loyalists began with the adoption of the Continental Association by the Congress in 1774 and continued with the work of various local committees and the colonial, and then state, legislatures.[2] During the period of the Revolutionary War a great jumble of legislation was passed by the thirteen states, with some superfluous goading from the Congress, and the result was that the disabilities suffered by Loyalists varied a great deal.[3]

All states passed at least one test law requiring inhabitants to take oaths, which usually involved abjuring George III and pledging allegiance to the new regime and faith in the Revolution. Categories of persons to whom the laws applied varied, but commonly included all adult males. Penalties for refusal included suspension from office, imprisonment, disfranchisement, barring from political office, withdrawal of legal rights, extra taxation, confiscation of property, banishment, and execution if any exiles should return. Many took the oaths demanded by one side or the other hypocritically, and, of course, the number of adherents to each side waxed and waned with the fortunes of war.[4] There were many other commonly found laws concerning the Loyalists that contained provisions for billeting troops with them, forcing them to accept payments in Continental paper money, levying fines of increasing severity for refusal to serve in the militia and for many other unpatriotic actions, restricting their freedom by censorship of speech and action, disfranchising them and barring them from office and from the legal and the teaching professions, exiling them to another part of the state, to another state altogether, or from the whole United States. The shifing of dangerous Loyalists to Whiggish areas was common, especially when a place was threatened militarily. Thus Rhode Island sent some of its Loyalists to the northern part of the state, and Connecticut received New York and New Jersey Loyalists. As early as 1777 every state save South Carolina and Georgia had made traitors of all who actively supported the British. The celebrated Pennsylvania "Black List" of 490 Loyalists attainted of high treason was made up largely of men who had left with the British forces. In the end a few were pardoned and several were executed.

In November, 1777, the Continental Congress recommended the confiscation of Loyalist estates, a suggestion already made by Thomas Paine, and in some places already acted upon. All states finally amerced, taxed, or confiscated much Loyalist property, and in addition New York and South Carolina taxed Loyalist property in order to compensate robbery victims. Some towns simply raffled off Tory property. Patriot officers requisitioned horses and supplies from Loyalists rather than Whigs, and, of course, there was much old-fashioned looting, particularly of the property of exiles.[5]

Like Henry VIII's dissolution of the monasteries, the disbursement of Loyalist property created a vested interest in revolution. Also the device of trying partially to finance the war with traitors' wealth was naturally very popular, if of limited success. Many Whigs, some of them racketeers, did very well by taking the advice of an Albany, New York, merchant who wrote: "I find myself justified by Experience in declaring that a judicious Purchase of forfeited Lands . . . is by far the most Eligible mode I know of Improving a Fortune in a Secure way." [6] One observer thought it common for Loyalist estates to sell for less than one quarter of their real value.[7]

Even the Loyalists themselves benefitted to an extent from the depreciation. One reported that his wife bought back the family property in New Jersey for "a mere song," while another noted that a Boston Loyalist managed to have a friend repurchase his estate for the equivalent of only one year's rent.[8]

Although the majority of active Loyalists suffered much loss of property, some attempted by various subterfuges to preserve their estates quite apart from having a wife or third party act as purchaser. One scheme was to make over one's property, or make a sham sale, to a sympathetic, moderate friend who had escaped suspicion.[9]

Much commoner was the device used by exiles of leaving their wives or relatives behind in order to keep a foot in both camps. For example, Benjamin Pickman fled from Salem, Massachusetts, in 1775, but left his wife behind to look after their property, to which he returned ten years later.[10] Some brothers may even have chosen opposite sides for such a reason. As the British claims commissioners commented on one split family, "it is possible that this may be a shabby family Compact . . . to preserve the property whether Great Britain or America prevailed." [11]

The over-all severity of the various laws against the Loyalists has been estimated as follows:

"Harshest"—New York, South Carolina.
"Harsh"—Massachusetts, New Jersey, Pennsylvania.
"Light"—Rhode Island, Connecticut, Virginia, North Carolina.
"Lightest"—New Hampshire, Delaware, Maryland, Georgia.[12]

With some exceptions, notably Georgia, laws were harshest in states where Loyalists were most powerful, and as the war progressed, the purpose of the laws changed from conversion to "revenge and hate." [13] Similarly, enforcement varied, and was usually severest where danger was greatest and civil war bitterest.

A prominent Southern Tory reported that in Virginia, where the Loyalists were weak and little problem, the property of those who joined the British army went to their wives and children "on the Spot . . . as if the Father was dead," and he noted that his own wife "had never been molested but on the contrary treated with the utmost Kindness and Respect." [14] Other Loyalists described being turned off their property with only the clothes on their backs.

But perhaps more typical was the fate of the Chandler family of Worcester, Massachusetts. Colonel John Chandler, a very prominent citizen of distinguished Massachusetts pedigree, dubbed "Tory John" and later in England the "Honest Refugee," fled from Boston with the British army to become a permanent, proscribed exile. For over two years his wife and family continued to enjoy their property undisturbed, until the Worcester Committee of Correspondence began a process that resulted in the confiscation of all but a third of their real and personal property, which third was reserved for Mrs. Chandler's use as long as she remained in the United

States. Her husband did not return (he was forbidden to by an act of October, 1778), and on her death special legislation was needed to secure her property for her children.[15]

A myriad of particularities could play a part in determining the extent of persecution. A well-liked or respected Tory (and there were a few such)[16] might well escape, as might someone whose skills were especially valued, for example, a doctor. Influential but quiet Loyalists were more apt to avoid penalties than those of lower social standing or those more vociferous in their beliefs.

The zeal of the patriots could be extremely capricious and, as always with witch-hunts, frequently ridiculous and heavy-handed. One citizen was accosted for naming his dog "Tory," the implication being that a Tory was forced to lead a dog's life.[17] In 1776 at Stratford, Connecticut, an Episcopal minister was brought before the local committee because he had officiated at a baptism where the child was named Thomas Gage. The committee viewed the action as a "designed insult" and censured the cleric.[18] In the same state Zephaniah Beardslee reported that he was "very much abused" for naming his daughter Charlotte, after the queen. It may be noted that Beardslee, apparently a very serious Loyalist, had also been found drinking the king's health. The frequent persecution of Tories for this activity, however, is not as picayune as it seems, because toasts presuppose groups in taverns and the chance of Loyalist plots and associations. Thus, Abraham Cuyler held a gathering in Albany, New York, in June, 1776, that featured drinking and the singing of "God Save the King." At last the enraged Whig citizens crashed the party and carried the royal merrymakers off to jail.[19]

Frequently old scores were settled or the unpopular chastised under cover of patriot enthusiasm. Crèvecoeur had a Whig explain: "This great land of Canaan cannot be purged of its ancient idolaters without abundance of trouble. Now the Jews had a much better chance because the Canaanites did not speak the same language. We must guess, and sift, and find out; no wonder if we make mistakes sometimes." [20] James Simpson summed things up rather well and gave an interesting example of the vagaries of circumstances:

> It is notorious that the conduct of the Americans, in proscribing the persons, and confiscating the Estates of their fellow Citizens, have been very little influenced by the rules of indiscriminate Justice, or strict Impartiality, a considerable Property, hath frequently been the cause of condemnation, but hath sometimes been the means of Salvation to the Owners of it, for when a person of extensive influence had a prospect or perhaps a certainty of a rich succession he would of course use his endeavors to prevent a measure which would destroy his expectations.[21]

The Loyalists suffered in many ways that were not the direct results of legislation or government action. For example, they were often required to illuminate their houses (an action forced on recalcitrants in England by the Wilkes mobs of the 1760's) to celebrate such an event as an American military victory.[22] Many social pressures were brought to bear, admittedly given encouragement (normally superfluous) by various legal or semilegal bodies. Thus a committee at Skenesborough, New York, published the name of a citizen who had opposed the Continental Association, announcing that "[we] hereby give notice to the public that he may treated with all that neglect and contempt which is so justly his due, for his incorrigible enmity to the rights of American Liberty." [23]

The results of Loyalism might simply be social ostracism —being sent to Coventry—as, for instance, happened to James Allen, who noted in his diary for February 17, 1777: "I never knew how painful it is to be secluded from the free conversation of one's friends"; and to George Watson, a mandamus councillor, when he entered a church at Plymouth, Massachusetts, and "a great number of the principal inhabitants left." Or it might mean serious loss of services, as when the blacksmiths of Worcester County, Massachusetts, refused to work for any Loyalists, their employees, or their dependents; or an economic boycott, as in Connecticut, where the local committee forbade "all Persons whatever viz. Merchants Mechanicks Millers and Butchers and Co. from supplying . . . John Sayre or Family with any manner of Thing whatever." Lawyers, teachers, doctors, apothecaries, and others often lost their customers and hence their livelihoods.[24] Mathew Robinson, a Newport trader, from the first branded as "a Rank Torey," suffered several indignities, including the pulling down of his fences by a "multitude . . . under colour of laying out a Highway" and climaxing in 1781 when, after *"a New England Saint"* charged that Robinson "drank the King's Health, and damn'd the Congress and call'd them damn'd Rebels and Presbyterians," he was imprisoned by the rebels without examination, this being even "against their own Bill of Rights." [25]

In many areas—for example, New York—the Loyalists were allowed to sell their property before departing, but such hurried, desperate sales were unlikely to net a fair price, and the result amounted to confiscation.[26]

All wars and revolutions cause great mental strain and suffering, most of which goes unmeasured. The history of the Revolutionary era is liberally punctuated with stories of Loyalists who succumbed to melancholia, became mad, died, or committed suicide.

Alexander Harvey, a Charleston lawyer, wound up in a private English madhouse, having been "driven to Distraction" by his experiences as a Loyalist; George Miller, a North Carolina merchant whose fright had conquered his Loyalist principles, was thrown "into Convulsions" by the strain of serving in the American militia; Peter Harrison's death came after the shock of Lexington, and with it America lost its greatest colonial architect; several Loyalists, including the wife of William Franklin, simply died of "a Broken Heart"; the widow of Dr. Robert Gibbs of South Carolina recounted that the prospect of the loss of his property "so preyed upon his Spirits" that he died. Andrew Miller, of Halifax, North Carolina, was estranged from all his friends by his Loyalism, which literally killed him; others chose suicide—Millington Lockwood of Connecticut was wounded in the head, lost his reason, and drowned himself, while some years later, in London, after years of fruitless waiting for compensation, an unnamed, ruined Loyalist shot himself in despair, blaming an ungrateful country.[27]

Although Americans at the time of the Revolution would clearly have found it odd, today one of the sharpest historical debates is over the question of how far the American Revolution was a *real* revolution. Even those historians who, noting the social dislocation, argue that the American Revolution was rather like the French Revolution stress the absence of the Terror. Mass executions there were not, a guillotine there was not, yet atrocities and terror there most certainly were. It is fitting that in the beginning the rebels "hoisted the Red Flag or Flag of Defence." [28]

Leaving aside civil-war aspects such as the execution and maltreatment of prisoners and the burning of towns (by both sides: for example, the Americans fired Norfolk and Portsmouth; the British, Falmouth and Fairfield), we can cite a great range of fates that awaited the Loyalists; they were catalogued by "Papinian" as tarring and feathering, rail riding,

> . . . chaining men together by the dozens, and driving them, like herds of cattle, into distant provinces, flinging them into loathesome jails, confiscating their estates, shooting them in

swamps and woods as suspected Tories, hanging them after a mock trial; and all this because they would not abjure their rightful Sovereign, and bear arms against him.[29]

Tarring and feathering (pine tar and goose feathers) became the classic Whig treatment of the Tories, and the British Government believed there was "no better proof of Loyalty" than suffering this punishment.[30] A famous instance of it occurred in Boston on January 25, 1774, and is worth recounting in some detail.

At about eight o'clock in the evening a club-wielding mob milled along Cross Street. Their objective was John Malcolm, a distinguished but hot-tempered veteran of the French and Indian War, a native Bostonian, an ex-overseas merchant turned royal customs official, and a highly unpopular man for many reasons connected with both his personality (he was inordinately quarrelsome) and his job.

His recent arrival in Boston had been preceded by the unpopular news that in 1771 he had helped the governor of North Carolina against those reputedly Whiggish rebels known as the Regulators and that in October, 1773, he had officiously seized a brigantine at Falmouth (now Portland), Maine. Malcolm waited, ready and armed, behind barred doors. Undeterred, the mob raised ladders, broke an upstairs window, captured their prey, dragged him onto a sled, and pulled him along King Street to the Customs House, or Butcher's House, as it was popularly known, where the spectators gave three mighty cheers.

Although it was "one of the severest cold nights" of the winter, so cold that both Boston Harbor and even the very ink as it touched paper had frozen hard, the wretched man was put in a cart, stripped "to buff and breeches," and dealt the punishment of tarring and feathering, which American patriots were soon to convert into a major spectator sport.

Malcolm, self-styled "Single Knight of the Tarr," as opposed to English Knights of the Garter, had already suffered the same indignity the year before for his conduct at Falmouth. He later claimed to be the first in America tarred for loyalty.

A contemporary description gives a good idea of how Malcolm and many others were treated:

The following is the Receipe for an effectual Operation. "First strip a Person naked, then heat the Tar until it is thin, and pour it upon the naked Flesh, or rub it over with a Tar Brush, *quantum sufficit*. After which, sprinkle decently upon the Tar, whilst it is yet warm, as many Feathers as will stick to it. Then hold a lighted Candle to the Feathers, and try to set it all on Fire; if it will burn so much the better. But as the Experiment is often made in cold Weather; it will not then succeed—take also an Halter and put it round the Person's Neck, and then cart him the Rounds."

Malcolm, flogged and otherwise molested at intervals, was paraded around various crowded streets with his neck in a halter and was finally taken to the Liberty Tree, where he refused to resign his royal office or to curse Thomas Hutchinson, the hated governor of Massachusetts.

The crowd then set off for the gallows on Boston Neck. On the way Malcolm gasped an affirmative when one of his tormentors asked if he was thirsty and was given a bowl of strong tea and ordered to drink the king's health. Malcolm was next told to drink the queen's health; then two more quarts of tea were produced with the command to drink to the health of the Prince of Wales.

"Make haste, you have nine more healths to drink," shouted one of the mob.

"For God's sake, Gentlemen, be merciful, I'm ready to burst; if I drink a drop more, I shall die," Malcolm implored.

"Suppose you do, you die in a good cause, and it is as well to be drowned as hanged," was the reply.

The nine healths, beginning with the "Bishop of Osna-brug," were forced down the victim's throat. Malcolm "turned pale, shook his Head, and instantly filled the Bowl which he had just emptied."

"What, are you sick of the royal family?"

"No, my stomach nauseates the tea; it rises at it like poison."

"And yet you rascal, your whole fraternity at the Custom House would drench us with this poison, and we are to have our throats cut if it will not stay upon our stomachs."

At the gallows the noose was placed in position around Malcolm's neck and he was threatened with hanging, but he still refused to submit, whereupon he was "basted" with a rope for a while, and finally, on pain of losing his ears, he gave in and cursed the governor. The stubborn, brave man was further carted around the town, made to repeat various humiliating oaths, and finally deposited back at his home just before midnight, half frozen, an arm dislocated, and, as he said, "in a most mizerable setuation Deprived of his senses." Five days later, bedridden and "terribly bruised," he dictated a complaint to Governor Hutchinson, which his injuries obliged him to sign with an X.

The frost and tar caused an infection that made his skin peel extensively. However, he was careful to preserve a piece of skin with the tar and feathers still adhering (the stuff was the very devil to get off), which he carried to England as proof of his sufferings when, somewhat recovered, he set sail on May 2, 1774, to try to gain compensation for his loyalty.[31]

Another Tory punishment that became traditional was the gruesome riding on a rail that sometimes followed tarring and feathering, but was severe enough in itself. It consisted of jogging the victim roughly along on "a sharp rail" between his legs. The painful effect of these "grand Toory Rides," as a contemporary called them, can readily be imagined.[32] Seth

Seely, a Connecticut farmer, was brought before the local committee in 1776 and for signing a declaration to support the king's laws was "put on a Rail carried on mens Shoulders thro the Street, then put into the Stocks and besmeared with Eggs and was robbed of money for the Entertainment of the Company." [33]

Persecution of the Loyalists came in many forms. In 1778 prisoners in Vermont were made to tread a road through the snow in the Green Mountains. The wife of Edward Brinley was pregnant and waiting out her confinement at Roxbury, Massachusetts, accompanied by "a guard of Rebels always in her room, who treated her with great rudeness and indecency, exposing her to the view of their banditti, as a sight 'See a tory woman' and striped her and her Children of all their Linen and Cloths." Peter Guire, of Connecticut, was branded on the forehead with the letters *G. R.* (George Rex). Samuel Jarvis, also of Connecticut, related that the following treatment made his whole family very ill:

That your Memorialist for his Attachment to constitutional Government was taken with his Wife and Famely, consisting of three Daughters and one little Son by a Mob of daring and unfeeling Rebels from his Dwelling House in the dead of Night Striped of everything, put on board Whale Boats and Landed on Long Island in the Month of August last about 2 oClock in the Morning Oblieging them to wade almost to their Middles in the Water.[34]

Probably the best-known mobbing in Philadelphia was that of Dr. John Kearsley, whose widow finally submitted a claim to the commissioners. Kearsley, a leading physician, pill manufacturer, and horse dealer, was a pugnacious American with strong Loyalist views. He was seized by a mob in September, 1775, and had his hand bayoneted; then he was carried through the streets to the tune of "Rogue's March."

Sabine reports that he took off his wig with his injured hand and, "swinging it around his head, huzzaed louder and longer than his persecutors." This display of spirit notwithstanding, he nearly died following this treatment, according to his widow. His house was later ransacked, he was arrested, and he finally died in jail.[35]

Atrocious punishments of Loyalists were sometimes carried out by local authorities in semilegal fashion—it was noted that the tarring and feathering of a New York victim in 1775 "was conducted with that regularity and decorum that ought to be observed in all publick punishments."[36] But just as often mobs, drumhead courts, and all the horrors of vigilante policing were found. Indeed it is possible that the term "lynch law" derives from Charles Lynch, a Bedford County, Virginia, justice of the peace who became renowned for his drastic, cruel action against neighboring Tories.[37]

The number of Loyalists subjected to cruel, often extralegal, punishments can only be estimated, and likewise the number of those murdered or executed "legally" will never be known, but no one familiar with the sources—Whig newspapers are full of accounts of executions—can doubt that it is substantial,[38] although the statement by a New York Loyalist that the rebels "made a practice of hanging people up on a slight pretence" is no doubt an exaggeration.[39] Probably only fear of reprisals kept numbers from being much larger than they were. The carrying out of the supreme penalty was usually reserved for some overt aid to the British such as spying, piloting ships, guiding troops to the attack, recruiting, counterfeiting.[40]

One of the most notorious executions of a Loyalist was that of John Roberts, a native-born Pennsylvania Quaker, who had aided the British occupying forces in Philadelphia and rather foolhardily had not departed with them. His trial was in 1778, and even many Whigs petitioned the authorities for a pardon, but in vain. A contemporary described the situa-uation thus:

> Roberts' wife, with ten children, went to Congress, threw them-selves on their knees and supplicated mercy, but in vain. His behaviour at the gallows did honor to human nature. He told his audience that his conscience acquitted him of guilt; that he suffered for doing his duty to his Sovereign; that his blood would one day be demanded at their hands; and then turning to his children, charged and exhorted them to remember his principles, for which he died, and to adhere to them while they had breath. This is the substance of his speech; after which he suffered with the resolution of a Roman.[41]

In 1792 the state of Pennsylvania restored Roberts' con-fiscated estate to his widow, Jane, a belated act of justice, for it seems Roberts had been a scapegoat, only one among so very many who had cooperated with the British.[42] Roberts' behavior would doubtless have made him a remembered hero had he suffered for the other side. Similarly, in Connecticut, Moses Dunbar was tried and hanged for accepting a British commission and recruiting troops at about the same time that Nathan Hale suffered the same penalty. Connecticut honors Hale but forgets Dunbar.[43] One of the more bizarre execu-tions was reported by the *Boston Gazette* for November 3, 1777, under the date line Fishkill: "Last Thursday, one Tay-lor, a spy was hanged at Hurley, who was detected with a letter to Burgoyne, which he had swallowed in a silver ball, but by the assistance of a tartar emetic he discharged the same."

But perhaps more moving across the years than accounts of atrocities are the more pedestrian misfortunes of war. Women in particular are always the great sufferers, being sep-arated from their husbands and sons, living in constant dread of bereavement. In 1780 Mary Donnelly petitioned the Brit-ish authorities in New York for relief. Her husband had been serving on board a privateer when "about seven months ago as my youngest Child lay expireing in my Arms an account came of the Vessil being lost in a Storm." Mrs. Donnelly was now destitute, "frequently being affraid to open my Eyes on the Daylight least I should hear my infant cry for Bread and not have it in my power to relieve him. the first meal I had eat for three days at one time was a morsel of dry bread and a lump of ice." [44]

On June 6, 1783, Phebe Ward, of East Chester, wrote to her husband Edmund, a native of the province of New York:

> Kind Husband
>
> I am sorry to aquant you that our farme is sold. . . .
> thay said if I did not quitt posesion that thay had aright to take any thing on the farme or in the house to pay the Cost of a law sute and imprisen me I have sufered most Every thing but death it self in your long absens pray Grant me spedy Releaf or God only knows what will be com of me and my frendsles Children
> thay say my posesion was nothing youre husband has forfeted his estate by Joining the British Enemy with a free and vollentary will and thereby was forfeted to the Stat and sold
> All at present from your cind and Loveing Wife
>
> phebe Ward
> pray send me spedeay anser.[45]

One of the most pathetic stories of all concerns Filer Dibblee, a native-born lawyer, and his family. In August, 1776, they fled from Stamford to Long Island, but a few months later the rebels turned Dibblee's wife and five children "naked into the Streets," having stolen the very clothes from their backs as well has having plundered the house. The family fled to New York City, where Dibblee obtained sufficient credit to settle at Oyster Bay, Long Island, but in 1778 the rebels plundered the family a second time and carried Dib-

blee as prisoner to Connecticut, where he remained imprisoned six months until exchanged. With further credit the
family established themselves at Westhills, Long Island,
where they were "plundered and stripped" a third time;
then came a move to Hempstead, Long Island, and in 1780
a fourth ravaging. Dibblee now, for the first time, applied
for relief from the commander in chief and received about
one hundred dollars. In 1783 the whole family moved to St.
John, New Brunswick, where they managed to survive a
rough winter in a log cabin, but Dibblee's "fortitude gave
way" at the prospect of imprisonment for his considerable
indebtedness and the fate his family would suffer as a conse-
quence. The result was that he "grew Melancholy, which
soon deprived him of his Reason, and for months could not
be left by himself," and finally in March, 1784, "whilst the
Famely were at Tea, Mr Dibblee walked back and forth in
the Room, seemingly much composed: but unobserved he
took a Razor from the Closet, threw himself on the bed, drew
the Curtains, and cut his own throat."

Shortly afterward the Dibblee house was accidentally
burned to the ground, was then rebuilt by the heroic widow,
only to be accidentally razed again the same year by an Indian servant girl.[46]

It is not surprising that imprisonment and escape loom
large in Loyalist annals. The most celebrated prison was in
Connecticut at the Simsbury (now East Granby) copper
mines, where the ruins still afford a dramatic prospect. The
isolated and strongly Whig back country of Connecticut was
considered a good spot to incarcerate important Loyalists
from all over the Northern colonies, and the mines, converted into a prison in 1773, were ideal. The "Catacomb of
Loyalty," to quote Thomas Anburey, or the "woeful man-
sion," to quote an inmate, contained cells forty yards below
the surface, into which "the prisoners are let down by a

windlass into the dismal cavern, through a hole, which answers the purpose of conveying their food and air, as to light,
it scarcely reaches them." The mere threat of the "Mines"
could make a Loyalist conform.[47] One prisoner regarded being sent there as a "Shocking Sentence (Worse than Death)."
The mines received such celebrated Loyalists as Mayor
Mathews of New York and William Franklin, who wrote of
his "long and horrible confinement" and was described on his
release as "considerably reduced in Flesh." [48]

In May, 1781, there was a mass breakout. The leaders of
the escape, Ebenezer Hathaway and Thomas Smith, arrived
in New York some weeks later, and their alleged experiences
were reported by Rivington's newspaper. Hathaway and
Smith recalled that they had originally been captured on a
privateer, sentenced, and marched the seventy-four miles
from Hartford to Simsbury. The entrance to the dungeon
was a heavily barred trap door that had to be raised

> by means of a tackle, whilst the hinges grated as they turned
> upon their hooks, and opened the jaws and mouths of what
> they call Hell, into which they descended by means of a ladder
> about six feet more, which led to a large iron grate or hatch-
> way, locked down over a shaft about three feet diameter,
> sunk through the solid rock. . . . They bid adieu to this world,

and went down thirty-eight feet more by ladder "when they
came to what is called the landing; then marching shelf by
shelf, till descending about thirty or forty feet more they
came to a platform of boards laid under foot, with a few
more put over head to carry off the water, which keeps continually dropping." There they lived for twenty nights with
the other prisoners, using "pots of charcoal to dispel the foul
air" through a ventilation hole bored from the surface until
the opportunity to escape came when they were allowed up

into the kitchen to prepare food and rushed and captured the guards.[49]

Some colorful Connecticut escapes in other places are also recorded. Nathan Barnum avoided appearing for trial in 1780 by inoculating himself with smallpox, whereupon he was "sent to the Hospital, where he was chained to the Floor to prevent his Escape, he found Means to bribe one of the Nurses, who not only brought him a File to cut off his Irons, but amused the Centinal, placed over him while he effected it. . . ."[50]

Samuel Jarvis and his brother got out of prison "by the assistance of Friends who had privately procured some Women's apparel which they Dressed themselves in, and by that means made their escape through the Rebel Army." James Robertson asserted that while he was in jail at Albany, the British attacked and set the building on fire, whereupon, unable to walk, he managed to crawl into a bed of cabbages "and chewing them to prevent being suffocated" was found three days later badly burnt.[51]

There was even a series of Tory hiding places between New York and Canada, rather in the fashion of the "Underground Railroad" of the pre-Civil War days.[52]

The treatment of imprisoned Loyalists ranged over the widest possible spectrum. Simsbury was notoriously the worst prison, almost the Andersonville of the time. Many Loyalists suffered close confinement in much pleasanter conditions; others merely underwent house arrest; others were only prevented from traveling; some were on parole and, if banished to some remote part of America, were boarded with reluctant Whigs. Some worked in the normal way by day and simply spent the night in jail. In 1776 Thomas Vernon, a fanatically early riser, was removed, with three other prominent Rhode Island Loyalists, from Newport to Glocester, in the northern part of the state, because he had refused the test oath. The foursome's journey and their few months' stay in Glocester were pleasant and gentlemanly, almost Pickwickian. The friends walked and admired the countryside, ate, drank, and conversed well in the local inn where they lived; they planted beans, killed snakes, trapped squirrels, fished, played Quadrille (a card game); they were very well treated by the ladies of the house and by neighboring females. Their chief complaints were the lack of books, some local abhorrence of Tories, particularly by the men (their landlord said "the town was very uneasy" at their being there), a few fleas, tedium from the lack of friends and family, and some stealing of their food by their far from genial host.[53]

One Whig member of the Continental Congress opposed even the condemnation of a Loyalist pamphlet because it was "a strange freedom that was confined to one side of a question," [54] but such enlightenment (or foolhardiness) was rare. Most active Whigs hated the Loyalists as "traitors." "I would have hanged my own brother had he taken part with our enemy in the contest," declared John Adams.[55] It was a common observation that the Whigs held the Tories "in greater detestation" than the British, that their "inveteracy" was "inconceivable," [56] and several Tory prisoners of the French attributed their harsh treatment to "misrepresentation" by the Whigs.[57]

Benjamin Rush was so incensed by British mistreatment of his father that he resolved to "drive the first rascally Tory I meet with a hundred miles barefooted through the first deep snow that falls in our country." [58]

And, of course, greed and envy played a part. Crèvecoeur, through fictional characters, expressed valid motives for the Whig desire to attack the Tories. He has Aaron Blue-Skin, "a new-made squire," declare, "Oh, how it pleases me to bring the pride of these quondam gentry down! This is fulfilling the Bible to a tittle; this is lowering the high and rewarding the low; this is humbling the proud; this is exalting the Christian, the meek man." A lady Whig adds, " 'Tis best these rich fellows should go, for they won't fight, and by decamping they leave plaguy good fleeces behind." [59]

Human suffering is always deplorable, but it is well to recall that the Whigs suffered from British and Tory persecution and would doubtless have suffered more if they had lost the war, as the harsh behavior of the one Loyalist legislature (in Georgia) that did meet during the war suggests.[60]

In Britain Loyalist exiles encountered some anti-Americanism, but it was not serious or comparable to national Francophobia—no anti-Americanism was observed during the notorious Lord George Gordon riots of 1780.[61] Although American property in Britain was not appropriated, the British, in fact, set some precedent for confiscation. As early as 1775 Parliament ordered the seizure of American ships and cargoes on the high seas; General Howe confiscated Whig property when he arrived in New York at the begininng of the war; [62] in 1780 Governor Robertson shared out rebel lands among Loyalists in New York; [63] and final victory might have meant an expropriation of American property reminiscent of that in conquered Ireland.[64]

The Whigs suffered as the Tories did—legal persecution, mob action, imprisonment (the British prison ships were particularly horrible and gave rise to effective propagandist literature),[65] and all the excesses of civil war. Adrian C. Leiby, the historian of the Hackensack Valley, for example, reports that there was barely a Whig family there that had not lost someone to a Tory raiding party.[66] There is at least one recorded tarring and feathering of a Whig by British troops—of one Thomas Ditson, Jr., in Boston in March, 1775.[67] In June, 1779, the *Virginia Gazette* reported the murder of a Whig captain by a party of Tories whom he had discovered robbing his house. A sentinel wounded him with a gunshot; then, after taking all the horses from the stables, the Tories pursued the captain into the house, where he was lying on a bed, and

> immediately thrust their bayonets into his body several times, continuing the barbarity while they heard a groan; and lest life might still be remaining in him, they cut both his arms with a knife in the most inhuman manner. The villain who shot him, had been his neighbour and companion from his youth.

The victim lived another two days.[68]

CHAPTER VI

The Unhappy Loyalists:
Exile and Compensation

⟨§ "Grating it must be to persons who have seen good days, to be forced to be begging a Subsistence from a Country for whose Cause they have lost everything, yet I must do them the justice to say that in all their Afflictions I never heard them regret their Attachment to England however they have suffered for it."

The Earl of Macclesfield, 1784.[1]

Eight of the thirteen states specifically banished particular listed Loyalists, but these eight states and the other five got rid of many more through fines, various social pressures, mobs, and so forth. Most displaced Tories initially found sanctuary within the British lines, and the great exodus abroad did not come until the years following the surrender at Yorktown.

At all times the British Isles contained a number of Americans who had come "home" for some reason: to attend a university or dissenting academy, to study law at the Inns of Court, to see to trade and business. A few, like the painter Benjamin West, who had arrived in 1763, came to follow a career for which there was little scope in America. In 1776,

according to the Reverend Jonathan Boucher, there were between two and three thousand Americans in Britain, and
while most of them had doubtless come for reasons such as
the above, some indeed had come as Tory refugees.[2]

Substantial refugee migration began in 1774 with the arrival from New England (which supplied most of the mi-
grants in the opening years of the war) of such worthies as
Governor Thomas Hutchinson, the Reverend Samuel Peters,
Samuel Curwen, Richard Saltonstall, and Sampson Salter
Blowers. But there had been an even earlier trickle; for example, John Mein, the Scottish anti-Whig printer of the
Boston *Chronicle,* fled as early as 1769, and his partner and
fellow Scot, John Fleming, left in 1773.[3]

All these early birds were scornfully denounced by those
Tories who stayed behind and took an active part during the
war. William Jarvis, of Connecticut, boasted that "he was not
one of . . . those loyalists who never took up a musqut in the
Cause of Government, and came to Great Britain to enjoy her
Munificence in Peace and safety." [4] David Faith, of West
Florida, wrote to Lord North, May 6, 1783: "My Situation I
flatter myself will appear to your Lordship very different
from those in General Called Loyalists, as most of them left
America at an early period without taking any Active part on
either side. . . ." [5]

By the end of the war there were probably between five
and six thousand Loyalists in the British Isles,[6] but many
of these (just how many is not known) were to depart. Some
returned to the United States; some started a new life in
Canada; others found a future in other parts of the British
Empire.

Let us examine first, however, what life was like for the
Tories while they were in Britain during the Revolutionary
period. Refugees who arrived in the British Isles were naturally drawn to London, not just because it was *the* great city

but also because it was the seat of government and hence the source of patronage, the place to agitate for pensions, places, and salaries. Then, as now, the cost of living in London was excessive—one witness claimed, with some exaggeration, that even "ten times as much capital" would not allow a man to support his family at the American standard they had enjoyed.[7] Accordingly, most Loyalists had to avoid fashionable neighborhoods and gravitated to fairly low rent areas—Pimlico was a favorite. Many others deserted the metropolis altogether for the cheaper provinces, from which they made special visits to town if their presence was needed for some reason. Thus in 1783 Robert Fowle, the ex-official printer at Portsmouth, New Hampshire, thanked the temporary support commissioners for an allowance of fifty pounds a year, but added snidely, "I shall retire to a cheaper part of the Kingdom more suitable to the Provision you have made for me." [8] The north of England was frequently mentioned in this connection, as was Wales, where, for example, Thomas Flucker, formerly secretary of Massachusetts, retired for the sake of economy.[9] Some of the Irish returned to Ireland for similar reasons, and one Loyalist even sent his family to France.[10] Samuel Curwen wandered from London to Bristol, Sidmouth, Exeter, and finally back to London.

The most popular city other than London was Bristol, the attractions of which, besides economy, included its close trading connections with America and its status as a port of embarkation as well as debarkation; it was, indeed, the city in which many of the exiles first arrived and was a convenient springboard for the anxiously anticipated return. Governor Hutchinson preferred Bristol to any other part of England because the people were "very like those . . . of New England." [11] In 1780 Samuel Curwen noted down a very distinguished list of fellow Massachusetts Loyalists who resided in Bristol, including such names as Oliver, Coffin, Hallowell,

Sewall, Faneuil, and Waldo.[12] The people of Bristol (that is, the voters) not only returned the great Edmund Burke, friend of America, to Parliament but also, in 1774, sent an American, Henry Cruger, born in New York, to represent them at Westminster for the next six years.

What did a Loyalist refugee face when he arrived in Britain? The degree of distress varied. There was the misery of the several who were shipwrecked off the coast and got ashore with only the wet clothes on their backs; a heavily pregnant Mrs. Elizabeth Ivey of Rhode Island almost perished off the Scilly Islands, while her "Indulgent Husband, two Sons, and two Black Servants" were indeed drowned.[13] And there was the affluence, albeit usually less than he was used to, of a royal governor returning home to a substantial pension or new office, or of a rich merchant who had considerable credit in Britain and might be able to turn some of his American assets into cash. In short, the price of exile was everything from utter destitution to mere dislocation for some of the lucky. A very few Loyalists became minor celebrities, at least for a time. Hutchinson was one; and at the end of the war Chief Joseph Brant (a visitor rather than an exile) was fêted by London society, quizzed by James Boswell, and painted in full Indian regalia by Romney. But most Loyalists at all levels found themselves in a strange environment with few or no friends or contacts.

Although a certain skepticism should be exercised when reading Loyalist petitions for help, private letters and diaries confirm that much of the destitution described was genuine. One Loyalist said he had literally "only one halfpenny" when he landed at Deptford.[14] James Molloy reported that he was "very little Better than in a Starving Situation," adding bitterly, "I could live very happy in America if I never had Joined His Majesty's Troops." [15] What did persons in such a predicament do? Most war exiles left their families behind, so with luck some of their goods or income might eventually reach them. Personal valuables—watches, rings, and so on—could be pawned in an emergency, and this expedient was often resorted to.[16] Government help, if not bountiful, was available. Commissioners were appointed to dispense temporary support, either annual pensions or small lump sums, to victims frequently officially confirmed to be actually starving and in rags.[17] Some Loyalist officials continued to receive their salaries; a few got new positions in Britain and the colonies that remained—most often in Canada but also in India and the Caribbean islands. Some clergymen got English livings; some aged veterans became "Chelsea pensioners," [18] while some younger ones were absorbed into the British army, though there were complaints that provincial ranks were not recognized and Loyalist officers had to begin again as ensigns. Jacob Williams, a native of North Carolina, arrived in London in 1784, but in 1787 it was reported that although he received fifteen pounds a year from the treasury, he had spent the last three years in the Marylebone workhouse.[19] Debt and the dread of imprisonment for debt followed many exiles like a lengthening shadow.[20] Several claimants did end up in the Fleet Prison or in various other "comptors," as such debtors' prisons were called.[21] Others died bankrupt, while friends who had buried them received funeral expenses from the commissioners.[22] At the beginning of 1784 Joseph Roca, referring to his "exquisite Distress" in "a Land of Strangers," petitioned the Government, in the person of Lord Sydney, thus:

> Destitute of Cloaths and foods I have a mere Refuge from the Inclemencies of the Season at Night, by the Charitable forbearance of a poor Woman to whom I am much indebted. From the Dependence I placed upon the Promises Your Lordship was graciously pleased to make me I have fought with Calamity—I have tired my friends and have more than parted

with my all but alas! I am human—My fortitude now fails me and I sink beneath the accumulating Weight of my Afflictions.[23]

In 1786 the Reverend Samuel Peters recounted a tale of woe to the claims commissioners on behalf of Thomas Cummings, a New Hampshire Loyalist, who was dying and owed forty pounds to his "humane" landlord, "a poor Gardner." Cummings, who had to support a wife and several children, was in desperate need of medical attention, but lacked the guinea per visit the doctors demanded. Peters, in asking for some extra cash for the family, noted bitterly that "severall Small Collections have been made for him and his wretched family among such American Loyalists as have small Pensions, as those who have large Pensions cannot spare sixpence for human Nature in Distress." [24]

The two foregoing examples are not the only ones that mention the kindness of English landlords; Nathan Barnum remarked that his two children were being cared for only "by Courtesy of a Quaker Family." [25]

Jolley Allen, a London emigrant who spent twenty-two years in Boston, where he amassed a large fortune, presents a dramatic case of suffering. Allen joined Howe and had to retreat, accompanied by his wife and six children, early in 1776 with the British. But he did not get very far. He was shipwrecked on Cape Cod and forced to live in a dilapidated cottage, the strain of which experience killed his wife. After some weeks Allen got a pass to visit the General Court at Watertown, during which time his children were "insulted." In Boston he too was "insulted," was unhappily surprised to find his former barber in possession of his property, and on reaching Watertown was confined while the General Court (as the Massachusetts legislature was called) spent a fortnight deciding what to do with him. The upshot was that Allen was sentenced to imprisonment, mobbed, his effects auctioned, and his children consigned to his brother's keeping. He finally managed to escape to London in March, 1777. After his long absence he found himself "a stranger," as returned emigrants usually do. Immediately he sought out his wife's sister, whom he found "doubly chained down, raving mad in Bedlam," and under the impression that the Allens had all perished in the Revolution. To add to his woes, the bills of exchange he had sent from Boston had not been cashed. Very depressed, he visited the New England Coffee House, haunt of his fellow exiles, where the sight of old friends did cheer him up somewhat. Allen immediately set about waiting on Lord George Germain to get aid and was lucky enough to receive a quarterly allowance, without which, he said, "I must have perished in London." [26]

It might well be asked why the suffering refugees did not simply follow their regular American pursuits in Britain. Some, of course, did just that, but many found it impossible. Those who were merely gentlemen were not trained to earn a living except by management of capital and of agricultural estates, both of which had often been lost. Mrs. Elizabeth Dumaresq, a once well-to-do Boston relative of Lord Shelburne and the Earl of Granville, was actually forced to enter domestic service.[27] Merchants, though skilled, found it hard to get back into business without connections and capital. Officeholders needed, and sometimes got, new offices, but they faced stiff competition from native Britons, a competition intensified by the Revolutionary abolition of so many American positions.

The Loyalist immigrant did not arrive in a colonial society teeming with new opportunities. On the contrary, he faced a more settled, more closed, more hierarchical society than America's, with much more poverty, and in many ways much less opportunity, and he often encountered prejudice against provincial Americans. Also, immigrant Britishers who had "bettered themselves" in America returned to find they were expected to resume their previous more humble stations.[28]

Some exiles, including Governor Hutchinson and Joseph Galloway, were consulted by the government for advice on American policy. Also, three Americans resident in England —Dr. Edward Bancroft, Paul Wentworth, and Rev. John Vardill—(they could hardly be called refugees because they left before the troubles began) were engaged in astoundingly successful and quite profitable espionage for the British, although, like most governments, Lord North's failed to take advantage of it. The combined efforts of Bancroft and Wentworth gave the British access to details of Franco-American plans from the beginning, including the Treaty of 1778, a copy of which was in London within forty-eight hours of its signing. Bancroft was a capable scientist and fellow of the Royal Society. A native of Westfield, Massachusetts, he emigrated to England in 1765 and, through a false public stance as a violent Whig and his cultivated friendship with Benjamin Franklin and Silas Deane (who was the first American negotiator with the French at the beginning of the war) became, according to Lewis Einstein, "probably the most remarkable spy of all time." Bancroft was recruited by Paul Wentworth, a New Hampshire relative of the governor of the same name. Wentworth, who also had not lived in America during the decade preceding the Revolution, was another friend of Franklin, and corrupted Silas Deane, finally getting him to oppose independence. After the war Dartmouth College, unaware of Wentworth's wartime activities, made him a trustee. The Reverend John Vardill, a native New Yorker, who was visiting England on official business for King's College when the Revolution broke out, stayed on and temporarily forsook the ministry for espionage, which he carried out from an office near the prime minister's residence in Downing Street, spying on American sympathizers in England and recruiting American agents, including (his greatest coup) a certain Maryland sea captain, Joseph Hynson, who was bribed to steal Franklin's secret dispatches from Paris to the Congress. The motives of these three American turncoats, or Loyalists, seem to have varied: office—the Regius Professorship of Divinity at King's College, New York—in Vardill's case; money in the case of Bancroft; and power, position, and social and political ambition in the case of Wentworth.[29]

Some professional men could find in England an outlet for their talents. Thus John Mein wrote anti-American articles for newspapers, as did several other Tories such as the Reverend Jonathan Boucher and Vardill, who, apart from his espionage activities, also wrote in support of Lord North.[30]

But professional men were not always accepted—Dr. Alexander Stenhouse of Maryland noted "how difficult it is for physicians of the greatest Eminence to gain the Confidence and Employment of any Community." [31] Enoch Hawkesworth, formerly a schoolmaster in Virginia, was forced into domestic service.[32] Things were sometimes—but not always— easier for skilled artisans. Isaac Heron, a New York Loyalist, returned to Ireland, where he tried to resume his trade as a watchmaker—in vain. He failed, he said, because of lack of capital, the number of long-established competitors, and finally because "his known Loyalty rendered him unpopular even in his own Country." [33]

Some Loyalists were the victims of fraud and confidence tricks. Henry Juncken, a German Quaker merchant from Pennsylvania, paid £135 for the lease of a London public house, only to find to his shock that it was actually "a house of ill-fame" not worth even £40.[34]

Without minimizing physical hardship, we must also consider the mental anguish of exile, which was more than likely the greater burden, especially to those who saw their prime

years dribble away during the long war and peace negotiations.[35] The Reverend Joshua Wingate Weeks, a loyal Anglican clergyman exiled from Marblehead, Massachusetts, wrote
in his London journal for February 19, 1779:

> Every object around me fills me with melancholy. Even the
> beams of the Sun do not shine with their wonted cheerfulness,
> places of amusement seem to wear a dismal gloom and even
> the house of God does not afford me that pleasure it used to
> do. I am like a man who has lost all his friends. . . . For my
> Wife, my Children, my friends are in a manner dead to me. I
> am banished from them and perhaps may never see them again
> untill I see them in the mansions of bliss, where I hope we
> shall all meet. [36]

The general result of exile in Britain was much despond-
ency and grief (sometimes fatal) and some insanity and
suicide.[37]

The loyal refugees were acutely dismayed to find that the
home country was not united in support of the American
war.[38] The war was very unpopular in many quarters, especially lower down in the social scale. There was difficulty recruiting soldiers (even some officers were loath to fight), and
some draftees were reported deliberately getting themselves
arrested for debt in order to avoid shipment to America.[39] A
yeoman farmer in Kent expressed a common attitude of his
class when he complained of "this unnatural War against our
best allies or friends the Americans," adding simply, "I do
not like this War." [40] There was even fund raising on behalf
of the Americans. An interesting letter, signed *Detector
Americanus,* in a London newspaper denounced the false accounts of the mistreatment of rebel prisoners that were being
circulated to promote collections.[41]

British radicals were generally sympathetic to the American Whigs. A cleric noted in 1784 that Scottish "people of

fashion" were bemoaning the loss of the war, but "the case is otherwise with the common people, who rejoice in that liberty which they are sensible they want, and which they hope to share." [42] The Irish, who suffered in fact many of the indignities claimed by the Americans, were generally deemed pro-rebel, just as they were usually Whig in America; one Irish Loyalist decided not even to risk returning to his native land because of his expected unpopularity, and an Irish sea captain was certain that "the common people of Ireland were almost unanimously in favour of the Americans." [43]

The refugees were probably not surprised at lower-class or Irish support for the rebels. Nor were they amazed by the moderating influence of what Robert Proud, referring to opposition politicians like Wilkes, Chatham, Burke, and Barré, called "a strong Party in England (once apparently its [the rebels'] sole Dependence), and mistakenly called the Friends of America." But Governor Hutchinson, calling for a clean shirt in which to meet his maker, died broken and depressed not long after Charles James Fox had demanded in March, 1780, that the payment of colonial governors' salaries should cease, "above all the pension to a late Governor, Mr. H., that firebrand and source of the American disputes." Chief Justice William Smith, the Whiggish Presbyterian from New York was downcast to find that his natural English friends—Nonconformist reformers—supported American independence. It certainly did irk the Loyalists that, as Samuel Curwen noted, "most of the middling classes" shared the pro-rebel feeling. In more general terms one refugee *cri de coeur* ran, "A Decayed Suffering Famaly has seldom the Pity, But has often the Contempt of the World." Like their brethren in America, the Loyalists were surprised to find that the British Government seemingly lacked vigor and enthusiasm, and that in the end even George III seemed to desert them: a Mrs. Wright, an expatriate from New Jersey, renowned waxworker and gossip-in-chief to the Loyalists, told William Smith: "The King pities the Loyalists but attributes to their Counsels and advice the late fatal War and says tho' they are to be helped they can't be satisfied and he wished the Nation rid of their Importunities." [44]

James Boswell shows that even some British Tories were pro-rebel. Despite the arguments of Dr. Johnson, Boswell was "inclined to the side of the provincials" and considered Lord North's policies "mad." [45] Many Englishmen, both Whig and Tory, coldly noted in the years following the Revolution that erroneous estimates of Loyalist strength (often from the refugees) had needlessly prolonged the war.

A recent scholar has noted "a wave of public sympathy" in Great Britain at the time of the peace treaty because of the harsh American treatment of the Loyalists (who were likened to royalist refugees from Cromwell) as regards their property and debts, but the wave soon subsided. In 1787 some British friends of the Loyalists introduced a bill into the House of Lords that would have prevented Americans from suing Loyalists in British courts for the recovery of debts. The bill was killed because British creditors of Americans feared retaliation, and some merchants even inserted the following comment on the Loyalists in a newspaper: "Go on, Sirs, until you have made yourselves as thoroughly odious to all ranks in this Kingdom, as you are in America." [46]

Even at the beginning of the Revolution it was reported from London, in words somewhat valid for the whole period, that the result of British coolness was:

The refugees who lately deserted their own homes to seek protection in England are very silent, keep close, and don't talk of American affairs, . . . as they find the spirit of the times likely to drive them back. N.B. An Englishman hates a coward.[47]

Americans in general suffered all along from a weakness of representation in Parliament. During the Revolutionary period (1760-1783) at most six Americans (or only four, if, as is possible, two—Barlow Trecothick and Paul Wentworth—were not born in America) sat in the House of Commons, and only three sat concurrently. Of the possible six only two, Henry Cruger and Trecothick, were particularly sympathetic to the American cause. And among British-born Members of Parliament only a very few, such as Thomas Pownall, the former governor of Massachusetts, took a serious interest in America. It was America's misfortune that in spite of the efforts of men like Cruger and Trecothick there was no lobby such as the West Indies or India possessed. Sir Lewis Namier and John Brooke bluntly conclude that Parliament's view of America must be characterized as ignorant.[48]

The Loyalists, then, certainly faced hostility in Britain. Even from their friends they met superciliousness and snobbery. Samuel Curwen, stung when he heard the colonists described as "cowards" and "poltroons," wrote this in defense of all Americans in December, 1776:

It is my earnest wish the despised Americans may convince these conceited islanders, that without regular standing armies our continent can furnish brave soldiers and judicious and expert commanders, by some knock-down, irrefragable argument; for then, and not till then, may we expect generous or fair treatment. It piques my pride, I confess, to hear us called *"our colonies, our plantations,"* in such term and with such airs as if our property and persons were absolutely theirs, like the "villains" and their cottages in the old feudal system, so long since abolished, though the spirit or leaven is not totally gone, it seems.[49]

The Loyalists were Americans, but Americans without a home. That was their tragedy. William Jarvis, banished from his native Connecticut, bemoaned being "cut off from every

near and beloved Connection [I have] on Earth"; Jonathan
Sewall reported that Samuel Porter (Harvard, class of 1763)
was physically ill with melancholy—"I am assured that he
can neither live nor die in peace but in Salem, his once happy
seat"; and Thomas Hutchinson, the loving historian of Massachusetts, wrote, "I would rather die in a little country farm-
house in New England than in the best nobleman's seat in
old England." 50

A petition from several Charleston, South Carolina, Loyalists said very nicely: "Although your Memorialists differ
from their fellow Citizens in political opinion, they still have
and ever shall retain a natural affection for the Country where
they have passed their happiest days and have their dearest
connexions." 51

On March 29, 1783, Major Walter Dulany, of the Maryland
Loyalists, wrote to the commander in chief in New York, Sir
Guy Carleton, about the prospect of being given a permanent
commission, explaining his position thus:

> My duty as a subject; the happiness which America enjoyed
> under the British government; and the miseries to which she
> would be reduced by an independance; were the motives that
> induced me to join the British Army; nor are there any dan-
> gers, or difficulties that I would not cheerfully undergo, to
> effect a happy restoration.
>
> But, at the same time, that I acted, with the greatest zeal,
> against my *rebellious* countrymen I never forgot that I was an
> American—If therefore, Sir, Independance should be granted,
> and the war still continued, I should deem it extremely im-
> proper to remain in a situation, obliging me to act either di-
> rectly or indirectly against America.52

It is not surprising that the refugees, their pride wounded,
found much to criticize in the mother country. This has often
been the case with visiting colonials of all periods who have
discovered that their romanticized picture of "home" is not

in accord with reality. Samuel Porter, of Salem, bluntly dubbed England "Sodom"; [53] another Loyalist called it "the land of liberty and pride," [54] and there was much "astonishment" at the shocking "Extravagances" of the population. "There is great Room for Censure upon the Abandonment of the People to Dissipation," wrote Chief Justice William Smith, who like many, was also surprised at the poverty of the common people compared with the greater prosperity of Americans, and predicted mass emigration if the poor could ever afford it and the rebel government became more "inviting." [55]

Echoing later visitors to London, Smith remarked on the number of prostitutes and beggars, adding the general observation that "nothing is done in this City but for money." In most ways Smith found New York, then a comparatively sleepy town, preferable to London, where the traffic noise kept him awake at ten o'clock at night and finally subsided only to resume after midnight when all the undesirable shows and diversions came out. In general, the stern Presbyterian, though he did succumb to the theater in the end, concluded that "the Luxury of the Times undervalues Piety." [56]

The Loyalist refugees represented, in a sense, the first great influx of American tourists, and many of them assiduously visited all the sights, but characteristically Edward Oxnard, after seeing the House of Commons, remarked that "the speaker's seat is greatly inferior to that of the speaker in the house of representatives in Massachusetts." [57]

As for the tripartite interaction between the Americans, the British, and the climate, nothing has changed. "The People of this Country to apologize for it when I complain of the Climate say it is an unusual season. It is constantly raw and wet . . . ," wrote William Smith.[58] In January, 1776, Samuel Curwen noted: "Almost as cold as ever I felt in New England"; and then: "The fires here not to be compared to our large American ones of oak and walnut, nor near so comfortable; would that I was away!" [59] In the month of August, 1784, William Smith wrote that he needed a fire in his room, and he added wryly, "I have not yet changed my Winter Cloathing." [60] In 1792 Benjamin Marston wrote to his sister in Massachusetts: "I am heartily tired [of England]. It is in most respects inferior to every country I have ever seen, —excepting what the Art, Skill and Industry of Its Inhabitants have done for it,—which has not yet,—nor never can— procure for it Bright Suns and Serene Skies." [61]

During his exile in London Dr. John Jeffries of Boston mainly attended his fellow countrymen, who, he said, "from difference of climate, chagrin, and various circumstances, are very frequently disordered." [62] In February, 1779, a visitor to Governor Wentworth of New Hampshire recorded: "I have found him very much dejected and pining for his native country." [63] Samuel Curwen's diary is punctuated with refugee funerals.

Typical of expatriates, it was sometimes the little things that were most telling. In 1783 Edward Chandler wrote: "Mrs. Chandler is of this opinion that the *Hams* in England are by no means equal in quality to those in America, particularly made in the Jerseys. . . ." [64] Visitors to England have often rebelled against the food. Some New England Loyalists had friends ship them native fruits and nuts.[65]

Some Loyalists did find things to praise in Britain. Jonathan Sewall noted, as did many, that in New England, the "Land of liberty," he had not enjoyed free speech, "though in the land of slavery my chimney sweep can condemn the conduct of the King's ministers, members of Parliament, and even of the King himself." [66] Governor Hutchinson was not the only refugee consulted, flattered, and entertained by the great in England. Some Americans were quite overwhelmed, even seduced, by the sophistication and culture of London, and none more so than Copley, the artist.[67]

It comes as no surprise that in London, the haven of the wealthy, or formerly wealthy, the Loyalists tended to stick together. They swarmed like bees around such leading refugees as Sir William Pepperrell and Thomas Hutchinson. The latter's household, presided over by his daughter Peggy, was usually alive with a Loyalist hum—in June, 1776, twenty-five American refugees were living under the Governor's roof.[68] Many Tories were welcomed and helped by Benjamin West, one of the most renowned artists in England and one of the two or three most famous Americans in the world at that time.[69]

In 1776 Samuel Curwen founded a New England Club, meeting at the Adelphi Tavern for a weekly dinner, which was attended by such prominent New Englanders as Hutchinson, Copley, Robert Auchmuty, and Samuel Quincy; and in 1782 Curwen noted, "We have an American Thursday dinner club at the New England Coffee-House"—which was in Threadneedle Street and which he had visited back in July, 1775, on his first day in London. This coffeehouse had originally been the rendezvous of merchants and colonial agents before the Loyalists took it over.[70] Other habitual gathering places included the Old Jewry meetinghouse, the St. Clemens coffeehouse, the Jerusalem tavern, and the Crown and Anchor in the Strand (also a dallying place for Boswell and Johnson).[71]

At these Loyalist meeting places the refugees indulged in such perennial *émigré* business as gossiping, petitioning, complaining, planning return and revenge, plotting tactics for gaining pensions, compensation, and places, quarreling with each other, meeting for the common good, and boosting morale. As one Loyalist reported of a fortnightly refugee club, "We talk freely of Politics, tell all the News, and are for the time happy." [72] It was in a London coffeehouse that Massachusetts-born Jacob Bailey, Anglican missionary on the eastern frontier of Massachusetts, read aloud the last verse of his "A Farewell to Kennebec" and "drew tears and sighs from many." [73]

Some Loyalists got a glimpse of George III, and a few of the prominent achieved the accolade of an interview. In January, 1784, William Smith, of New York, went to the King's levee at St. James's Palace along with at least three other Loyalists—Jonathan Odell, the New Jersey poet; Colonel Oliver DeLancey of New York (a feuding enemy of Smith); and Governor William Tryon. Smith exchanged a few words with His Majesty, but only after he had exhibited a certain, perhaps symbolic provincial clumsiness, getting his sword tangled in the legs of the man behind him while bowing.[74] George III also talked with Hutchinson, Samuel Shoemaker (as we have seen), and many others and maintained a cordial, rather touching, concern for these most loyal American subjects.

Most Loyalists who became exiles did not leave America until after Yorktown, so they often experienced the first tribulations of life away from home in some alien part of America. It might be banishment to the back country of their own or another colony or, more likely, life with the British army. Thus many Loyalists lived at some time under British protection.

Life within the British lines was rather similar to Loyalist life in Great Britain except there was far more opportunity for direct participation in the war. In New York Tory activity may be followed in the greatest Loyalist newspaper, Rivington's *Gazette,* where one reads advertisements announcing innumerable loyal meetings (often of Loyalists from individual colonies—they tended to stick together to look after their particular interests) to be held in taverns and inns (where petitions, toasts, complaints, and plots would be form-ulated). Also there was a host of loyal occasions—plays, shows, concerts, balls, displays, lectures, sports events, and celebra-tions of all kinds. Rivington tried to keep up morale—an increasingly difficult task as the disastrous years wore on and housing and supplies grew scarcer—by publicizing Whig set-backs, many of them purely imaginary. Thus Franklin and Washington were reported dead, Robert Morris was a de-fector, and hordes of Russian Cossacks were on their way to help George III put down the rebellion.

Proximity to the admired imperial authority was not alto-gether happy, however. New York remained under military rule, which could be harsh (many Loyalists suffered from the enforced billeting of troops), and this was never withdrawn in favor of civilian government.[75]

Loyalists in New York could never experience the *sum-mum bonum*, the sight of George III, but in the winter of 1781-1782 the King awarded them the next best thing, a visit from his son, the future William IV, "the Sailor King," then serving an apprenticeship as a midshipman with Admiral Digby's fleet. The Prince, undismayed by patriot kidnapping plots, plunged into New York's social whirl, much increased by the war, and in characteristically ludicrous fashion also plunged into the water and almost drowned while skating.[76]

In America during the war the British Government was aware of its responsibility toward the Loyalist refugees. Mil-itary commanders and governors in the thirteen colonies, Florida, and Canada cared for them, granted supplies and even pensions and cash. In New York Clinton disbursed rebel lands to Loyalists; certain government revenues and fines were appropriated for them; and there were also charitable collections and lotteries.[77]

George Deblois, Jr., of Massachusetts, asserted, rather

naïvely perhaps, that throughout the war he had always lived in "a Garrison Town where such Loyalists as applied for Support were seldom or never refused it." [78] Those Loyalists who served in the armed forces or some auxiliary branch were, of course, usually paid for their sevices, and many royal officials continued to draw their salaries. Other Loyalists were able to continue their normal pursuits, and some merchants and traders, far from suffering from the war, made large profits dealing with the British forces. In occupied areas much abandoned Whig property was appropriated for Tory use.

In Britain, long before the peace treaty and the setting up of commissioners to consider permanent compensation, the Government recognized a responsibility to the refugees. Some were disabled and had no alternative but to turn to the Government's bounty. William Jarvis had lost the use of both his legs through wounds received while serving as an officer in the Queen's Rangers and, as he put it, "had also sacrificed at the Shrine of Loyalty no inconsiderable property and Prospects." [79] In granting temporary support, the commissioners certainly gave special consideration to wounds and ill-treatment suffered in the cause of loyalty.

But not only the disabled refugees found themselves in need of aid. Samuel Curwen wrote in December, 1776; "My little bark is in imminent hazard of being stranded unless the wind shifts quickly, or some friendly boat appears for its relief. In plain English, my purse is nearly empty." [80] Two ensigns petitioned Lord Sydney, October 11, 1784, saying that they had "the unhappy Alternative of perishing for Want in a Country where they are unknown, or of throwing themselves on the Bounty of the Crown." Some years later, in May, 1787, James Carson claimed that he had made seven hundred pounds a year as a merchant in South Carolina, but now, he said, "How changed is my situation! tho I can not accuse my self with misconduct or imprudence"; on July 12, 1783, Roger Morris asserted that his family's "only future permanent Income must depend upon what we may receive from Government." [81]

For Curwen, at least, the wind did shift, in the form of one hundred pounds a year from the Royal Treasury, but not all were so fortunate. It was necessary to prove one's loyalty and losses, which was not always easy. Nathan Barnum, of Connecticut, petitioned frantically, saying that the only way he could get proof was to return to Connecticut, but he could only return if he could get a Government allowance, and he could only get an allowance if he had proofs of his loyalty. . . . [82] Many refugees asked for, and sometimes got, money to return to America to look after their affairs or to cover the cost of passages for their families from America to Britain. [83]

By October, 1782, 315 refugees in Britain were getting annual payments totaling £40,280 as "a means of maintaining the Claimants . . . untill their fate shall be decided," and added to this, between £17,000 and £18,000 was dispensed annually in occasional payments for loss and hardship. [84]

The awarding of temporary pensions was not always well investigated or free from political intrigue, so John Eardley Wilmot and Daniel Coke were appointed to investigate the pension roll in late 1782, and they succeeding in eliminating eighty-one Loyalists and reducing the complete payment to £25,800 per annum; but meanwhile, from new petitions, 428 new names were added, at a cost of £17,455 per annum. Many of these temporary support allowances were continued until well after 1790. [85] The investigators admitted that "ours is the very unpleasant task of literally giving bread to those who want [i.e., need] it," and they gave short shrift to the wealthy, like Lord Dunmore, who tried to join the bread line. [86]

In the eighteenth century anyone seeking favors from an

individual or a government official had to engage in obsequious supplication. The Loyalists, often destitute *émigrés*, were frequently in this position. Today the Public Record Office in London is replete with groaning shelves of the paper remains of Loyalist demands addressed to Government offices and officials, great ministers, and more humble civil servants. The Loyalists went through months and years of petitioning, footslogging, and interviewing, sometimes with success, sometimes to no avail.

The Reverend Jonathan Boucher recalled that on reaching London late in 1775 he immediately got recommendations from Lord Dartmouth and the Bishop of London,

> ... by both of whom I was encouraged to hope something might be done for me. I was weak enough to cherish these hopes for years to no purpose; and I might, if I pleased, fill the remainder of my volume with an account of various plans and projects I formed by means various acquaintances and connections I was at infinite pains to form with men of rank and in power, not all of them romantic and unreasonable, but which however all came to nothing. . . .[87]

Boucher, though, did get a pension and finally a curacy.

Joseph Roca wrote to Lord Sydney, the secretary of state, October 12, 1784, to say that he was literally "starving," adding: "Permit me my Lord to observe that it is now one year and half past that I have been doing nothing but frequently troubling your Lordship and Office with Memorials and intreaties." [88]

Even the lucky ones had to put up with vexations. Samuel Curwen noted in his *Journal* for July 10, 1784:

> To the Treasury; found the American door besieged by a score of mendicants like myself, waiting their turns—though I thought my early attendance would have entitled me to No. 1, I was glad to stand No. 21; so great was the crowd that I was more than once about to depart and leave them.[89]

At this point it is appropriate to return to the career of John Malcolm, the much-tarred former customs man from Massachusetts.[90] Malcolm left Boston for England in the spring of 1774 and at once commenced an unending round of solicitation and supplication. He petitioned Lord North, Lord Dartmouth, even succeeded in placing a petition in the hands of George III, and eventually was awarded a pension of £100 per annum. Meanwhile, in the autumn of 1774, Malcolm and Robert Rogers, another expatriate, ran unsuccessfully in the popular Middlesex constituency, for seats in the House of Commons, appropriately enough as Tories, against Serjeant Glynn and John Wilkes, renowned Whig sympathizers with the American cause, or "mock patriots," as they were dubbed by the two aspiring Loyalist legislators.

Emigrés are notoriously quarrelsome with each other. Malcolm found time to continue a dispute with Francis Waldo, a fellow official, concerning a customs matter at Falmouth, Maine, in 1773, and in the process fell out with Governor Hutchinson. In about 1780 Malcolm was appointed an ensign at £60 per annum in a Company of Invalids (i.e., invalid soldiers) at Plymouth. In 1782 Loyalist temporary pensions came under review; Malcolm petitioned the Marquis of Rockingham, the head of the new ministry, and in April, 1782, came up to London to present his case. The commissioners reduced his pension to £60 per annum, but he was still left with a comfortable total income of £120 per annum.

In February, 1783, Malcolm had failed to rceive his quarter's salary (delays in payments were a constant Loyalist complaint), and, of course, he promptly wrote to the claims commissioners:

Pray Gentlemen what is the reason of it? . . . I hope it is not thro' your means or if it should be so pray let me know of it immediately that I may go in Person to my Gracious Sovereign King George the third now on the Throne of this Realm for whom I suffered so much in the Continent of North America and there lost my all in this World, which was a very handsome genteel Estate and there became a Bankrupt for my good King and this Country's Sake. And I pray, shall I now be left forsaken by my King and this Government?

He went on to say that he had had no promotion in the Invalids and "daily" expected his "helpless" family to arrive from America and could not support them on his ensign's pay. Finally he requested some franks for his correspondence and as a postscript mentioned that his recent official journey "of 244 Miles from hence cost me between 11 and 12 Pounds but I hope you will soon make it up to me." He later tried to get himself promoted to the rank of captain. Malcolm died in November, 1788.[91]

The humiliating defeat at Yorktown led early in 1782 to the resignation, first, of Germain, then, of Lord North; to a consideration of abdication by George III; and finally to the formation of a new ministry under Rockingham (shortly succeeded, on his death in July, by Shelburne), which was committed to making peace and splitting the Franco-American alliance. Sir Guy Carleton replaced Clinton in New York, with conciliatory orders to avoid battle and salvage what he could, while Richard Oswald was sent to Paris to begin peace talks with Benjamin Franklin. Because of the basic friendship of the new ministry with the United States, and the skill of Franklin, the upshot was a premilinary treaty in November, 1782. The formal Peace of Paris, which recognized the United States' independence, fixed the country's boundaries (the Mississippi River was made the western boundary), and settled other points at issue, including the Loyalist question, was signed on September 3, 1783.

The Loyalist question was the most difficult part of the entire negotiations, and almost sank them. The Americans felt an understandable animosity toward their enemy brothers,

while the British Government saw the national honor involved in the fate of these loyal sons who had been encouraged to pledge their lives and futures in the royal cause and
had been assured of continued protection.

Oswald had at first proposed that the Americans compensate the Loyalists for their losses, but as one of the Americans
remarked, "It is strange that you should insist on *our* rewarding People who have been plundering and burning and cut-
ting our Throats," adding, "But it would be very hard to
oblige *us* to do it, even if you had conquered us; and you will
please to recollect that you have *not* conquered us." [92] Also,
if the Loyalists were to be compensated, so should Americans
who had lost property and slaves at the hands of the British
and the Tories.[93]

All that the British were able to get for the Loyalists in the
final treaty was contained in the fifth and sixth articles. Under the terms of Article Five, the Congress would "earnestly
recommend to the Legislatures of the respective States" that
the Loyalists be allowed twelve months in which to regain
their rights and property, which the legislatures were asked
to restore; and, as provided by Article Six, further confiscation and persecution were to cease.[94]

Both sides knew that the two articles would be dead letters,
but from the British point of view at least the initiative lay
with the Americans; and as it happened, the states did not
accept the Congress's recommendation, Loyalist property was
not restored, and persecution and confiscation continued.[95]
An immediate shout of betrayal went up. In Parliament, Pitt,
echoed by Burke, Sheridan, and Lord North, now out of
office, charged that the government "had abandoned the
unhappy Loyalists to their implacable enemies." [96] From
among the Loyalists themselves, Joseph Galloway fired off a
pamphlet criticizing Article Five, but Shelburne, who certainly did not relish Articles Five or Six, just replied, *"I had*

*but the alternative to accept the terms proposed, or continue
the war,"* [97] adding, "A part must be wounded that the whole
of the Empire may not perish." [98]

Ever since Yorktown the Loyalists had had to consider the
impossible, the unthinkable—the triumph of the rebel United
States. Many remained convinced that although the rebels
had won military success, the upstart republic would soon
succumb to political and economic anarchy, a view that per-
sisted, in the face of most of the evidence to the contrary,
until well into the nineteenth century, and died only as the
Loyalists died.

As the Anglo-American peace talks progressed, the Loyalists in exile, or sheltered by the occupying British army, became more and more apprehensive, distressed, and even
hysterical. There was a widespread Loyalist furor in America
and Britain that even managed to unite radicals like Samuel
Curwen with conservatives like Peter Oliver.[99] From New
York on August 6, 1782, Benjamin Thompson wrote to Vis-
count Sackville (as Germain was now styled), "You cannot
conceive . . . the distress that all ranks of people have been
thrown into by the intelligence of the Independence of America being acknowledged by Great Britain, and the loyalists
being given up to the mercy of their enemies," and he described the Loyalist attitude as "little short of actual rebellion." [100] In London in February, 1783, the exiles elected
delegates to combat the provisional treaty,[101] but even less
than Shelburne were they able to reopen the war, or change
the attitude or resolves of the Americans.

The vast majority of Loyalists had originally regarded
their exile as temporary and had expected to return as victors
as soon as the British had quelled the rebellion, but as rebel
success became more and more evident, and finally when the
peace treaty in fact abandoned them, the exiles had to change

their way of thinking. Many agreed with Samuel Curwen, who by March, 1783, had despaired of the treaty and Loyalist attempts "to counterbalance the dreadful evils consequent on ministerial neglect," and they echoed the question he put to a former Massachusetts neighbor, "What think you of returning to your late abode, Salem?" [102] Similarly, at the beginning of 1783 the Reverend Jacob Duché was so keen to get back to Philadelphia that he was prepared to sacrifice the three hundred pounds a year he got as chaplain to a charitable English institution; and in March the Reverend Charles Inglis announced that although he had opposed the Revolution from "principle and conscience," he would now accept the result.[103] Duché did finally return, but Inglis finished his life as the first Anglican bishop of Nova Scotia. To some who could not, or for various reasons did not return, the hope remained as a pipe dream, replacing earlier dreams of the failure of the rebels. As late as 1793 Count Rumford informed a friend: "I think it very probable that both you and I shall end our days" in America; "Great Britain is not a place for you, nor for me. . . ." [104]

Not only in Britain was the desire to return home expressed, but also wherever Loyalist *émigrés* were to be found, particularly in Canada. In Halifax in December, 1785, the claims commissioners meeting there noted that many Tories had returned to the United States, and some years later it was said that ever since 1786 lands in Nova Scotia had decreased in price because of "the immense number of Loyalists" who had gone back.[105] (It should be stressed, of course, that the great majority of Loyalists were never exiled and at the end of the war had no wish to leave America. Peter Van Schaack told a Whig friend in April, 1783, that he was "among the great number of Loyalists who wishes to stay." [106]

The number of Loyalist *émigrés* who returned at the close of the war was quite considerable, though it was certainly a small proportion of those exiled.[107] Benjamin Franklin was moved to write to Francis Maseres, June 26, 1785, with his customary eye for irony, that the American Republic "cannot be a tyrannical one, as your loyalists represent it; who at the same time inconsistently desire to return and live under it." [108]

A writer in the *Boston Gazette,* February 10, 1783, recalling the crimes of the "Savage Britons, and more savage Refugees," recommended that anybody in Boston thinking the Tories should be allowed to return ought to be sent to join them in exile. The same newspaper, in its May 5, 1783, edition, quoted a correspondent to the *New Jersey Gazette* who frankly called the peace treaty clauses concerning the Loyalists "a forlorn hope," advised all Loyalists to quit America, and promised continued persecution, arguing that the Tories were the very cause of the outbreak and protraction of the war (if Americans had been united, the British would have stepped down as they had during the Stamp Act crisis). He told the Loyalists: "You shewed no mercy to your country, and you will have judgement without mercy."

Both Franklin and Washington felt quite savagely toward the Loyalists. They shared a prevalent, probably majority, view, which was stiffened in some cases by the fears of those who had acquired Loyalist property. Neither the end of the fighting nor the signing of a peace treaty meant the end of persecution for the Loyalists. In some places it only increased, and a Loyalist committee was soon able to present to the British Government a list showing, state by state, the laws passed in violation of the treaty.[109] David Colden wrote from New York, September 15, 1783:

The spirit of persecution and violence against the unhappy loyalists does not appear to abate in any degree, since the cessation of hositilies. They are not suffered to go into the country even to take a last farewell of their relations. Committees are formed throughout the country, who publish the most violent resolves against the loyalists, and give instructions to the legislative bodies, directly repugnant to the treaty. We are told that these commitees have allarmd the people in power, who wish to suppress them, but know not how. The people have been taught a dangerous truth, that *all power is derived from them*.[110]

The reception awaiting returning Loyalists varied with different individuals and from place to place, but everywhere it could be unfavorable. In Connecticut Stephen Jarvis tried to visit his father, but threats of violence forced him away.[111] In July, 1783, two returned loyal Rhode Islanders were imprisoned and deported.[112] On January 15, 1785, John Sym advised his friend Archibald Hamilton not to return to Virginia because "you would be arrested for every Shilling you owed, before you was twenty four Hours in this State." However Sym also stated, "As to your own personal security you would have nothing to fear in Virginia. In Carolina, I hear it is otherwise." [113]

It was indeed. In South Carolina at least one Loyalist, a man called Love, was lynched at Ninety-Six in 1785,[114] and earlier it was reported that a Tory named Maxwell had returned to Georgia and "in a few days, *he was not in being*." [115] There was violence all over America. Early in 1783, Cavalier Jouet was ejected from New Jersey by "a number of fellows who came about [him] with sticks and whips"; and John Hinchman, returning to his home after the peace treaty, was mobbed, which treatment gave him a palsy stroke.[116]

The following three examples may serve to illustrate further the extreme terrorism some returning Loyalists encountered. At the end of 1783 a New Yorker ventured to Wallkill to visit his parents, was captured, had his head and eyebrows shaved, was tarred and feathered, and was forced to wear a hog yoke and a cowbell around his neck and a cap of feathers on his head. Finally, he was sent back to New York, adorned with a placard depicting Benedict Arnold, the Devil's imps, and a Tory driving off a cow.[117]

Just after the signing of the peace treaty, Prosper Brown, a Saybrook Loyalist, returned to New London on his way home, whereupon a mob hung him up by the neck on a ship at the wharfside, took him down, stripped him and gave him the cat-o'-nine-tails, tarred and feathered him, hoisted him naked from the yardarm for a quarter of an hour's exhibition, and then put him on a boat for New York without his belongings and with a warning not to return on pain of death.[118]

In May, 1783, it was reported that one Triest, a Loyalist who had been with the British forces, hearing news of the peace treaty, returned to his family at Townsend, Massachusetts,

> . . . but having forfeited the protection of the citizens of America, was taken with a hard-spike under his crotch, and a halter round his neck, as the *only reward* of merit suitable for such traitors, he was hung at the mast head of a sloop from eight o'clock in the evening until twelve next day; he was then taken down, put in irons, and sent in a boat with his family to Bagwaduce, having first signed a paper not to return on pain of death.
>
> N.B. Ropemakers are desired to reserve some hempen cravats, as they will soon be in fashion.[119]

If there was widespread animosity from radical Whigs against returning Tories, there was also a considerable demand for leniency as well as encouragement to return from the moderate Whigs.

General Benjamin Lincoln voiced regret to his wife that the Boston newspapers were full of so much virulence against the Tories: "We are not only driving from us many men who might be very useful, but we are obliging them to people Nova Scotia."[120]

Such sentiments were echoed by many patriots, including Charles Carroll, John Jay, Christopher Gadsen, Timothy Pickering, and Patrick Henry, to name a few. Nathanael Greene exclaimed that "it would be the excess of intolerance to persecute men for opinions which, but twenty years before, had been the universal belief of every class of society." [121] Most commonly, political, social, or economic utility was stressed. Thus Alexander Hamilton opined, "We have already lost too large a number of valuable citizens," [122] and he agreed with John Jay and others that harsh treatment of the Loyalists was bad for business.[123]

Connecticut, and some other states, rapidly adopted a conciliatory policy after a brief burst of vindictiveness. (Actually, Connecticut had even been rehabilitating Loyalists *during* the war: a proclamation of May, 1777, offering pardon to Loyalists who would take an oath of allegiance before August 1 was followed by a similar one in May, 1779, and "hundreds had recanted before 1783.") [124] This was particularly the case in New Haven, where the motives seem to have been primarily economic—a desire to escape the orbit of New York and Boston. In May, 1783, Ezra Stiles noted that "a subscription Paper" was going about that would invite wealthy Tory merchant families from New York City to settle in New Haven; in March, 1784, the town meeting voted in favor of allowing the return of Tories in the interests of business; [125] and by this time voters of Loyalist sympathies were clearly an important element in elections.[126]

Like Connecticut, New Jersey had a campaign, following the peace, to encourage Loyalist merchants to return, in order to strengthen the state's economy.[127] In North Carolina, many conservatives, such as William Hooper, an aristocratic signer of the Declaration of Independence, urged moderation, and in 1783 many of the less notorious Loyalists were pardoned, but the sale of Tory estates continued until 1790.[128] In Virginia Patrick Henry led a campaign for moderation.

In short, examples of harsh treatment can be matched by examples of leniency, and of the two, it was usually the kinder treatment that came as a surprise to returned Loyalists. Ward Chipman wrote in his diary of Boston in 1783: "We immediately found how groundless our fears had been of meeting with anything unpleasant or disagreeable and determined to visit all our friends publickly in the morning." [129]

Samuel Curwen noted in his *Journal* that in England in November, 1783, Captain Nathaniel West brought "a message from the principle merchants and citizens of Salem, proposing and encouraging my return," a request to which Curwen soon acceded.[130]

If in South Carolina a returned Loyalist was lynched at Ninety-Six, Charleston was the scene of opposite sentiments. In 1787 Governor George Mathews successfully argued against such worthies as Edmund Rutledge that General Andrew Williamson, dubbed the "Arnold of Carolina" because of his doubtful behavior at the siege of Charleston in 1779 (after a brilliant career as a patriot officer), be allowed to remain, and Williamson's property even escaped amercement. The same year Loyalist William Cunningham, accurately known as "Bloody Bill" because of his guerrilla exploits during the war, was able to die peacefully in his native land.[131] William's cousin Patrick, an outstanding Loyalist soldier, came back to Charleston in 1785, and although he was fined 12 per cent of his property and denied political rights for seven years, he served two terms in the state legislature during that time.[132] James Humphreys, a leading Tory newspaper editor, was one of several outstanding Loyalists who returned to Pennsylvania. Thomas Robinson, the most important Delaware Tory, returned to his home after successfully petitioning the governor in 1786 and correctly pointing out that although his politics had differed from those of his fellow countrymen, he had helped them, had collected and preserved the New Castle County records, and was now "desirous to spend the Evening of his Life among the Friends of his Earlier Years in his native Country. . . ." [133] The former loyal governor of Maryland, Robert Eden, died in Annapolis in 1784 while trying to recover his estate, and in the same state Philip Barton Key, uncle of the author of "The Star-Spangled Banner" and a zealous Loyalist army captain on half pay, managed to return home, practice law, get elected to the legislature, and finally in 1806 to become a member of the United States Congress. In New York State, a scene of great bitterness and persecution at the time of the peace treaty, an inhabitant of Albany reported in November, 1785, that most exiles from that area had returned and "live Quiet and unmolested"; and it is calculated that throughout the state during the "critical period" (1781-1789) of American history, eleven out of sixty political leaders had been Loyalists.[134] In 1790 Henry Cruger, the leading American Member of Parliament during the Revolution, returned permanently to his native New York, and two years later he was elected to the state senate at Albany.

Most states were remarkably quick to adopt a lenient policy toward the Loyalists, and even those, like New York and New Jersey, that had suffered greatly from civil war, and had therefore passed drastic laws, had repealed anti-Tory legislation by 1788. North Carolina confiscated Tory estates as late as 1790, but otherwise was lenient and pardoned many Loyalists as early as 1783. Throughout America many Loyalists' estates were returned. Generally, states that had suffered the least civil war—such as New Hampshire, Massachusetts, and Rhode Island—or that had very few Loyalists—such as Virginia—were the first to cease persecution and prepare to readmit exiles.[135]

Nevertheless, some particularly obnoxious Loyalists found it took a longer time to gain readmittance, and others were permanently forbidden to return. Joseph Galloway was refused permission to return to Pennsylvania in 1793, and no really active Loyalist (except perhaps Thomas B. Chandler) returned to New Jersey, while those who had not actually aided the British—for example, Chief Justice Frederick Smyth —had no difficulty.[136]

Meanwhile, it was generally recognized in Great Britain that in view of the peace treaty and the hollowness of the Congress's recommendations, permanent compensation would have to be given to genuine Loyalists for losses caused "by the commotions of the Empire." [137] One contemporary noted that "the fate of the exiled Loyalists was a melancholy damp to the general satisfaction" with the treaty, while the solicitor general rashly volunteered, "Tax me to the teeth, and I will cheerfully stint myself to contribute their [the Loyalists'] relief"; and Shelburne, looking on the bright side, argued "that without one-fifth of the expense of one year's campaign, happiness and ease could be given to the Loyalists. . . ." [138]

Needless to say, the Loyalists shared this attitude and agitated for compensation as soon as peace became a prospect. "The suffering Loyalists of North Carolina" met at the London Coffee House in March, 1783, and set up a committee to consider their losses, a course of action also taken by émigrés from other colonies.[139] During the same year the exiles as a whole came together and formed a committee, containing an agent from each colony, that produced a learned pamphlet, *The Case and Claim of the American Loyalists impartially stated,* demanding compensation. A Loyalist petition to William Pitt noted that the peace treaty had "brought Security and comfort to the rest of the nation," but had left the Loyalists "nothing but a well-founded claim on the justice of Parliament." [140]

Parliament did indeed find the claim "well-founded." In July, 1783, following a Compensation Act,[141] it appointed a five-man commission, formed by selecting three men to help John Eardley Wilmot and Daniel Coke. Since October, 1782, Wilmot and Coke, as we have mentioned, had been investigating those Loyalists receiving or claiming temporary support in an attempt to effect economies.[142] London hearings got under way, Coke and Wilmot sitting at Newcastle House, Lincoln's Inn Fields, while two of the other commissioners, Colonel Thomas Dundas and Jeremy Pemberton, were dispatched to Nova Scotia to hold hearings, and the fifth commissioner, John Anstey, was sent to New York to gather information. They remained in session at various centers in the New World until 1789.

The claims commissioners had to classify those they accepted as Loyalists into six divisions according to the degree of Loyalist zeal displayed, and they had to record the details and authenticity of the losses claimed. The only losses considered legitimate were quite rigidly defined—for example, damage by British troops, the loss of escaped slaves, trading setbacks attributed simply to the dislocation caused by the Revolution, Loyalist debts to American citizens [143] were excluded; property owned at the beginning of the war and lost directly through loyalty, the loss of salaries for royal offices, and loss of professional income were allowed.[144]

Never was it intended that the full amount of acceptable losses be paid, and after a time a complicated schedule, drawn up by Pitt, was used to decide the proportion granted—normally well under half.

The question arises, Apart from the fact that the government felt unable to give full compensation even by its own definition, did the Loyalists receive just treatment? It is clear that the commissioners' presence was widely advertised, although some Loyalists in Canada arrived too late or entirely missed the hearings. A Loyalist living in an outlying area who had lost only a small amount might well find it more trouble than it was worth to journey to Montreal, Quebec, Niagara, Shelburne, St. John, or Halifax. Those who reached the commissioners found the investigations very thorough indeed, so much so that many echoed Burghley's famous condemnation of the Court of High Commission as savoring too much of the Inquisition. For example, the following question may well have been asked of that numerous class of Loyalists who had begun the Revolution on the Whig side:

> When you deserted the American Cause in which you took a decided part and went within the Kings Lines for protection or came to Great Britain professing yourself a Loyalist, was it from Conviction of the heinousness of your Offence, or from Apprehension you had that the Kings Troops would finally subdue America, in which case your Estate if not your life would have become forfeited?[145]

A pamphlet (of which the current income tax guide is reminiscent), printed in London in 1783 and explaining to Loyalists how to go about submitting their claims, apparently sold well at a shilling a copy.[146]

There was particular complaint that the commissioners examined privately whomever they wished without the claimant's being present or even informed. Further, the commissioners did not allow the claimants to have lawyers to represent them.[147]

The commissioners who awaited a claimant were well primed, having gathered much background information from leading Loyalist witnesses, and they continued to make full use of local experts, such as William Shoemaker and Joseph Galloway for Philadelphia, or William Franklin for New

Jersey, and they also consulted a special committee of important Loyalists, one from each colony.

Unless too ill or too old, the Loyalist claimant was called alone into a private room and questioned under oath; he was required to produce as much written corroborating evidence as possible—deeds, proof of confiscation, and so on; debts and mortgages were noted; witnesses' statements were asked for either by oral testimony or letters of support, and anyone who might have a firsthand knowledge of a claimant's circumstances might be questioned. The aim was to establish what had been lost *specifically* by loyalty and then to come to a fair appraisal of the cash sum—thus the commissioners had to be familiar with the differing values of the various colonial currencies, and had to be able to appraise everything from, say, a brass bedstead in Boston to thousands of acres of frontier land in Pennsylvania to a town house on Broadway in New York.

Successful fraudulent claims were probably rare. The commissioners, with their grave sense of responsibility and fear of spending public funds wantonly, did not err on the side of leniency.

They gave short shrift to obvious fakers with "moonshine" claims, and this probably frightened many others; [148] there were simply too many witnesses about to give the lie to outrageous claims, and the commissioners encouraged the receipt of accusations from the malcontents who were always particularly evident among *émigrés*. For example, one Dennis Carleton in London in June, 1784, communicated to the commissioners the following information concerning certain Loyalists claiming compensation for losses: one fellow Loyalist had left his wife in New York during the war to hold on to his property and then was able to sell it, another "is a Gainer rather than a Loser by the War," another lost nothing at all, and yet another's wife still possessed her husband's allegedly lost property. And then Carleton revealed his motive—his own earlier claim had been turned down, and he now hoped for a more favorable reception. Not, perhaps, the noblest of reasons, but such "informers" did serve to prevent fraud.[149] Finally, in a more regular fashion, the refugees themselves took action: in July, 1783, the North Carolina Loyalists met in London to gather information so that fraudulent claimants would be unable to impose themselves on the commissioners.

The records of the claims commissioners are replete with documents: transcriptions of viva voce examinations and written evidence from exiled Loyalists and others designed to give the commissioners background information on the values of property and amounts of income in America, containing warnings of possible frauds, and also offering many suggestions for useful questions to pose to claimants. Thus we have, undated, unsigned, "Unconnected Hints for facilitating an enquiry in the Losses of the American Loyalists," "Questions proposed by Major McLean to be asked the American Loyalists," a letter dated August 7, 1783, from Jack Hood offering advice on ways to calculate Loyalist salaries, and this letter from Lord Dunmore of October 7, 1783, listing possible abuses:

> By claiming property held by Wife, Brother, Sister, Child or some other Connection for the Claimant.
> Persons who remained there till drove out by weight of Rebel Taxes.
> Persons who fled from an abhorence of a Military Life.
> Others I fear have fled from their Creditors in America.[150]

A reading of the claims proceedings reminds one of Smollett's Mathew Bramble, who wrote of a certain country squire, "There is not a family in the country, nor a servant in his own house, nor a farmer in the parish, but what knows the utmost farthing that his lands produce. . . ."[151]

Apart from the disappointment that even recognized losses were not repaid in full, there was also a good deal of Loyalist complaint about the commissioners' use of "private information," [152] about their seemingly arbitrary disallowances of various individual parts of various claims, and, whether it was sour grapes or a legitimate grievance, about one's evaluation compared with someone else's. Anthony Stokes, formerly chief justice of Georgia, protested on October 23, 1784, that he was only awarded fifty pounds a year, which was the same amount awarded to "some of the most obscure Loyalists from America, whilst several, who held offices inferior to mine, have an Allowance of a hundred a year." [153]

There was much complaint, including various tracts and a petition to Parliament, about delays in examination and payments. Delays were hardly surprising. A mere few weeks after the two commissioners had begun work in London in 1783, 2,063 petitions had been received, and at the same time Wilmot and Coke had to continue to deal for the next year and a half with claims for temporary support, often from the same persons who claimed full compensation. The volume of claims was so great that temporary support cases were heard only in the evenings.[154] The records that have survived constitute a forbidding mass—tens of thousands of letters, petitions, affidavits, and memorials. When Chief Justice William Smith submitted his claim on March 22, 1784, he was told it would be two years before it could be dealt with.[155]

The commissioners faced years of grinding labor to get through all the claims, and by 1788, when they were beginning to wind up their work, *five years* had passed since Parliament had officially recognized its obligation, and perhaps *twelve years* had passed since the unfortunate Loyalist had lost the property in question; in the meantime, in a strange country, his situation might well have become desperate.

But most historians agree that Britain acted generously

and well. The strongest criticism should probably be directed against what one writer has called the "culpable dilatoriness" of the government [156]—even the appointing of the commissioners was delayed (until the government could determine whether the peace treaty would have any meaning), and later, when the amount of work was realized, more manpower could well have been assigned to deal with the claims.

The two chief commissioners, Wilmot and Coke, were both able lawyers and Members of Parliament who had followed an independent line during the Revolutionary War, generally opposing the government's American policy. Thus it is not surprising that the Loyalists distrusted the Whiggish bent of their inquisitors. Indeed, Coke admitted during the debate in the House of Commons in June, 1786, that he had begun his work rather disliking the Loyalists, but he added that his experience in dealing with them had won him over to their side.[157]

In many ways the commissioners were very reasonable. They could understand equivocal or early Whig behavior far more easily from those who were American-born than from British emigrants. And in the case of John Rose, a long-time resident of South Carolina, they commented, "He had been so long in this Country [America] that he might almost have been excused if he had adopted their Prejudices." [158]

On the other hand the commissioners did retain many of their own prejudices as eighteenth-century gentlemen. Official Britain has seldom relished emigrants. In the case of John Cumming, who emigrated to New York with 200 fellow countrymen in 1774, the commissioners grudgingly admitted that he was a Loyalist and granted him sixty pounds a year, but could not forbear to remark that he "was no friend to this Country in carrying out so many Emigrants." [159]

From a twentieth-century point of view, and from an eighteenth-century American point of view, the commissioners were immensely snobbish. They were continually amazed at the way people relatively low on the social scale could better themselves in America. Characteristic of their attitude was this comment, made in reference to one James J. Rice, a waiter and tavernkeeper of Philadelphia who had become an officer in the New Jersey Volunteers: "It has been his Misfortune that the Troubles put him for a time into the situation of a Gentleman. And he is probably unwilling to return to his former Occupation which certainly is open to him here as it was in that country." [160] In the case of Adam Grave of Maryland, the commissioners awarded him thirty pounds per annum, but added:

In giving that Assistance to him we beg leave to be understood to measure it out to his Station in Life [he was not a "gentleman," but a modest German farmer] more than to his comparative merits and Sufferings because many have greater Allowances who have infinitely less merit with this Country.[161]

Most wars provide unusual opportunities for advancement. One such case occurred in Georgia: In their decisions, the commissioners reported that Richard Davis, a baker, went to Georgia "only two or three Years before the troubles, where (instead of suffering by the war) he got into Situations created by the War which he had no right at any time to have expected." These "situations" were Clerk of Market at eighty pounds per annum, and Clerk to the Chief Justice at fifty pounds per annum. The commissioners continued, "he comes with a very bad grace" to claim compensation for the loss of offices, and added, "He probably will be able to get his bread in this Country by following his old trade of Baker which is much more fit than to be Clerk to a Chief Justice." One wonders whether Davis wished he had chosen the other side and remained in America.[162]

As for loyal Negroes, all of whom the commissioners considered to be ex-slaves, a usual comment, accompanying a
refusal of aid, was "he ought to think himself very fortunate in being in a Country where he can never again be reduced to a State of Slavery" (a reference to Somersett's case
of 1771-1772 in which Lord Mansfield ruled that slavery
could not exist in Britain).[163] There were too few Negroes in
Britain at this time to create a racial problem. In fact, many
Negroes had a novelty value as servants. But others did suffer
unemployment; some were taken as slaves despite Somersett's case; others were impressed into the navy; and some
were shipped off to Sierra Leone in 1787.[164]

There is some discrepancy in the sources as to the number
of claims presented and the total amount of money granted.
However, the following seems to be close to the truth: 5,072
claims were presented on both sides of the Atlantic. Of these,
954 were withdrawn or disallowed; the remaining 4,118
claimants (1,401 in Canada) asked for something over £8,000,-
000,and were paid something in excess of £3,000,000. The
approximate figures for actual payment have been translated
as between fifteen and twenty million dollars. Van Tyne estimates the total cost to Britain of compensation and resettlement in Canada as at least thirty million dollars.[165] To this
may be added £25,785, paid annually in pensions to 204 Loyalists for losses of official or professional income, as well as
annual payments to 588 widows, orphans, and other deserv-
ing cases. Payments such as these continued well into the
nineteenth century. Finally, another type of aid (and one that
the commissioners often recommended) was the use of patronage: a few officers were granted new commissions, and
about 500 volunteer officers got half pay; royal officials were
paid arrears, and a few lucky ones obtained new offices in
Britain or the colonies.[166]

There were not enough offices to go around. The independence of the United States helped see to that, but the republic did offer some scope. Thus Sir John Temple, John Hamilton, and Phineas Bond were all Loyalists who returned to America as consuls after the war. Canada and the West Indies also accommodated quite a number of Loyalists. Examples in Britain itself include George Chalmers, who was appointed First Clerk of the Board of Trade, and Benjamin Thompson, who was made Undersecretary of State for the Northern Department in 1780, an important stage in his variegated career.

Were the Loyalists fairly dealt with, then? They got even less than half of what they were allowed to ask for, and many were a long time in getting that. But all manner of recompense was made. At one extreme, Sir John Johnson got a little less than half the approximately £100,000 he claimed in compensation for his lost property; [167] Chief Justice William Smith, by no means the best compensated, got new crown offices worth £1,300 per annum (he had had earlier a temporary pension of £400 per annum), plus a cash payment of £1,200 for property losses, and, as a matter of fact, he still retained much valuable property in America. At the other end of the scale, John Stinson, a modest New Hampshire farmer, was awarded £190 in full for the loss of his farm; Shadrack Furman, a Virginia Negro, got a pension of £18 per annum, which would probably just about sustain life in London; and Scipio Handley, a Charleston Negro, was paid £5 in full for the loss of his few chattels.[168] Naturally, it was better to be rich than poor, white than black.

Probably very few Loyalists escaped being considerable financial losers (not to mention emotional losers), but by the standards of the day the British Government had spent a large sum of money, and certainly American Whigs who had suffered depredations from British Loyalist attacks were not recompensed in a comparable way.[169] In 1784 Colonel Beverley Robinson of New York, who was treated rather well, wrote that the London claims commissioners "seem to take great pains and pay attention to our unhappy situation," adding, "they have a troublesome and difficult task." [170] Chief Justice William Smith found Wilmot and Coke "polite" but somewhat "imbarrass'd." [171] When compensation decisions had been largely completed in 1788, a Loyalist committee, headed by Sir William Pepperrell, expressed, with apparent sincerity, its gratitude to the king, and Benjamin West drew his celebrated (unfortunately now lost) allegorical picture depicting the beneficence of Britannia. [172]

However, 1788 was not the end of Loyalist claims and agitation. Some attempted to get relief or change their status after the commission had been dissolved, [173] and payments and complaints continued into the nineteenth century until all the Loyalists had died.

The British Government, in its way, had granted compensation for losses of property and pensions for losses of income, but there remained resettlement and the granting of land in other parts of the Empire for the majority of the exiles, for whom Great Britain was no refuge. This is partly the subject of the next chapter.

CHAPTER VII

Diaspora

❧ "From Hell, Hull, and Halifax, may the good Lord preserve
us."
—*An old Yorkshire saying, referring to Halifax's notorious
seventeenth-century guillotine, applied in the eighteenth
century to the New World Halifax.*

The Revolution led to a great diaspora, turning the Loyalists
into wanderers. Thus Virginia-born Colonel David Fanning
retreated from North to South Carolina and thence to East
and West Florida, the Bahamas, and finally Nova Scotia. Daniel Leonard, before he died in London in 1829, aged ninety,
the dean of English barristers, had sojourned in Halifax and
Bermuda (as chief justice, 1782-1806), with return visits to
his native Massachusetts in 1799 and 1808.

To go back to the beginning, there had been a trickle of
Loyalist emigration after the Stamp Act crisis, and there certainly was talk of an exodus from Boston as early as August,
1775,[1] talk that became a reality in March, 1776, when about
a thousand Massachusetts Loyalists sailed with the retreating
British to Halifax, Nova Scotia. This was the first major dispersal, being followed by a large exodus from Philadelphia in
June, 1778, and a very small one from Newport in October,

1779. Large numbers fled with the evacuation of Savannah and Charleston in 1782, and 1783 saw the great and final departure of many thousands of refugees from the doomed oasis, New York City. Meanwhile, a less dramatic but constant dispersal by land had been going on for years into the Floridas and Canada.

Probably between 80,000 and 100,000 Loyalists finally fled from the United States. A few remained in Great Britain; some of the Europeans, mainly Germans, drifted back to their homelands; some Loyalists settled in the Caribbean islands; but about half of the total number of exiles wound up in Canada, which makes it by far the most important country of refuge. In 1783 Canada, in the modern sense, did not exist; (but it is useful to retain the word as a general geographic description for British North America). There were simply two Canadian provinces: Nova Scotia, comprising the area now called the Maritimes—that is, Nova Scotia, Prince Edward Island (then called St. John's Island), and New Brunswick; and Quebec, the original New France, which also included the largely unoccupied westward region of the Great Lakes.

Nova Scotia became the home of a majority of the Canadian refugees—about 30,000 people was Governor John Parr's estimate at the beginning of 1784, and the number probably rose to 35,000.[2] A maximum of 10,000, though 6,000 to 7,000 is perhaps nearer the mark, settled in the province of Quebec.

In 1783 Nova Scotia (or Acadia) had been British, with the exception of Cape Breton Island, since the Treaty of Utrecht of 1713. But the growth of the area had been slow because it was a frontier war zone between British and French America. In 1749 Halifax was established by government action (the only American colony Britain ever founded this way) as a counterpoise to the French fortress of Louisbourg on Cape Breton Island, and a few British and New England settlers were attracted. In 1755 and the years following, the exigencies of war and the intransigence of the original ten thousand French settlers (the Acadians) caused the British to deport many of them. The Seven Years' War ended in 1763 with the complete surrender of France in North America, and Cape Breton Island passed into British hands. But the consolidation of the British hold on the Maritime area did not lead to mass settlement, although a few New Englanders had settled along the Bay of Fundy during the war and others soon penetrated the valley of the St. John River and also established fishing villages on the southern or Atlantic shore. Prior to the outbreak of the American Revolution, the whole Maritime population remained a good deal less than twenty thousand, yet a general assembly had been meeting in Halifax since 1758!

The dominant group of settlers in Nova Scotia during the Revolutionary War has since been dubbed the "Neutral Yankees" or "His Majesty's Yankees." Economic self-interest, strategic considerations, and remoteness from conflict kept these transplanted New Englanders at least neutral.

The effect of the mass arrival of the Loyalists, largely by sea from New York in 1783, though there had been a trickle since 1774, was dramatic and important. The population was doubled; the "Neutral Yankees" and the remaining French elements were overwhelmed; and most of the coastal areas of the peninsula, Cape Breton, and St. John's Island received some settlers. The two chief settlements were the valley of the St. John, including the city of the same name (incidentally, the only present Canadian city founded entirely by Loyalists), and Shelburne on the southern shore of the peninsula, which reached a very temporary population of ten thousand.

The Loyalist influx caused the partition of Nova Scotia. The Loyalists themselves (partly because they disliked the original inhabitants) and Governor Parr agitated for it, and in August, 1784, New Brunswick, which probably received about fourteen thousand permanent Loyalist settlers,[3] was created. In the same year Cape Breton was also detached, all conceivably part of a British policy of divide and rule.[4] Colonel Thomas Carleton (brother of Guy) became the first governor of New Brunswick and remained, at best, a tolerable incumbent for the next thirty years. Several Loyalists received New Brunswick government posts: the Reverend Jonathan Odell became provincial secretary, Jonathan Bliss was made attorney general, and Ward Chipman was solicitor general. In 1785 Fredericton was chosen as capital of the colony, and immediately, in ambitious American fashion, the Provincial Academy of Arts and Sciences, the future University of New Brunswick, was founded in that city. In November the first election was held, and the Loyalists proved themselves good Americans by making it a very violent contest, at least in St. John.[5] However, New Brunswick's subsequent early history was one of rather unruffled, uneventful oligarchy. It has been argued that in some ways the Loyalist tradition in New Brunswick (and to a degree throughout Canada) had a baneful influence. The dependence on the British Government during the Revolution and early settlement caused a permanent lack of initiative, an unhealthy scramble for office, a tradition of "political" jobbery and amateurish "mediocrity," and a morbid absorption in politics that hindered economic growth, especially industrialization.[6]

The future of the Maritimes—the assimilation of the Loyalist refugees, the concomitant economic and political growth —is a new chapter of Canadian history and beyond the scope of this book. Suffice it to say that the coming of the Loyalists in effect created the Maritime Provinces, especially New Brunswick, which became known as "the Loyalist province" (St. John was and still is known as "Canada's Loyalist City"), while in other areas the Loyalists remained an essential part of the population.[7]

As in Nova Scotia, Loyalists had been drifting into the colony of Quebec since the beginning of the war; indeed a few arrived as early as June, 1774. It was the natural refuge of New Yorkers: in 1776 Sir John Johnson (who became superintendent of Canadian Indian affairs in 1782) led his tenants to Montreal and formed the King's Royal Regiment, while Colonel John Butler's Rangers had their headquarters at Niagara. Such units as these, allied to the Iroquois, engaged in partisan forays into New York, but by 1780 the Loyalists were in retreat and the sympathetic governor of Quebec, General Frederick Haldimand, was caring for them at camps near Three Rivers and Sorel.[8]

Most Loyalist refugees went to the Maritimes, but up to ten thousand, as we have said, found their way into the province of Quebec. Some arrived by bateaux via Nova Scotia and the tedious push up the St. Lawrence; a few came from Florida up the Mississippi to Detroit; many trekked overland with hand carts via the shores of Lake Champlain, or across the Iroquois land to the upper St. Lawrence, or crossed Lake Ontario from Oswego to the northern Canadian shore; while others made their way west along the southern shore of Lake Ontario and crossed into Canada over the Niagara River. The loyal Iroquois themselves (including Joseph Brant) fled across Lake Ontario and finally settled part of the northern shore and the land between lakes Ontario and Erie. Very few refugees remained in the French part of Quebec. A few settled at Sorel and at a spot on the Gaspé Peninsula, where they were destined to be assimilated into the French majority.[9] Most white Loyalists congregated in three principal areas—the Niagara peninsula, where hundreds of Butler's discharged men formed a nucleus; around Cataraqui (Kingston) and the Bay of Quinté on the northern shore of Lake

Ontario; and along the upper St. Lawrence between Lake Ontario and Montreal, to which area Haldimand had directed Loyalists from the camp at Sorel.

As in Nova Scotia, a new population produced a new province and laid the foundations of modern, democratic, English-speaking Canada, which had previously been mainly a conquered alien territory. The Loyalist settlement was largely to the west of the old French area of the lower St. Lawrence, which did not succumb to Loyalist influence and has remained tenaciously Gallic. In 1791 the British Government, led by the younger William Pitt, did the logical thing and, by an order in council, split Quebec into two provinces, Upper and Lower Canada. Upper Canada (destined to become Ontario, the richest of all Canadian provinces) thus was a direct result of the Loyalist immigration. The Constitutional Act of 1791 set up legislatures in both provinces, each with a popularly elected lower house, thus beginning constitutional political development. It should be stressed, however, that, as in the Maritimes, with the bitter lesson of the American Revolution fresh in their minds, the British authorities did not make the executive branches of these provinces—the governors and their ministers—responsible to the assemblies. The "lesson" of the Revolution was that imperial control should be stricter, not lighter, and Pitt made a point of trying to set up an "established" church with special "Clergy Reserves" of land that could be used to endow benefices.[10] From the start, Nova Scotia was given a bishop, with responsibility for the rest of Canada, something the old American colonies had never had, though they had feared it.

The first lieutenant governor of Upper Canada was the well-known commander of Loyalist soldiers, John G. Simcoe. Simcoe, an able executive, saw it as part of his mission to attract to Upper Canada the many Loyalists (a majority of the population, he believed) who remained unhappily in the United States. Accordingly, he offered two hundred acres of free land to anyone who would take the oath of allegiance to the king. As it was, Upper Canada lay athwart the natural frontier advance from the United States. The result was something of a speculative land boom as many Americans swarmed in—a migration partly from Loyalist motives until the year 1798.[11] By 1812 four fifths of the 100,000 inhabitants of Upper Canada were American-born, but only one fifth had arrived with or were descended from the original Loyalists. The rest were the so-called "late Loyalists," or simply, regular American frontiersmen.[12] Thus, as elsewhere in British North America, the Loyalists were vastly outnumbered by later settlers, but they had founded the province, and their conservative influence could never be quite obliterated. Upper Canada was the main area of western resistance to the United States during the War of 1812 (although not all Loyalists stayed loyal), and the Loyalists have remained an element in Anglo-Saxon Canadian nationalism, especially in its anti-American, pro-monarchy, pro-Empire form.[13] In spite of all the Americans of non-Loyalist origin in Upper Canada, that area's anti-Americanism was stronger than that found in the Maritimes, which have always had close ties with the United States. It is significant that six members of New Brunswick's first assembly, which met in 1785, returned to the United States before the first session was completed! [14]

Generally in Canada the Loyalists and their traditions have been viewed as a stabilizing force: the aristocratic ruling cliques of the nineteenth century, such as Upper Canada's "Family Compact," were partly inspired by Loyalism and memories of the dangers of republican democracy; Loyalist sentiments moderated the 1837 rebellions and "dominated the struggle for responsible government"; Canadian westward expansion was celebrated for its law and order in contrast to the rip-roaring boisterousness of the American frontier.[15]

At the beginning of the Revolutionary War there had been satiric patriot talk that Loyalists were to be sent to Hesse to replace those Hessians killed in battle,[16] but the problem as it confronted the British of what to do with the Loyalist refugees was real. In 1778 there was a rather preposterous scheme put forth suggesting that part of Maine be set aside for Loyalist settlement.[17] And there was a genuine but abortive plan, proposed by an ex-New Yorker, to establish a Loyalist settlement in the Australian lands recently discovered by Captain Cook.[18] Some Loyalists forlornly hoped for partition of the thirteen colonies. William Franklin suggested as late as November 12, 1782, that the British army retain certain areas, such as New York City and Charleston, as a surety of fair treatment for the Loyalists,[19] while a few months earlier South Carolinian Loyalists had demanded partition, arguing by analogy that only seven of the seventeen Dutch provinces had gained independence from Spain in the seventeenth century.[20] At the peace negotiations there was a British demand for a western American area to be reserved for the resettlement of the Loyalists,[21] and there was even talk of putting them on the "wastelands" of England,[22] but it was generally realized that for most Loyalists new homes, outside of both the United States and England, would have to be provided. The majority looked to Canada (which remained British in spite of American demands at the conference table) as the obvious place—comparatively close, geographically similar to the northern colonies at least, potentially loyal (even the French and "Yankees" had been neutral during the war), and with land enough, but not offices, for all.

But meantime the Loyalists had to look out for their immediate future. It was generally agreed that those who had been particularly active would be unable to remain in, or return to, the United States. As a petition of Loyalist officers to General Guy Carleton put it: "The personal animosities that arose from civil dissensions have been so heightened by the Blood that has been shed in the contest, that the Parties can never be reconciled." [23] Thus these officers asked for pensions, half pay, and lands and provisions in Canada, and in fact members of many Loyalist regiments, including their dependents, were shipped there and given a new start in life, and land in accordance with their rank, at the government's expense.[24]

New York City was under the command of the sympathetic Carleton, who carefully corresponded with Governor John Parr of Nova Scotia concerning arrangements for the refugees, and who adamantly refused American demands for an immediate evacuation, which would have meant abandoning some Loyalists. Throughout 1782 and 1783 most British ships in the vicinity had to make three or four trips to Nova Scotia in order to take off all who wanted to go.[25] In 1783 it was even necessary to charter American boats.[26] The city teemed with Loyalists from all over America who were putting their affairs in order as best they could and making hurried preparations for the journey north, which was their "last hope of remaining British." [27] James Rivington made frantic appeals for the payment of delinquent subscriptions, and his *Gazette* was full of advertisements announcing the appointment of attornies representing Loyalists' estates, property for sale, and shipping accommodations available.[28]

Frederick Smyth wrote from New York in September, 1783, that the approaching winter would be hard for the Canadian settlers, adding, "I hope government will give them every possible assistance." [29] The British Government, in the persons of Carleton and Brook Watson, his helpful commissary general, did a good deal—free passage and transport of property were offered to all Loyalists who were free of debt and had lived within the British lines for twelve months; provisions, medicine, tents, blankets, clothes, and tools were provided in New York or on arrival in Canada and for the next three years.[30] In some cases government rations were continued as late as 1792.[31] As early as 1776 in Halifax and 1778 on the shores of Lake Peter, Loyalists had been receiving rations. As the disasters of the war increased, and with them the influx of Loyalists, General Frederick Haldimand of Quebec dispensed supplies generously and wisely, Governor Parr of Nova Scotia doing so less wisely.[32] Most important of all, as soon as it could be surveyed, land was given by lot to the refugees, the amount varying from place to place and with the rank of the individual.

Most of the refugees were utterly dependent on this government support: some petitioners stated no more than the stark truth when they claimed that apart from government supplies they were "without a Shilling in [their] Pockets." [33] The problems of starting a new life in the bleak north were lessened in many cases by the refugees' self-discipline: many regiments stayed together, and some refugees banded together in heterogeneous groups, like the 920 persons at Frontenac who "formed themselves into Companies, each . . . under the Direction of a Captain, for the more effectual Execution of their general Design, and for their mutual Support," the design in this case being trade with the Indians.[34]

The usual form of government aid is well illustrated by the following memorandum: [35]

New York 14 June 1783.

Necessaries and Provisions given to Loyalists gone and going to Nova Scotia, who are realy Poor Viz

Arms

for 1 Man
- 1 Spade ⎫
- 1 Axe   ⎬ to each family
- 4 Yards Woollen Cloth
- 7 Yards Linen
- 2 Pairs of Shoes
- 2 Pairs of Stockings
- 1 Pair of Mitts

for 1 Woman
- 3 Yards of Woollen Cloth
- 6 Yards of Linnen
- 2 Pairs of Stockings
- 1 Pair of Mitts
- 1 Pair of Shoes

for 1 Child above 10 Years old
- 2 Yards of Woollen Cloth
- 6 Yards of Linen
- 1 Pair of Stockings
- 1 Pair Mitts

for 1 Child under 10 Years
- 1½ Yard of Woollen Cloth
- 3 Yards of Linen

Six Months Provisions for each Person from the Time of their Arrival.

N.B. Men, Women and Children above 10 Years, at full Allowance
Children under 10 Years, at half Allowance
hopes were given them that should their wants demand further Aid of Provisions. Government would Grant it if in their Power ⎬ Brook Watson

The British Government, as we have mentioned, dispatched two of the claims commissioners, Colonels Dundas and Pemberton, to Canada to examine Loyalist claims in the same way that cases were heard in London. But it is certain that only a small proportion of the Loyalists actually presented claims. The losses of the majority were moderate and thus did not merit the trouble and expense of preparing a claim and journeying to Halifax, St. John, or Montreal. Some did not even know that it was possible to submit a claim; others were too late.[36]

Van Tyne calculated that the British spent $5,000,000 to start Nova Scotia, and by 1787 had spent $4,000,000 on Upper Canada, all this not including the disbursement of free land. The grand total, including compensation, was at least £30,000,000.[37]

Almost every aspect of eighteenth-century life was considerably more dangerous than it is today. Travel, especially by sea, was very hazardous. The overcrowded voyage of up to three weeks from New York to Nova Scotia was generally very trying, with rough seas, dreadful food, disgusting accommodations. Many Loyalists suffered shipwrecks. One dramatic example occurred in November, 1783, when the transport *Martha*, laden with Loyalist families from Maryland, sank off Seal Island in the Bay of Fundy, drowning 250 persons, a few members of the crew being the only survivors.[38]

For those lucky enough not to have been shipwrecked en route, conditions in Nova Scotia must sometimes have made them almost wish they had been. On January 25, 1783, an advertisement in Rivington's *Gazette* sang the praises of St. John's Island by discounting the rumors that there was nothing to eat there except insects that otherwise would eat the settlers, and by describing the isle as a veritable fertile paradise with a climate such "that Fevers and Agues are unknown." At about the same time the patriot *Boston Gazette* commented that the Loyalists were about to flee to "the frozen desarts of Nova Scotia, there to drag out the residue of a life more intolerable than death." [39] Of the two hyperboles, the patriots' was the more accurate.

The *Boston Gazette* for September 22, 1783, published an extract of a letter from Port Roseway that described the refugees as "the most miserable set of beings that it is possible to conceive of," cursing "both King and Congress." The *Boston Gazette* is not necessarily the most unbiased source for descriptions of Loyalists, but it is a fact that Shelburne, the artificial boom town at Port Roseway, boasted ten thousand sanguine inhabitants in 1783, which population had dwindled to a forlorn few hundred two or three years later.[40] Shelburne did have a good harbor, but it was frozen in winter; the soil was infertile, and the land needed to be cleared of trees. Many of the well-to-do settlers were unsuited to the task; many of the discharged soldiers, unlike those groups mentioned earlier, lacked discipline; and the whole population was exceptionally quarrelsome and factious. The end of government supplies in 1787 was the *coupe de grâce*.[41]

The majority of free or emancipated Negroes who had fought for the British were taken to Canada. About three thousand went to Nova Scotia,[42] but it is clear that they received much less than fair treatment. For example, several hundred "Black Pioneers," commanded by a mulatto, Colonel Stephen Bluck, settled at Port Roseway, but they were carefully placed in "Birch Town," four miles away from the main settlement at Shelburne.[43] After seven years in Canada Thomas Peters, late sergeant in the "Black Pioneers," was deputed to go to London to present the Negroes' complaints. In general, he said, their condition was "extremely irksome and disadvantageous," partly because of the failure to receive the land they had expected, but more particularly because of "a public and avowed Toleration of Slavery"—even acknowledgedly free Negroes had no civil rights, and some had actually been enslaved.[44] Early in 1792 Peters led more than a thousand of his compatriots to Sierra Leone in West Africa. Their subsequent history was turbulent, but the best scholar on the subject asserts that "without the Nova Scotians the Colony would have failed." [45]

For whites, too, life in Nova Scotia left something to be

desired. Of course, *émigrés* rarely enjoy having to move, and those who had built up any sort of life for themselves in America were obliged to start over again from scratch in Canada and, especially if they were getting on in years, could not be expected to relish the experience, however favorable the conditions. But conditions were in many ways unfavorable. In 1784 a Loyalist complained, "all our golden promises are vanished in smoke. We were taught to believe this place was not barren and foggy . . . but we find it ten times worse. We have nothing but his Majesty's rotten pork and unbaked flour to subsist on. . . . It is the most inhospitable clime that ever mortal set foot on." [46] Criticism of the climate was repeated continually. Rufus Chandler wrote in May, 1787: "It is now more than six months since I arrived in this country, the weather has been so Extreme Cold that we have continued froze up the whole time and are heartily tired of Nova Scotia." [47]

The climate was a worse shock to Southerners. On December 9, 1785, a group of North Carolina Loyalists petitioned the British Government in words that, typical of such petitions, betray an underlying bitterness and disillusionment: "your Memorialists are extremely Sorry, that their most gracious Sovereign has been compelled from the rigours of necessity to cede his late refractory Subjects all that Happy, Temperate, and Southern Climate in America to which your Memorialists and their numerous adherents have been accustomed." They continued that in Nova Scotia they "found it altogether impossible, in the present state of finances, to clear the ground, and raise the necessaries of life, in a Climate to southern Constitutions inhospitable and Severe." [48] Accordingly, they wanted to go to the more congenial Bahama Islands.

As James Cable, a Connecticut refugee, said in reference to Nova Scotia: "The difficulties attending the Settling of the

Country . . . [are] great, the People in general being poor and very unequal to the Task, Cattle and other Articles dear, Winters long and tedious." [49] A disabled New Jersey Loyalist, Weart Banda, told the claims commissioners of "his wound rendering him incapable of those Exertions for their [i.e., his family's] Support which the rude face of this Country absolutely requires." [50] In short, in spite of the small but organized population that already existed and the long settlement of some places by the time the Loyalists arrived, Canada was still a poor, backward, frontier place with a severe climate. The Maritimes have remained comparatively poor to this day, so it is not surprising to find one Loyalist writing in 1791 that Annapolis, in Nova Scotia, "is still the seat of Harmony and friendship, I wish I could add wealth," and that Parrsborough, also in Nova Scotia, "is by no means a flourishing settlement. . . . To set down at Parrsborough for the sake of a Good house, is like a hungry man setting down to a table well set out with a variety of empty plate and Dishes." [51]

Conditions were best for modest farmers, for the few rich officeholders, and for ex-officers (because they received half pay) and were worst for the comparatively few professional men. But some of the half-pay officers did not fare well. It was reported that the financial security made the recipients idle and morosely introspective and prevented them from joining in the clearing of the wilderness.[52] Rufus Chandler found that there were too many "starved Lawyers"; there was no money to be made in law. Dr. Azor Betts related that he was forced to clear land because the New Brunswickers were too poor to support a medical practice.[53] Joshua Chandler, formerly a wealthy Connecticut gentleman, was loath to go to "the Deserts of Nova Scotia" because "not one of the Famaly are used to Labour," and he believed that he himself was too old to begin.[54]

And the story of Filer Diblee's family—whose earlier misfortunes we have already recounted—provides a most poignant example of Loyalist sufferings in Canada. Diblee himself, a former representative in the Connecticut general assembly, had been driven to despair by the strains of remaining loyal and had committed suicide in 1784. On November 17, 1787, Mrs. Diblee, the daughter of a well-known Stamford, Connecticut, family, wrote to her Loyalist brother, William Jarvis, then living in exile in Pimlico, London.

Kingston, New Brunswick
Nov^{br} 17.87

Dear Billy

I have received your two Letters and the Trunk, and I feel the good Effects of the Clothes you sent me and my Children, and I value them to be worth more than I should have valued a thousand Pounds sterling in the year 1774. Alas, my Brother, that Providence should permit so many Evils to fall on me and my Fatherless Children—I know the sensibility of your Heart—therefore will not exaggerate in my story, lest I should contribute towards your Infelicity on my account—Since I wrote you, I have been twice burnt out, and left destitute of Food and Raiment; and in this dreary Country I know not where to find Relief—for Poverty has expelled Friendship and Charity from the human Heart, and planted in its stead the Law of self-preservation—which scarcely can preserve alive the rustic Hero in this frozen Climate and barren Wilderness—

You say "that you have received accounts of the great sufferings of the Loyalists for want of Provisions, and I hope that you and your Children have not had the fate to live on Potatoes alone—" I assure you, my dear Billy, that many have been the Days since my arrival in this inhospitable Country, that I should have thought myself and Family truly happy could we have "had Potatoes alone—" but this mighty Boon was denied us—! I could have borne these Burdens of Loyalty with Fortitude had not my poor Children in doleful accents cried, Mama, why don't you help me and give me Bread?

O gracious God, that I should live to see such times under the Protection of a British Government for whose sake we have Done and suffered every thing but that of Dying—

May you never Experience such heart piercing troubles as I have and still labour under—you may Depend on it that the Sufferings of the poor Loyalists are beyond all possible Discription—The old Egyptians who required Brick without giving straw were more Merciful than to turn the Israelites into a thick Wood to gain Subsistance from an uncultivated Wilderness—Nay, the British Government allowed to the first Inhabitants of Halifax, Provisions for seven years, and have denied them to the Loyalists after two years—which proves to me that the British Rulers value Loyal Subjects less than the Refuse of the Gaols of England and America in former Days—Inhumane Treatment I suffered under the Power of American Mobs and Rebels for that Loyalty, which is now thought handsomely compensated for, by neglect and starvation—I dare not let my Friends at Stamford know of my Calamatous Situation lest it should bring down the grey Hairs of my Mother to the Grave; and besides they could not relieve me without distressing themselves should I apply—as they have been ruined by the Rebels during the War—therefore I have no other Ground to hope, but, on your Goodness and Bounty—

I wish every possible happiness may attend you, and your amiable Wife, and Child—and my Children have sense enough to know they have an Uncle Billy, and beg he will always remember them as they deserve.

I have only to add—that by your Brother Dibblee's Death—my Miseries were rendered Compleat in this World but as God is just and Merciful my prospects in a future World are substantial and pleasing—I will therefore endeavour to live on hopes till I hear again from you—I remain in possession of a grateful Heart,

> Dear Billy
> your affectionate Sister,
> Polly Dibblee [55]

Man, in the form of government officials, could ease the Loyalists' plight, even if the Canadian environment and climate were beyond his powers. But unfortunately not all the persons in authority performed as well as Carleton. There were legitimate complaints about poor arrangements for the reception of the Loyalists (at St. John virtually nothing had been done); the surveying and dispensing of land was too slow and sometimes unfair (the six hundred Loyalists on Prince Edward Island were notoriously cheated); supplies of food, timber, tools, and sawmills were not always sufficient, the result being that some unfortunates had to spend their first winter in tents or bark huts. There is a traditional story in Halifax that during that first winter the cabooses (the deck kitchens) had to be taken off the ships in the harbor to house the immigrants.[56]

A lady Loyalist recalled her arrival at primitive St. John in 1783: "I climbed to the top of Chipman's Hill and watched the sails disappearing in the distance, and such a feeling of loneliness came over me that, although I had not shed a single tear through all the war, I sat down on the damp moss with my baby in my lap and cried." [57]

In the early years of the Revolution Governor Legge of Nova Scotia, despite many other shortcomings, dealt well with the refugees, notably those who had fled from Boston in 1776, who were given cash. The Governor also attempted to regulate the prices of supplies, which were in danger of skyrocketing.[58] Later Governor Parr, a run-of-the-mill administrator from Ireland who took office in 1782, certainly faced greater difficulties, but the situation overwhelmed him, and there was reasonable complaint that he was unequal to the job. Also, Parr, in contrast to the military commander, General Henry Edward Fox, a younger brother of the celebrated Charles James Fox, was not particularly sympathetic to the Loyalists, who upset his quiet, comfortable routine.

Antagonism was widespread among the existing, far from fanatically loyal, inhabitants of Canada, who could hardly be expected to relish the sudden Tory descent. In 1786 Colonel Dundas, the claims commissioner, noted laconically that the Loyalists of Nova Scotia had "experienced every possible injury from the old inhabitants." [59] For their part, the Loyalist arrivals in the Maritimes, possibly with some justification, considered themselves superior: Edward Winslow referred to "the languid wretches who formerly inhabited the country," and Dundas called them a "despicable race." [60]

As for the Loyalists' reception in the province of Quebec, though all was not perfection, Governor Haldimand, as we have noted, proved a much abler administrator than Parr. Haldimand began land surveys in the autumn of 1783 (but they were done too quickly, and the result was numerous lawsuits), and Sir John Johnson was charged with moving the refugees from the camps by bateaux to their new western settlements. Haldimand did not hesitate to disobey his orders from England and gave the Loyalists full rations instead of half. The worst refugees he had to deal with were certain land-grabbers who left their families to be provided for at government expense while they roamed off. Many of the dissatisfied returned to the United States.[61]

The story of disillusioned emigrants, described in the preceding pages, is as old and as new as the history of emigration, and, of course, one finds no letters of praise among the claims records, which naturally stress the bleak side. But even at first some Loyalists, especially the better-off ones with jobs, found things favorable in Canada. On November 29, 1783, Sarah Winslow wrote from Halifax that "we are not only comfortably but eligably situated in a good house." [62]

In December, 1786, Colonel Dundas reported to Earl Cornwallis that in general the Loyalist settlements in Nova Scotia "surpass anything I could expect to have seen in a climate which is seven months winter." [63] Nova Scotia possessed two excellent natural resources—fish and timber—and an eager, protected market—the British West Indies, which remained an underlying source of economic strength. Already in 1783, within one year of its settlement, St. Andrews, a town founded by Maine Loyalists just over the United States border on the St. Croix estuary, was engaged in a flourishing export trade.[64]

In 1802 Edward Winslow looked back at the history of the Loyalists in New Brunswick. The early settlers had existed on a primitive frontier level in crude huts with rough wooden furniture and implements, clearing the land and desperately raising a few crops. During the first six years things improved a little, but at the end of fifteen or sixteen years the result of "immense labor" was a prosperous farming community living in snug log cabins without major grievances. "Enquire among 'em," suggested Winslow. "Are you oppressed with taxes? No. Does anybody interrupt you in matters of conscience? No. Do the laws afford you sufficient protection? Why yes." [65]

The western settlements of Upper Canada were more isolated than the settlements in the Maritimes, partly because of the rapids in the St. Lawrence. There was famine from 1788 to 1789, but by 1791 the worst was over, and the rich soil, as good as any in America, presaged a comfortable future.[66]

Throughout Canada, timber, game, and fish were a plentiful blessing. Nature was most bountiful in the practically virgin wilderness of Upper Canada. There forests of such hardwoods as walnut, oak, and elm, though valuable in the long run, were obstacles, being difficult to destroy, or float to a market. From the start wild geese, turkeys, and deer gave excellent eating, and the salmon were reportedly so thickly massed in the streams that they could be speared by anyone with so much as a pitchfork. The climate proved healthy enough, although malaria and insect pests were found in the west, and the isolation of the long hard winters could be trying and even dangerous when someone fell sick.[67]

The daughter of a Loyalist reminisced in 1861, with pardonable pride, that in the early days "men women and children all went to work clearing the land. There were none to make improvements in Canada then but . . . Loyalists and they with their hoes planted the germ of its future greatness." [68]

It used to be thought that the Loyalists in the Maritimes tended to be wealthy aristocrats or professionals from Massachusetts, Harvard graduates being particularly numerous. And this in contrast to the humble settlers from New York and Pennsylvania in Upper Canada, many of whom were illiterate, signing documents with the traditional X. It is now clear, partly through the work of Esther Clark Wright, that the majority of refugees in the east were also humble, American-born, and usually farmers, who were far more likely to have come from New York, New Jersey, and Connecticut than Massachusetts. The presence of a few distinguished former Massachusetts citizens led earlier to erroneous generalizations. The typical refugee, a strong, uncomplaining, backwoods farmer, or a humble artisan, with the necessary pioneer skills, proved a much more useful addition to a population engaged in opening up the wilderness than most Harvard alumni.[69] Of course, Canada as a whole did gain some very talented leaders, for example, Sir John Johnson, Chief Justice William Smith, Stephen Jarvis, Edward Winslow, Edmund Fanning, Jonathan Sewall, and Bishop Charles Inglis, to name a few at random.

One expert on the Canadian refugees argues that feelings of bitterness about the Revolution and its aftermath usually gave way rapidly to a desire to forget, and finally, about five years after the peace, to feelings of reconciliation.[70]

But reconciliation was not always the case. A contemporary account of the War of 1812 and the part played in it by the Canadian Glengarry Regiment on the border between Ontario and New York contains the following incident:

> In this regiment there were a father and three sons, American U. E. Loyalists, all of them crack shots. In a covering party one day the father and one of the sons were sentries on the same point. An American rifleman dropped a man to his left, but in so doing exposed himself, and almost as a matter of course, was instantly dropped in his turn by the unerring aim of the father. The enemy were at that moment being driven in, so the old man of course (for it was a ceremony seldom neglected,) went up to rifle his victim. On examining his features he discovered that it was his own brother. Under any circumstances this would have horrified most men, but a Yankee has much of the stoic in him, and is seldom deprived of his equanimity. He took possession of his valuables, consisting of an old silver watch and a clasp knife, his rifle and appointments, coolly remarking, that it "served him right for fighting for the rebels, when all the rest of his family fought for King George." It appeared that during the revolutionary war his father and all his sons had taken arms in the King's cause, save this one, who had joined the Americans. They had never met him from that period till the present moment; but such is the virulence of political rancour, that it can overcome all the ties of nature.[71]

As late as 1861 a Loyalist's daughter looked over the border with satisfaction at the growing storm of civil war—"The God of Heaven," she argued, was conscious of the unfair treatment the Loyalists had received and thus "the sword of vengeance is now . . . drawn over the American people (now they know how to appreciate loyalty). . . ."[72]

Reviled or forgotten in the United States, the Loyalists are venerated in Canada as founding fathers. In 1789 Lord Dorchester (as Sir Guy Carleton was now known), governor in series of all British North America, ordered that the Loyalists—defined as those who had joined the royal standard before the peace treaty of 1783—should, with their descendants, have "a Marke of Honor," the right to affix the letters *U.E.,* for United Empire Loyalists, after their names, and their sons and daughters were to receive two hundred acres of land (sons on reaching twenty-one, daughters on getting married). Something of a Loyalist cult developed in the mid-nineteenth century, and as late as 1894 the "distinction" *U.E.* was reportedly "treasured." [73] The Loyalist tradition is certainly very much alive in eastern Canada to this day, and even the skeptical will find themselves easily convinced by a visit there.

Like Canada in the north, the Floridas (East and West) in the south remained in British hands throughout most of the war and were a natural haven for Loyalists, especially from adjoining areas. The primitive Floridas had been ceded to Britain by Spain in the Treaty of Paris in 1763 and had been only partially settled by a few discharged British soldiers and others, which fact, added to their geographic remoteness, explains their failure to join in the American Revolution.

West Florida, comprising much of present-day Alabama and Mississippi, and the more isolated of the two provinces, was beyond the reach of the mass of Loyalist refugees, but as early as July, 1775, Lord Dartmouth designated it as a Loyalist asylum and instructed Governor Peter Chester to aid bona fide refugees and grant them land. This offer counterbalanced the normal flow of western migration with a Loyalist influx that probably doubled the population during the following five years, bringing it to six thousand inhabitants, most of them white. Almost all the thirteen colonies were represented, but the majority of settlers came from Georgia, South Carolina, and Virginia.[74]

During the Revolutionary War a West Florida Loyalist regiment was organized, but in spite of the additional presence of British regulars and a body of Pennsylvania and Maryland Loyalists, Pensacola, and with it the whole province, fell to the Spanish in May, 1781. What happened to the West Florida Loyalists is not entirely clear, but few stayed under the restored Spanish rule. Some probably accompanied the retreating garrison to New York; some arrived in Jamaica in 1783: one way or another most made their way to areas of British control.[75]

East Florida is more important in Loyalist annals than the western province. A few Southern Loyalists wandered into East Florida with the beginning of the war. One nervous Boston Irish customs man, Daniel Chamier, arrived in June, 1775, as the very first refugee.[76] Early in 1776 Lieutenant Colonel Thomas Brown, a prominent Georgia Loyalist, was able to form the East Florida Rangers, who were to become engaged in much bloody back-country fighting in the South. But there was no mass influx until the evacuations of Savannah and Charleston in 1782. Perhaps the Loyalist immigration brought about five thousand whites and eight thousand blacks.

East Florida was an obvious refuge for slave-owning Loyalists—as some Georgians in East Florida told Carleton, they could not go to New York because of their Negroes, "on whose labour the future subsistance of our families depends." [77] There were also many merchants among the East Florida Loyalists, but the majority were probably backwoods farmers. As elsewhere, the British Government, acting in this case through Governor Patrick Tonyn, aided the refugees as best it could with provisions, tools, and favorable land grants.[78]

But East Florida, geographically such a perfect spot for Southern Loyalists, was to prove itself merely a temporary haven. Governor Tonyn first heard of the possible evacuation of the province in June, 1782, and at the end of the year it was definite—by the peace treaty both the Floridas were returned to Spain and the inhabitants given eighteen months to sell their property and clear out if they wanted to. For the few original British inhabitants who had come in after 1763 this was bad enough, but for the Loyalists, still reeling from the British evacuation of Georgia and South Carolina, it was disastrous. Many Loyalists noted that the news of the cession emboldened the "Banditti who infested the Province" to greater desperate thievery, while others said they had to leave so soon that the crops were left unharvested, their slaves' work unrealized. One Loyalist said news of the cession made debtors default; another noted the difficulty of finding any buyers for his property but Spaniards, who could not be trusted to pay; another had to sell his property for half its value.[79] In short, as a Tory put it, "The People's consternation on this News [of the cession to Spain] is not in the power of the ablest Pen to describe." [80]

But the pen of one group of East Florida Loyalist petitioners made the attempt in a memorial of October 20, 1784. That memorial declared

. . . [we] whose fortunes have been Sacrificed and we bereft of our slaves, Abandoned by our Sovereign, Deserted by our Country, are Reduced to the Dreadful Alternative of returning to our Homes to receive insult worse than Death to Men of Spirit, or remain in constant dread of assassination, go to the inhospitable Regions of Nova Scotia, or to the Bahama Islands, where without Slaves, Poverty and wretchedness Stares us in the Face, or last of all deny our Religion and renounce our Country and become Spanish Subjects.[81]

Virtually all people of British or American origin left East Florida with most of their slaves rather than submit to Spanish rule. Some simply lit out into the back-country, but the greatest number, probably over 3,200, went to the Bahamas; nearly as many returned to the United States, while 1,850 proceeded to Jamaica, Dominica (Lord Sydney instructed the governor in November, 1785, to grant lands to 700 Loyalist families who had fled from East Florida),[82] and other islands; 880 went to Nova Scotia, something less than 300 to Great Britain.[83]

Thus the West Indies' population was considerably augmented by the evacuation of East Florida. But the islands had been gaining Loyalist *émigrés* since the begining of the war, directly from the rebellious colonies, and then particularly from the evacuations of Savannah, Charleston, and New York, while some disillusioned exiles had come from Nova Scotia to the southern islands. The exact figures will never be known, but the West Indies clearly gained many thousands of white Loyalists and their slaves. Most Loyalists went to the Bahamas and Jamaica, but Dominica, St. Vincent, and Bermuda deserve mention among the other more popular areas.

The British cabinet was aware of the need to compensate the East Florida Loyalists as early as July, 1783, but an act of Parliament was not passed until 1786, this designating two commissioners to investigate, and also empowering the governments of those British American colonies to which the Loyalists had fled to gather the necessary information. Loyalists, in general, in the Caribbean were eligible for compensation, but they had to travel to London or Canada to present their claims. Many did receive compensation, and others were rewarded with various offices in the West Indies; for example, William Browne of Salem, Massachusetts, became a very successful governor of Bermuda in 1782, and Daniel Leonard became chief justice of the same colony; in the Bahamas, William Hutchinson of Massachusetts, a nephew, it seems, of Governor Hutchinson, held office, William Wylly of Georgia had a distinguished legal career, and Stephen De-Lancey of New York was chief justice; Samuel Quincy of Massachusetts held legal office in Antigua; Nathaniel Coffin of Boston was a customs official for many years in St. Christophers; and James Robertson of New York became chief justice of the Virgin Islands.[84] Lord Dunmore, as governor of the Bahamas, wrote from Nassau to Lord Sydney, August 8, 1788, requesting that Philip Dumaresq, a Boston Loyalist, be appointed provost marshal: "I found him here reduced to a real State of Beggary, with a large family of Children, who to my knowledge have been often crying round him for bread when he had not a morsel to give them." [85]

The population increase was the most important result of the Loyalist dispersal from East Florida and other American points to the West Indies.

Governor Wright of Georgia regarded Jamaica as the best market for exiled Loyalists' slaves. Probably 400 white families and 5,000 blacks reached the island after the evacuation of Savannah, and 1,278 whites and 2,613 blacks following the evacuation of Charleston. Kingston was the favorite place of settlement. Thus Loyalist migration added considerably to Jamaica's rapidly growing population, which increased from about 213,000 in 1775 to 290,000 in 1787. The Loyalist refugees in the West Indies escaped the freezing winter of Nova Scotia and enjoyed the famous Caribbean climate, but in Jamaica the early years especially were disastrous, with hurricanes, famine, and the dislocation of trade with America. The part played by the Loyalists and their slaves in the subsequent history of Jamaica is rather obscure. They were too few to dominate, even temporarily, as they did in Canada. The island, anxious to attract settlers, welcomed them with favorable land grants, and in the years that followed, the Loyalist slaveowners were a further element of violent opposition to British plans to ameliorate the condition of the Negroes and finally abolish slavery.[86]

Perhaps fewer Loyalists and their Negroes went to the Bahama Islands than Jamaica, but proportionally they increased the population there much more, and hence had a more pronounced effect. A low minimum would seem to be 1,750 whites and 4,200 blacks, which more than doubled the original population, while a recent authority puts the total influx at 8,000, thus tripling the population and raising the proportion of Negroes from one half to three quarters.[87]

The Bahamas, lying so close to the continent across the Florida Channel, were a natural Loyalist bailiwick, a fact emphasized by a minor, but remarkable, Loyalist exploit. In May, 1782, these ancient British possessions had fallen to the force of Spanish arms, but in April, 1783, Major Andrew De-Veaux, a South Carolina Loyalist, led an almost insultingly small expedition from St. Augustine, Florida, and recaptured New Providence, the most important island of the Bahamas, in the last real action of the Revolutionary War.[88] DeVeaux's exploit could inspire a Hollywood melodrama with its mixture of daring and bloodless bluff. By it, he established himself as a local hero and carved out large estates in New Providence and Cat Island for himself.[89]

Following the Spanish defeat, there was a major Loyalist influx, especially of Georgians and South Carolinians and some North Carolinians. A group of the latter Loyalists, including also some disillusioned with Nova Scotia, wrote in a petition to Lord Sydney in February, 1785, that they "conceive the Bahama Islands to be the only place at present

within the British Dominions in America the most likely to
afford them, an opening the most promising, for present, and
future advantages." [90]

The Bahamas also received many Northerners—in 1783
1,400 Loyalists left New York bound for Abaco.[91] One observer was able to report to London in 1784 that "the Bahama Islands are now growing respectable and of conse-
quence . . . from the Number of Loyalists settling there." [92]
Most arrived during 1784 and 1785, but a trickle continued
until 1789. As elsewhere, the British Government arranged
for free transportation and special granting of land to the
refugees. They settled everywhere, but mainly in New Providence and the Out Islands, Great Abaco perhaps receiving
the most. Entirely new areas and islands had to be given representation in the assembly, government extended, and seats
reapportioned. To expedite the granting of land in the Bahamas, the British Government had the army carry out a
survey in 1783 and took steps to buy out the heirs of the
original owners, the lords proprietors, a move consummated
in 1787, although land was in fact dispensed from 1783 onward.[93]

As in Nova Scotia, the Loyalists rapidly found themselves
in opposition to the old inhabitants and, in this case, also to
Governor John Maxwell. While finding merit in the comparatively modest Loyalist farmers with between ten and a
hundred slaves, Maxwell found the rest quite troublesome:
"They demand everything immediately—land, stores and employment, in fact they almost wish to take over the government." As was happening in Nova Scotia, there were loud
complaints that land, provisions, and general welfare were
not being provided,[94] and in 1784 the refugees formed a board
to "preserve and maintain these Rights and Liberties for
which they have left their Homes and their Possessions." [95]
Anyone who thinks that the Loyalists were quietists or docile

subjects need only look at their rambunctious quasi-revolu-
tionary politicking in the Bahamas. By February, 1785, Maxwell had sought the comfort of England, and by the end of
1786 the old ruling party was in a minority, completely outnumbered by the unwelcome Tories. As good Americans, they
continued to press for increased power for the legislative assembly and were anything but passive accepters of the pre-
rogative of Maxwell's successor, Lord Dunmore.

The effect of the Loyalist immigration, other than political, was, despite complaints of excessive heat and thin soil, a
spectacular commercial and agricultural growth, many Loyalists finding a temporary prosperity in cotton growing, which
unfortunately ended by 1815 owing to the chenille bug and
American competition. Plantations were started as far afield
as the Turks and Caicos Islands. The increase in the number
of slaves led to a harsher slave code, and, as in Jamaica, increased opposition to British slavery reforms. In 1786 an official reported from New Providence that

> it is with great Pain of Mind that I, every day, see the Negroes,
> who came here from America, with the British General's Free
> Papers, treated with unheard of cruelty, by *Men* who call
> themselves *Loyalists*. Those unhappy People after being drawn
> from their Masters by Promises of Freedom, and the King's
> Protection, are every day stolen away from this Islands,
> shipped, and disposed of to the French at Hispaniola.[96]

The invigorating arrival of the Loyalists began the modern
era of the history of the Bahamas. The first permanent newspaper, the *Bahama Gazette,* was founded in August, 1784, by
John Wells of Charleston, the Loyalist son of a Scottish immigrant printer.[97] The best historian of the islands reports
that most prominent Bahamians today are descendants of
Loyalists. But not all prospered. One pathetic footnote was
added to Loyalist history in 1903 when an American geo-

graphical expedition visited two small islands, Spanish Wells (off Eleuthera Island) and Hopetown (off Great Abaco), where they found two forlorn colonies of poverty-stricken Loyalist descendants who had maintained their racial purity at the cost of a horrifying inbreeding that had produced idiots, dwarfs, and various diseases and physical deformities. The one thousand white inhabitants of Hopetown were almost all descendants of one person, Wyannie Malone, a Loyalist lady who had fled from South Carolina in 1785.[98]

CHAPTER VIII

Conclusion

ع§ "Feb. 24. To theatre to see Mrs. Cowley's new play; unfortunately it was hissed off the stage before the conclusion of the last act; being in its progress of acting alternately and frequently hissed by its foes and cheered by its friends; the latter proved the minority, and therefore unsuccessful, as all in minorities are in state and church, as well as theatres."

Samuel Curwen, London, February 24, 1781.[1]

There is a pervading, griping, quarreling, recriminating, often pathetic stridency about the Loyalists that is commonly found among *émigrés*. As a group they are one of history's complete losers. Some other loyalists have had the satisfaction of returning: the monarchy was restored in England in 1660, and in France in 1815. The South lost the Civil War, but the South endures.

Reasons why the Loyalists failed have already been given. Militarily, much of the blame rests with the British, who fatally overestimated the number of their friends.[2] But the Loyalists themselves had many weaknesses. One wrote in 1776 that the rebels had the disadvantage of knowing that the *"halter is round their necks."* Actually, fear was a Whig asset, while the Loyalists' knowledge of "the goodness of their cause," as the same writer put it, and their reliance on British aid, led to a fatal complacency.[3] Many historians have wondered why the Tories did not organize themselves before 1774, and why, when they did so afterward, it was done so very weakly and without coordination. To ask the question is to read history backwards. War and independence were not expected initially; as I have been at great pains to stress many Loyalists (especially the ablest) were Whigs at first; the initiative automatically remained with the radicals.

Tory leadership and organization rarely even approached Whig quality. The caliber of either an individual like Samuel Adams or an institution like the Committees of Correspondence was entirely lacking. The Tories never achieved much intercolonial liaison. In the all-important early stages there was no cooperation between such figures as Joseph Galloway, Chief Justice William Smith, and Thomas Hutchinson. The inept, vain Galloway quarreled with his potentially strong ally, John Dickinson, while Hutchinson pretty well abandoned the leadership of the Tories.[4]

In 1780, when the Revolution was virtually over, *Anglo-Americanus* reminisced on the failure of Loyalism in the province of New York. The last legal assembly had disapproved of the Congress and was "in general supported by the men of property." But two thousand "armed tatterdemallions" had marched from Connecticut and disarmed and persecuted the Loyalists. The writer, showing little understanding of the "New-England monster," independence, continued that it would never have come about but for liberty poles, committees, associations, congresses, and so on, which, he revealingly added, "at first were laughed at and despised by the Magistrates." [5] Too many Loyalists simply gaped in astonishment as the Revolution ran its course, as if the sun had suddenly started to rise in the west and set in the east. Even when finally roused, they did not act boldly or decisively;

they lacked the quality attributed by the Reverend Charles Inglis to Tom Paine—"that daring, decided spirit which seldom fails." [6] Reduced finally to despair, they could only hope that their reward would come "in a future life." [7]

For most Americans the Loyalist position—loyalty to a king and country thousands of miles away, and to a system that had not been working very benevolently for over a decade—was far less attractive than the Whig offer of being fully master of one's own house. As Daniel Leonard sagely put it as early as December, 1774, "the Tories' plan supposed a degree of subordination, which is rather an humiliating idea; besides there is a propensity in men to believe themselves injured and oppressed whenever they are told so." [8] Self-government (which the colonies virtually had by now) was far more the natural, practical way of things than imperial interference, and in a way it was the Loyalists who were the innovators. Their arguments were far too legalistic and theoretical, even too sophisticated and idealistic, for the masses.

George Washington's statue stands in Trafalgar Square, London; Lord Chatham's (William Pitt's), in Charleston, South Carolina. The South is dotted with statues of Civil War heroes. One searches the United States almost in vain, however, for memorials to the vanquished of the first civil war. One reason is that the South occupied a quite well defined geographical area, while the Loyalists were everywhere, delineated more mentally than geographically. In this sense the Loyalists are more akin to the Copperheads of the Civil War. Thus unlike the Southerners, they could not maintain a tradition, except in Canada. Many of the active fled abroad, and those who remained in the United States were scattered; they usually stayed quiet, but some accepted the republic and plunged into its politics, mainly it seems on the Federalist side, though there are examples of former Loyalists who became Antifederalists and Jeffersonian Democrats.[9] Either way, the Loyalists accepted the orthodox version of the republic's history.

That version of history, especially in the shaky days of the early republic, maintained, of course, that there really had not been any Loyalists, that the Revolution had been a glorious united uprising for the ideals of the Declaration of Independence and the constitution of 1789 against a tyrannous Britain. Despite its colonial roots, the American republic claimed to have started unanimously and from scratch in 1776 —*Annuit coeptis novus ordo seclorum,* as the one-dollar bill puts it; hence the Loyalists, by claiming the emperor had no clothes, denied the very basis of the nation. Therefore it is no paradox that traditionally the Civil War has been treated more objectively than the Revolution in American historiography and popular memory.

British historians joined American historians in sweeping the Loyalists from sight, and against such a formidable combination Canadian historians could hardly be heard. The Whig school of British history, dominant until quite recently, did not like George III or his ministers and lauded Chatham, Barré, Wilkes, Burke, and all the eighteenth-century critics of British policy in America. It came to be argued that the American Whigs were merely reacting (as Englishmen were increasingly to do later) against George III's attempts at "despotism." Thus the Loyalists were rather an embarrassment. And in their own time they were too weak and resented by (and resentful of) British society to make their views stick. When Burke enunciated his classic conservative theories in 1790, it was too late to aid the Loyalists, and he did not use them as an illustration. Earlier the whole philosophic position of Loyalist conservatism had been weakened by the failure to produce any thinker comparable to the member for Bristol.

Traditionally, until the twentieth century, when American history finally cut loose from legend, the chief source of "facts" for the Revolution had been the British *Annual Register*, written by Burke and the Whigs. Thus, Britons and Americans encountered an anti-Loyalist version of history without even realizing it, and histories of the Revolution from the 1780's through George Bancroft's classic volumes of the mid-1800's to the works of John Fiske and Sir George Trevelyan at the turn of the century reflected this.[10] The historical perspective of most scholars has greatly improved in recent years, but all in all neither Americans nor Britons have suffered from any overdose of historical truth as far as the Loyalists are concerned.[11]

The Loyalists are of manifest importance in the history of the United States if only for their large number, although the precise division of the population into Whigs and Loyalists has always been disputed. Almost all Loyalists in a position to voice an opinion continually and confidently claimed they were an overwhelming majority virtually everywhere. Many Whigs, including Washington, agreed that the Loyalists were powerful. Conversely, many other Whigs thought the Loyalists a deluded few, a view partially shared by a British expert, Wilmot, the claims commissioner, who stated in 1783 that Loyalists were more like one fifth of the population than the four fifths "some have asserted." [12]

One reason for the different estimates of Loyalist numbers is the difficulty, or rather impossibility, of definition. A contemporary definition ran, "A Tory is a thing whose head is in England, and its body in America, and its neck ought to be stretched," [13] but essentially a Tory was one who stayed loyal to George III and opposed American independence. The trouble is that many colonists preferred not to make a decision or were truly neutral. One Long Islander reported that when a questioner asked whether he was Whig or Tory,

"I told him I was for peace." Many other Americans were equivocal, sometimes changing sides as the fortunes of war fluctuated. Others were quietist, biding their time, only expressing their loyalty with a secret prayer for the king, a muted curse for the Congress.

Thus when it comes to numbers, a great deal depends upon definition, there being many gradations below the active, dedicated, consistent Tory. The exiled Loyalists, easily defined, are simplest to assess. My educated guess is that 100,000 exiles, as suggested at the time by Phineas Bond of Philadelphia, is quite accurate. The total number of Loyalists in the population has traditionally been put at one third, following John Adams, but if *active* Loyalists are meant, this proportion is a maximum, probably too high: the true figure would seem to lie somewhere between a minimum of 13 and a maximum of 30 per cent of the whole population, or between 15 and 36 per cent of the *white* population. (These figures include men, women, and children.) [14]

Precise numbers will never be known and are comparatively unimportant. The essential point is that the number of Loyalists was very substantial. R.R. Palmer has noted (on the basis of a lower estimate than 100,000) that the American Revolution expelled twenty-four *émigrés* per thousand of the population, compared with a mere five per thousand in the French Revolution.[15] By 1961 only 100,000 *émigrés* had fled the Cuban Revolution, and even if it is admitted that actually 250,000 would have liked to leave if they had been able to, the proportion would still be less than that in the case of the Loyalists! [16] In 1780, 8,000 Tories were in the regular army, while Washington's army numbered only about 9,000, and at best reached 30,000. Around 1900 the Boers in South Africa, with one tenth the colonial American population, managed to put 60,000 men in the field against the British.[17]

The *relative* strength of the Loyalists, colony by colony,

can be suggested with some assurance. Roughly in descending order of *proportionate* numbers, we find Georgia, New York, and South Carolina as Loyalist strongholds; powerful but considerably behind come New Jersey and Massachusetts, followed, with middling numbers, by Rhode Island, North Carolina, Connecticut, Pennsylvania, and New Hampshire; weak in Loyalists are Virginia, Maryland, and Delaware. The area of Vermont, not yet a state, lay largely within New York's borders. Vermonters, seeking independence, negotiated with the British and thus gained a reputation as Loyalists, but the fact is that Vermonters sought concessions from both sides—as a Loyalist informed the British, they "did not join the Congress but were [also] violent against Great Britain." Loyalists and many others discontented with life in the thirteen new states found an "asylum" in Vermont during the war.[18]

In general, certain towns contributed most heavily to the Loyalist ranks, and produced far greater proportions than rural areas. By proportionate numbers of Loyalists (roughly in descending order) the great Tory towns were: Savannah (par excellence), Charleston, Boston, Norfolk, Annapolis, New York, Baltimore, Portsmouth (New Hampshire), Newport, and Philadelphia. The majority of Connecticut's Loyalists were found in small towns in Fairfield County, and many New Jersey Loyalists lived in Perth Amboy. In Virginia, in addition to Norfolk, other centers of Loyalist strength that should be noted are Portsmouth, Gosport, Williamsburg, and Petersburg.

In terms of absolute numbers, rather than proportions, New York (colony and city), well in the lead with three or four times more Loyalists than any other colony, produced at least a third of those who were active, and in descending order the rest follow thus: South Carolina, Massachusetts, New Jersey, and Pennsylvania (strong); North Carolina, Connecticut, Virginia, and Georgia (middling); then Maryland, Rhode Island, New Hampshire, and Delaware (weak).

Apart from enjoying *relative* strength, the Loyalists, active or secret, were probably a majority in no colony (certainly never an effective majority). Only in Georgia, New York, and to a lesser degree in Pennsylvania did they pose any kind of serious threat to the Revolution.

It is not my purpose to try to determine the number of Whigs, active or otherwise. Suffice it to say that they were generally more numerous, invariably more powerful, and in sum more talented than the Loyalists. As for neutralists, including members of important pacifist sects like the Quakers, there were many—one third of the population, according to John Adams—but they can hardly be considered Loyalists.[19]

Another problem in ascertaining the number of Loyalists is local variation. Therefore a quick survey of each colony noting the strength and composition of the Loyalists is in order. Following that, we shall examine the over-all composition and structure of the Loyalist movement.

①*New Hampshire.* The Loyalists were weak. The majority lived in Portsmouth, tended to be wealthy officeholders or professional men, were native-born, and largely devoid of talent, apart from the youthful future Count Rumford.

②*Massachusetts.* The Loyalists were the most numerous here of all the New England colonies. They were usually native-born, often well-to-do, centered on Boston and environs (with smaller concentrations at Falmouth [now Portland], Maine,[20] and in central Worcester County), and generally were in commerce, royal service, or a profession. They included many outstanding citizens, often from old, honored families: Thomas Hutchinson, affectionate historian of his native state; John Singleton Copley, the best colonial artist; John Mein, printer; John Lovell, master of the Boston Latin School; the Reverend Jacob Bailey, Anglican poet and writer;

Chief Justice Peter Oliver, Jonathan Sewall, Daniel Leonard, and James Putnam, all eminent lawyers; Drs. John Jeffries and William Lee Perkins, the former a pioneer anatomist, the latter a pioneer medical lecturer. Among leading merchants are found Jolley Allen and the Deblois family. Finally, a general list includes Sir William Pepperrell, grandson of the man who took Louisbourg, Timothy Ruggles, Edward Winslow, Richard Saltonstall, and John Coffin.

In short, there is no reason to quarrel with Moses C. Tyler's assertion that the names of the Massachusetts Loyalists read "almost like a beadroll of the oldest and noblest families concerned in the founding and upbuilding of New England civilization." [21] No other colony could match Massachusetts in the quality of her Loyalists, but even there the Whigs, in general, excelled. The Tories could not equal such patriots as John Adams, Samuel Adams, James Otis, and Josiah Quincy, and they remained an impotent minority sustained only by British support. An estimate, made at the time of Lexington, that the Whigs outnumbered the Loyalists four to one is probably accurate.[22]

③ *Rhode Island.* The Loyalists, mainly American-born, wealthy, commercially, officially, or professionally employed, were centered almost exclusively in Newport, but were a weak percentage of the whole population even there.

There were few loyal Rhode Islanders of exceptional merit, but the following Newporters may be noted: Thomas Vernon, Richard Beale, John Nicoll, Nicholas Lechmere— all customs officers; Drs. Haliburton and Hunter; an old Newport trading family, the Brentons (Benjamin and Jahleel); the Wanton family (Joseph and Joseph, Jr.—the only important Loyalist politicians); and Martin Howard, Jr., the loyal pamphleteer who fled the colony after the Stamp Act.

④ *Connecticut.* The Loyalists were numerically rather feeble, mostly native-born, quite widely scattered geographically, but with the concentration toward the coast, particularly in the eastern towns on the Long Island Sound, notably Stamford, Norwalk, and New Haven, but even these towns were over-whelmingly Whiggish. A wide spectrum of urban and agrarian occupations is found, but there is a slight tendency toward commerce, a definite tendency toward modest wealth. Probably the only Connecticut Loyalists worthy of special mention are Benedict Arnold and the Reverend Samuel Peters, who after the Revolution became the first Episcopal bishop in the United States.

⑤ *New York.* Ranked seventh out of thirteen in total population, yet unquestionably the great Loyalist stronghold, New York produced as many members of the British armed forces as the rest of the colonies combined and at least half of the total American Loyalists. Even in New York (including the city) the Loyalists were probably not a majority, and certainly never in a position of power, because the Whigs had little difficulty in controlling the province, and only long British military occupation made New York City the Loyalist mecca.

Loyalist strength was found particularly, of course, in New York City, and also in Long Island (especially the western part) and Staten Island, then up through the heart of the province on the east bank of the Hudson as far as the southern boundary of Albany County, thence on both sides of the river to Lake Champlain (with concentrations around Albany and Saratoga), and along the Mohawk into Tryon County.

By nationality New York Loyalists were evenly divided between native- and foreign-born, the latter mainly from the British Isles (especially Scotland), plus some from Germany. The typical rural Loyalist was a modest farmer from the Hudson or Mohawk valleys; from New York City came the wealthy merchants, professional men, and royal-office holders.

As for talent, only Massachusetts can compare. Among royal officials the following should be named: Governor William Tryon; Lieutenant Governor Cadwallader Colden, a versatile, scientific Scot, also his son David and his grandson, Nicholas; Chief Justice William Smith and his fellow judges, the historian Thomas Jones and George Duncan Ludlow; John Tabor Kempe, the attorney general; Robert Bayard, judge of admiralty; Beverley Robinson, a judge and great landowner; James DeLancey, member of the celebrated family that dominated New York politics before the Revolution; David Mathews and Abraham Cuyler, mayors of New York City and Albany; Sir John Johnson, Guy Johnson, and Daniel Claus—all Indian agents; and Philip Skene of Crown Point. Among lawyers we find Henry Van Schaack; among soldiers, John Butler, Joseph Brant (the Indian chief), and Oliver DeLancey; among the numerous merchants, Isaac Low and John Dawson; among Anglicans, the celebrated polemicist clerics, Seabury, Inglis, and Cooper, and the entire faculty of King's College; among the great landlords, Roger Morris, Frederick Phillipse, and John Harris Cruger.

New Jersey. The Loyalists were quite strong, more so than in any New England state, but nevertheless were unable to prevent a Whig take-over. The Loyalists, mainly native-born, were strongest in the seaboard north, or East Jersey, especially in the Raritan Bay area centered on Perth Amboy, site of the royal administration. Farmers of modest means predominated, but there was a substantial minority of commercial, professional, and office-holding folk.

The Loyalists comprised a creditable number of the colony's men of talent. Two native-born Anglican clergymen, Thomas Bradbury Chandler and Jonathan Odell, were outstanding as writers, Chandler as a pamphleteer, Odell as a satirical poet. William Franklin proved himself an able governor but, fatally for his cause, lacked significant political support.

Cortlandt Skinner, a lawyer and large landowner, organized the New Jersey Volunteers, a successful Loyalist regiment, while Daniel Coxe, another martial lawyer, helped form the West Jersey Volunteers at Philadelphia during the British occupation. Other leading lawyers who were loyal were David Ogden and Daniel Isaac Browne, while Abraham Van Buskirk, an eminent physician, Robert Drummond, an important merchant, Richard William Stockton, of the well-known Princeton family, and James Moody, daring soldier and spy, may also be mentioned.

(7) *Pennsylvania.* This colony was not the great Loyalist bastion it is often claimed to be by historians; instead it was the stronghold of moderates, neutralists, and pacifists (mainly Quaker). Active Loyalists were proportionately fewer in number than in Massachusetts or Rhode Island and were concentrated in Philadelphia, but even there the *proportion* was less than in Newport, Norfolk, or Boston.

A Pennsylvania Loyalist, a member of a small minority, probably lived in Philadelphia or in one of the three eastern counties—Philadelphia, Bucks, or Chester. He was somewhat more likely to be an immigrant from the British Isles than native-born, was unlikely to be a Quaker or a German despite their large numbers in the province, and was likely to be in commerce (though Philadelphia, unlike Boston and New York, lost few leading merchants), or perhaps a professional man or officeholder; but if he lived in the country, he was probably a farmer of more modest means than his urban compatriots.

Although vastly inferior to the Whigs in talent, the Loyalists did manage to put up a fairly respectable showing, thanks to such men as Joseph Galloway, the leading American Tory theorist and pamphleteer; the Allen family, led by Chief Justice William Allen; Samuel Shoemaker, Quaker mayor of Philadelphia and confidant of the claims commissioners;

James Humphreys, one of the few loyal newspaper printers; the Anglican Reverend Jacob Duché, dubbed the clerical Benedict Arnold because, as we have seen, he began as chaplain to the First Continental Congress, and his fellow clerics, Thomas Coombe, poetaster, and the Reverend Thomas Barton, helper of Rittenhouse and pioneer mineralogist (his son Benjamin was a leading American scientist of the early nineteenth century); [23] Christopher Sower, Jr., a rare German Loyalist and printer; Phineas Bond, member of an old Pennsylvania family who returned after the war as British consul; Joseph Stansbury, the poet; Charles Stedman and Robert Proud, both historians; Isaac Wharton and John Parroch, merchants; Edward Shippen, lawyer; and Dr. John Kearsley, a leading physician and horse dealer.

(8) *Delaware*. There is much doubt about the Loyalists here, largely because the colony was overshadowed by its neighbors and because there was no dominant town for the British to occupy and thus encourage Loyalism. Apathy and neutralism were very strong in Delaware, but it seems that undeclared Loyalists were numerous and active, widespread throughout the population geographically, somewhat likely to live in northern New Castle County, and rather equally balanced between the foreign- and native-born. Active Loyalists tended to be wealthy commerial people. The only one worth singling out is Thomas Robinson, a rich man of affairs who was the colony's leading citizen.

(9) *Maryland*. With the exception of those who lived on the eastern shore of Chesapeake Bay, the Loyalists, very weak in numbers, were mainly immigrants (since 1763) from the British Isles, likely to be professional, commercial, or office-holding residents of Annapolis and Baltimore (though the Loyalists of Frederick County in the west should be noted). Loyalist strength in the two towns seems to have been pro-

portionately much less than in Boston, but greater than in Philadelphia or Newport.

In general Maryland Loyalism barely counted as a serious force, although a few outstanding individuals may be mentioned: most of the famous Dulany family; the Reverend Jonathan Boucher, the leading Maryland Anglican cleric, who was also a writer and the sometime teacher of Washington's stepson; George Chalmers, an active British-born lawyer and later historian of America; William Eddis, the governor's secretary and author of the well-known *Letters from America;* and James Chalmers, commander of the Maryland Loyalists and writer of *Plain Truth,* his rebuttal to *Common Sense.*

10)Virginia. Proportionately and in absolute numbers, the Virginia Loyalists were among the weakest of all Loyalist factions in America. What Loyalists there were in Virginia were overwhelmingly British, mainly Scottish, immigrants centered on the tidewater area of Chesapeake Bay, especially Norfolk (which had a high proportion but probably not a majority of Loyalists), Portsmouth, Gosport, Williamsburg, and Petersburg. Two counties on the Chesapeake peninsula, Accomoc and Northampton, were noted as loyal areas. Virginia Loyalists were generally wealthy, and usually in commerce (the colony's merchants were almost unanimously loyal), but there were also a number of professional men and officeholders. Apart from some leading merchants, Virginia Loyalists were largely undistinguished, but among British immigrants the Reverend John Camm, the president of the College of William and Mary, and two members of the faculty, the Reverend Thomas Gwatkin and the Reverend Samuel Henley, should be mentioned, as should a few outstanding native-born Loyalists: John Connolly, who in the spring of 1776 led an abortive expedition to rally the Loyalists in the west at Fort Pitt; Jacob Ellegood, a leading planter who organized and commanded the Queen's Loyal Virginia Regiment; John Randolph, who succeeded his Whig father Edmund as attorney general; the Corbin family; John Randolph Grymes, who commanded the Queen's Rangers for a time; and two members of old Virginia families, Ralph Wormley and William Byrd III, the latter being the wastrel holder of a famous name.

(11) *North Carolina.* The Loyalists commanded middling numbers, a lot less than New York or Georgia, a few more than Connecticut or Pennsylvania. A North Carolina Loyalist was most likely a recently arrived yeoman farmer from the Scottish Highlands who was of moderate means and living in an inland county, or less probably he was a somewhat richer British merchant or officeholder living in Wilmington and around the Cape Fear estuary, or in New Bern, the seat of government.

The majority of merchants were loyal, men like Lewis Henry de Rossett, Alexander Telfair, Thomas Macknight and his partners, and George Miller, later a British consul in the Southern states; a few very rich men, like council member Henry McCulloch, can be found among the Loyalists; three vigorous soldiers, Colonels Edmund and David Fanning and John Hamilton, were from North Carolina; and Martin Howard, Jr., who left Rhode Island in 1764, became chief justice of the colony; but in general the future Tar Heel State brought forth few Tories of real note.

(12) *South Carolina.* Proportionately, the number of Loyalists here ranks just behind the two leaders, Georgia and New York; in absolute numbers, South Carolina produced more Loyalists than any colony save New York. The city of Charleston was second only to Savannah as a strong Loyalist town. But throughout South Carolina the Loyalists were outnumbered and easily overpowered by the Whigs.

The great majority of the Loyalists were immigrants (British, plus a few Germans at Ninety-Six), often quite recent arrivals. A wide range of occupations and economic levels is found, but the tendency was toward wealth. Geographically, the Loyalist strongholds were three towns and their environs: Charleston, Camden, and Ninety-Six.

The impressive number of South Carolina Loyalists is not matched by a similarly impressive array of talent, although the following should be mentioned: two exceptional soldiers, Patrick Cunningham and William Cunningham; the able native-born governor, William Bull; William Powell, a rich Charleston merchant; James Boisseau, a leading native-born planter; Dr. Alexander Garden, after whom gardenias are named; Robert Wells, proprietor of a fine Charleston bookshop; James Simpson, the attorney general; and William Wragg, a prominent council member and, incidentally, one of the very few Americans commemorated in Westminster Abbey.

(13) *Georgia.* Most Loyalists were wealthy planters, professional men, and officeholders from Savannah; most were also immigrants, often quite recent, from the British Isles. Proportionately, George as a whole and Savannah were the most loyal places in America (with the possible exception of New York). Indeed, Georgia may have been the one colony where Loyalists were a majority, but even here it is doubtful.

Georgia Loyalists included some fine men. Governor James Wright and Lieutenant Governor John Graham were very able, and other active, influential public figures included the following members of the legislature: David Zubly, Jr., Alexander Wylly (a onetime speaker of the Georgia house), Josiah Tatnall, John Simpson, Basil Cowper (a leading moderate), and James Habersham, a pioneer schoolteacher and merchant. Lieutenant Colonel Thomas Brown was an active soldier, and the half-Indians, Lachlan and Alexander McGillivray, helped keep the Creeks loyal. Finally, the Reverend

John J. Zubly was a leading Southern pamphleteer, although his main energies before independence were on the Whig side.

Only in New York, Massachusetts, and to a degree in Georgia can the ruling class be said to have been substantially represented in the Loyalist ranks. And only in Massachusetts and New York can the Loyalist factions be said to have included a notable amount of outstanding talent, although Pennsylvania and New Jersey, to a lesser extent Georgia, and (because of a few isolated cases) Maryland and South Carolina should also be mentioned.

In discussing Loyalist talent, reference has been made largely to the higher ranks of society. But there were hundreds of Loyalists in humbler stations who could be singled out if there were space. Let us mention a few, literally at random. There was Donald McDonald, a Scot, who, as the claims commissioners put it, commenting on his military service at the battles of Cross Creek and Moore's Creek Bridge, "tho' a Taylor acted with great Spirit"; [24] James Cotton, in whom Governor Martin of North Carolina found great merit, "which, in a man of rather vulgar life and character, and especially in a native of New England, I cannot but estimate very highly";[25] Malcolm Love, a blacksmith and miller of Cross Creek, North Carolina, who refused a rebel commission and raised thirty-five men whom he commanded at Moore's Creek, where he was wounded and captured, finally making his escape, however; [26] William Warden, a native Bostonian and hairdresser by trade, who, loyal since the Stamp Act, became an Associated Loyalist when the British troops arrived and had to leave with them for exile in Canada in 1776; [27] Evan Roys, a humble native farmer of Berkshire County, Massachusetts, who was forced into the rebel militia in 1777, but escaped with his two sons and served the rest of the war in the British army.[28] Finally, although his brother was a Whig, James Craige, a native-born carpenter, as a selectman strove to keep his town of Oakham, Massachusetts, from rebellion, joined the British in Boston in 1775, was evacuated with them, and served the rest of the war in the Quartermaster's Department.[29]

When it comes to the general question of who the Loyalists were, there is a temptation to take refuge in a Whig answer, "They are a motley mess," [30] but we can hazard a more precise, if less dogmatic, description.[31]

The Loyalists seem to have been about equally divided between immigrants and native-born Americans, but as the former made up a minority of the population, they contributed proportionately more. About 90 per cent of the immigrants were from the British Isles, with Scotland the major country of origin, while Germany supplied almost all the non-British immigrants. The Scottish Loyalists lived chiefly in New York and to a lesser extent in North Carolina, South Carolina, and Virginia; the English were widely scattered; the Irish were mainly in New York and South Carolina; and the Germans lived almost entirely in New York, South Carolina, and Pennsylvania.

In New England and New Jersey the Loyalists were usually native Americans; in New York, Pennsylvania, and Delaware they were quite evenly divided between the native- and foreign-born; in the South they were usually immigrants.

Although there were some loyal Irish regiments, the subordinate position in the Loyalist ranks taken by the Irish relative to the Scots is supported by contemporary testimony. The Marquis de Chastellux wrote that "an Irishman, the instant he sets foot on American ground becomes, *ipso facto*, an American." By contrast the Scots were uniformly suspect, especially in the South, where, as creditors and merchant interlopers, they were particularly disliked, and it was proclaimed, "Our common toast is, a free exportation to *Scotch-men* and Tories." Henry Hulton, writing from Boston, as early as 1770 considered that although "the disease [of opposition to Britain] has been universal thro' the British dominions let me except [Scotland]; her sons have kept free from the general contagion [and] proved themselves good subjects and supporters of Government and order." [32] It was fitting that Jonathan Trumbull made the arch-Tory squire, M'Fingal, a Highland Scot.

An analysis of the occupations of those Loyalists who submitted claims to the British is given below, and it may reflect the structure of Loyalism in general.

Occupation	No. of Claimants	% of Claimants
Farmers	1,368	49.1
Commerce		
(a) Artisans	274	9.8
(b) Merchants and shopkeepers	517	18.6
(c) Miscellaneous inn-keepers, seamen, etc.	92	3.3
Combined commerce	883	31.7
Professions		
(a) Lawyers	55	
(b) Teachers and professors	21	
(c) Doctors	81	
(d) Anglican clerics	63	
(e) Other clerics	7	
(f) Miscellaneous	26	
Combined professions	253	9.1
Officeholders	282	10.1

These figures show the leading group of Loyalists, by occupation, to have been farmers, and actually the farmers were underrepresented when it came to submitting claims; we can safely say, then, that a majority of Loyalists were certainly farmers or landowners. There were major rural, inland pockets of Loyalists, chiefly in New York (mainly in Tryon, Albany, Charlotte, Westchester, and Dutchess counties); and in North Carolina most Loyalists were from the back country, particularly Cumberland and Anson counties. There were minor rural concentrations in South Carolina in the two inland districts of Camden and Ninety-Six, and also in Maryland and to an extent in Delaware.

If most Loyalists were farmers, still a very sizable minority of Loyalists were in commerce or a profession, or held an official position, and accordingly they usually lived in the towns, most of which were on the coast. Thus, because nine tenths of the colonial population was rural, Loyalism had a distinctly urban and seaboard tinge.

Everywhere the commercial element—that is, the merchants, shopkeepers, artisans, and the like—whatever its percentage in terms of the whole population, contributed a greater percentage to the ranks of the Loyalists. In over-all figures the Loyalists in this category still remained a minority of the whole commercial population—yet a much larger minority than farmer Loyalists. Only in New York City, Virginia, and North Carolina were a majority of the merchants clearly Loyalists, and in New York only a small minority were sent into exile.

Among the Loyalists in the professions, doctors easily outweigh all other groups, especially teachers. Nearly four times as many loyal doctors as teachers are found. (The relative proportions of doctors and teachers in the total population are not clear, but doctors probably slightly outnumbered teachers.) The true proportion of Loyalist doctors is probably much higher, because doctors were so badly needed during the Revolution that often their Toryism did not result in persecution.[33] Doctors were divided in their allegiance like everyone else. Therefore in Boston one must match the loyal Dr. John Jeffries with the famous patriot Dr. Joseph Warren; while in Charleston, South Carolina, Dr. Alexander Garden is balanced by Dr. David Ramsay, the Whig historian. The heads of King's College, New York, and of the College of William and Mary, Virginia, were Loyalists, but faculties, with the exception of King's College's, were generally Whig, and Loyalist alumni seem to have been a minority at all colonial colleges. About one sixth of the alumni of Harvard were Loyalists, making it probably the most loyal college,[34] though King's College was not far behind.[35] The College of New Jersey, the College of Philadelphia, and the College of William and Mary produced few Loyalist graduates. More than twice as many lawyers as teachers were loyal, but lawyers as a whole seem to have been rather evenly divided.

In general, it is difficult to say how great a proportion of the professional people were Tory, but Moses Coit Tyler believed that a "clear majority" were so inclined. He may have been right.

In the colonial legislatures an overwhelming majority of members were Whig, but in the upper houses one half to two thirds of the councilors (a rich minority group close to the royal governors) seem to have remained loyal.[36]

Perhaps one out of ten hard-core Loyalists held a royal or proprietary office. Major-office holders provide the only part of the population where a majority clearly remained firmly opposed to the Revolution. Joined by a few rich farmers, planters, merchants, and professional men, the officeholders gave the Loyalist movement its leadership and dynamism, such as it was.

Among the Loyalists one can easily point to such persons as William Prince, a Southern Negro slave, who served the British for six years,[37] and to Samuel Montgomery, who rented a very modest farm in Georgia, which he abandoned to join the British army.[38] Or one can look at the rich and powerful: a Hutchinson in Boston, a DeLancey in New York. There were many thousands of poor Loyalists, greater in number than rich ones, but the richer segments of society contributed proportionately more heavily, especially to the activists. The Loyalists in some areas recruited heavily from the poor people, particularly in New York and Connecticut, and to a lesser extent in Pennsylvania; in the South and also in Massachusetts the Loyalists were drawn more from the rich.

A word remains to be said on religion. Religion was not usually the key to Loyalism, with the exception of Anglicanism in certain colonies.[39] It was a serious factor in Massachusetts, Rhode Island, New Jersey, and especially New York. There was an Anglican tinge to Loyalism in New Hampshire, Connecticut, and Maryland. Most of the Northern clergy were loyal, but there were significant exceptions, such as the Reverend Edward Bass, Anglican missionary at Newbury, Massachusetts, who dropped the prayers for the king, was allowed to remain, and finally became the first Episcopal bishop of his native state,[40] and the Reverend Robert Blackwell of New Jersey, who was a very definite Whig.[41] In Pennsylvania and the South, the clergy was much divided—in South Carolina the majority was actually patriot. If the Anglican clergymen were by no means unanimously loyal, it is to be expected that the congregations were usually divided. But largely because of the doctrines and outlook of the Church of England and its fashionable appeal to the wealthy, this church supplied a higher proportion of Loyalists than any other. It is not surprising that as New York filled up with Loyalist refugees, the city's Anglican churches proved too small and the governor had to make "the great Court Room, in the City-Hall" available for services.[42] But it seems unlikely that a majority of Anglicans was Loyalist. It must be remembered that the Anglican Church claimed more signers of the Declaration of Independence than any other, and generally it produced a large share of the leading Whigs in the middle colonies, and especially in the South, though none in New England.

Conversely, the Presbyterian Church produced hardly a Loyalist, with the exceptions of Chief Justice William Smith, of New York, and Chief Justice William Allen of Pennsylvania. The Calvinist churches were normally patriotic, but always there were exceptions, such as the Reverend Jonathan Ashfield, of Deerfield, Massachusetts, who provocatively, after the Boston Tea Party, held a village dance with tea as the featured beverage. When he died in 1780, he had been deprived of his salary, of firewood, and of the use of his church.[43]

The Methodists, most of whom lived in the Southern colonies, were accused of Loyalism, but very few seem to have followed John Wesley's conservatism in that way.[44]

The Quakers were often called Loyalists at the time, and have been sometimes since, and they were certainly much persecuted by the patriots. Some Quaker merchants traded with the British, and a few even fought for them.[45] But the chief cause of Whig suspicion was the refusal of most Friends to fight. However, a contemporary, Brissot de Warville, wrote that the Quakers "were treated by both sides with confidence. The spies, encouraged by this, at length habited themselves as Quakers and several were actually hung in that costume." [46] In fact the Friends were generally neutral, not Tory. This seems also to have been true of the other pacifist sects.

Most of the comparatively few Roman Catholics (mainly Irish) in America were Whig, but the British were able to raise more than one American Catholic regiment, including a New York unit of Scottish Highland Catholics, this group as a whole being generally loyal.[47] Most of the few Jews in America are held to have been Whig, but two distinguished Jewish families were loyal: the Harts in Newport, the Lucenas in Savannah.[48]

In view of the foregoing numerical and descriptive account of the Loyalists, the American tradition of purblindness must be rectified. It is hard to say what other legacies besides prejudice the Tories bequeathed to American history. Did the persecution and mobbing of the Loyalists contribute significantly to American traditions of violence and lynch law? [49] It is possible. Has the myth of patriot unanimity and righteousness fostered in Americans a tendency to see issues in terms of "black or white," and to hold narrow views on colonial and monarchial matters? [50] Certainly the Loyalists evoked deep hatred at the time, even, uncharacteristically, from George Washington. In the early years of the republic many Americans denounced the Tories violently, even hysterically, sometimes, it was charged, in order to "wipe the stigma of toryism from their own characters." [51] At the beginning of the 1850's Horace Greeley noted that some voters equated the failing Whigs of the day with the Tories of the Revolution.[52] As late as 1861 it was thought effective in the South to attack General Winfield Scott's Unionism as latter-day Toryism. In short, from the Revolution until the Civil War radicals in American politics saw the Loyalists, Federalists and Whigs as a continuing, baleful aristocratic force. There were also less successful attempts to turn the tables. The Democrats under Andrew Jackson were branded as Tories by Henry Clay and others in opposition who deliberately adopted the name Whig in order to equate Old Hickory with George III. In the presidential election of 1844, Young Hickory, James K. Polk, faced the perennial charge that his grandfather, Ezekial Polk, had been a Loyalist during the Revolution.[53] And, of course, closely connected with the Loyalists is American Anglophobia, a tradition maintained in the 1920's by Mayor Thompson of Chicago when he advised that "the King of England keep his snoot out of America," [54] and more recently and more sophisticatedly by Franklin Delano Roosevelt, who nourished a deep suspicion of British imperialism.

It has been argued that various political results have stemmed from the ouster of the Loyalists, from the origin of the American practice of judicial review [55] to the hegemony of the Virginia "dynasty" of early presidents to the growth of the temperance movement in New England.[56]

A huge amount of Loyalist property, notably land, was confiscated and sold. Did this have any effect on the subsequent development of America? In particular did it lead to a wider distribution of property, to democratization? Did poorer people get land, or was it merely transferred to the already wealthy? Nobody knows all the answers, and a good deal of backbreaking research remains to be done. It is clear that the degree of democratization varied from place to place, and it is impossible to generalize confidently. However, the trend of recent research has been to dampen an earlier broad enthusiasm for the leveling effect of the sale of Loyalist estates and to see it as at most a long-run result.[57]

It is certain that many families came to the fore because of the economic and political opportunities offered by the Revolution, especially by the flight of the Loyalists and royal administrations, which created a vacuum that had to be filled. But usually these newcomers were already quite well-to-do, if of second rank. Thus the Cabots and the Lowells moved into Boston from Essex County.[58]

It is argued that American conservatism lost its natural allies and organic base, and hence, in the usual European sense of the word, was never a serious force. There may be truth in this. It is suggested that by the permanent expulsion of up to one hundred thousand Loyalists, the United States escaped the bitter divisiveness that such countries as France have suffered from returned *émigrés*.[59]

Some Loyalists were certainly entirely out of tune with the new republic, two adamant but likable examples being the Byles sisters. Probably only Massachusetts could have produced such ardent patriots as James Otis and Samuel Adams, or such dyed-in-the-wool Tories as the Byles sisters, Catherine and Mary. In them flowed the distinguished blood of the Mathers and the Cottons. They dwelt in Boston with their father, Mather Byles, the poetry-writing Congregational minister and Tory punster (he dubbed the sentry posted over him his "observe-a-Tory"), who died in 1788 in poverty and disgrace. In the years after the Revolution the sisters carried on in a dream world, maintaining their home on Nassau Street (now Tremont) as a kind of Loyalist museum, with themselves as the chief exhibits. They also had a chair that had belonged to their grandfather, Lieutenant Governor Tailer, on which they would seat republican guests and then ask if the guests could sit comfortably under the Crown, pointing to a carved crown in the center of the chair.

Among their souvenirs and royal portraits (which Catherine said helped make up for the fact that she could no longer hear public prayers for the royal family), the sisters, sipping "loyal tea," relived the festivities of the Boston siege when Earl Percy and Lord Howe visited them, berated the "Yankeys," and corresponded with their far-flung Loyalist relatives. Catherine even wrote to George IV on his accession, assuring him of continued loyalty. Later she grandiosely attributed the lack of an answer to a letter she had written to William IV to the possibility that the King "has been told that I am Aunt to an abominable Yankey, and his Majesty is loth to encourage such a connection." In 1835 the authorities removed part of the sisters' house to make way for a street. The ladies were pained, but hardly surprised. It was simply "one of the consequences of living in a Republic." But they made sure that when they died their property would find its way out of the United States to more congenial—and loyal—resting places.[60]

The Reverend Calvin White is also worth recalling. White, a descendant of John White (who came to Massachusetts in 1632), was born at Middletown, Connecticut, in 1762 and died at the age of ninety-one a few years before the Civil War. It is revealing that this Yale graduate was at first a Congregationalist but was converted to the Anglican faith, and finally in 1822 embraced Roman Catholicism, a logical end, perhaps, to his spiritual journey. In the years following independence White remained an unrepentant aristocratic Tory. He never voted or recognized the republic in any way except to pay taxes. It is related that as late as 1850, while out driving near Orange, New Jersey, he was shown a spot known as "Tory Corners" because it had been a Loyalist stronghold, whereupon "the old man uncovered his head and bowed in reverence." [61]

But White, the Misses Byles, and their ilk were eccentric, isolated individuals, stranded on the beach by the receding tide of the British connection, representing no significant forces in the American community. Most of the inflexible had fled permanently—such men as Jonathan Sewall, who changed the spelling of his name to Sewell to distinguish himself from the patriot branch of the family. His son, Jonathan, a chief justice of Lower Canada, relented sufficiently to accept an honorary degree from Harvard, but he kept the new spelling of his name.[62] James Putnam was very bitter, and when asked if he wished to leave New Brunswick and return to the United States, he replied, "No, thanks to the Devils who have robbed me of my property I do not wish to live with or see such infernals." [63]

However, it is one of the main contentions of this book that most Loyalists had far more in common with the patriots than otherwise.[64] Alexander C. Flick, the authority on New York Loyalists, concludes that the Loyalists "if anything, in the days before the revolution . . . were more active than the Whigs" in working for reform.[65] One Loyalist, Benjamin Marston, exiled to London, followed quite a radical course, becoming active in the antislavery movement (many Loyalists attacked the hypocrisy of slave-owning Whig leaders). Marston wrote in 1791, "I am sincerely tired of England," and a year later confided to his sister that he was actually glad the Loyalists had lost, because the world had been improved by the American Revolution—Europe was in a ferment that would finally end all "Usurpation," and man would be left "master of himself." Not, however, that he praised the American rebel leaders any more, he explained, than he would praise Judas for aiding Christianity.[66] Some Tories remained somewhat pro-American as late as 1812, when they refused to fight against their homeland.

Although the legislature of Canadian Loyalists at Fredericton, New Brunswick, was bedecked with life-size portraits of George III and his queen, the often Whiggish political history of that, or any other, Loyalist area does not suggest that America had lost a group that was essentially alien. If the Loyalists were to prove themselves not really so far from the Whigs, similarly the American Revolution, though it was a *revolution*, was comparatively moderate and did not really move the patriots that far away from their British past. It is symbolic that in 1776 the rebels changed their flag from plain red to a more sober thirteen stripes (bespeaking a less violent and more studied attitude).[67] Another symbolic happening was the sale of Governor Hutchinson's burial plot on Copp's

Hill, Boston, to a patriot, who erased Hutchinson's name from the stone, but retained the Governor's "armorial bearings." [68] And all the American presidents until Jackson were, of course, very much "gentlemen" in the British tradition.

In short, most exiled Loyalists would have found the American republic quite congenial. The United States would not have been much endangered by them; rather the United States was weakened by the great loss of Tory talent (after all, even though the Loyalists could not match such Whig luminaries as George Washington, Samuel Adams, and the rest in the quality of their leadership, still there were among the Loyalists men of great stature in their respective fields).

Unquestionably the exile of the Loyalists deprived America of a great deal of ability and of much artistic patronage. Most of the outstanding Loyalist exiles have been mentioned earlier. On the cultural side any list of very distinguished *émigrés* should include, among others, Copley the painter; Count Rumford the scientist; Jonathan Boucher, Charles Inglis, Chief Justice Smith, Jonathan Odell, and Joseph Galloway, all able writers; and Peter Harrison, the pre-eminent architect of colonial America, whose death at New Haven in 1775 had been hastened by the Revolution. It is most significant that neither Thomas Jefferson, in his *Notes on Virginia* of 1782, nor the Reverend Samuel Miller, in *A Brief Retrospect of the Eighteenth Century* in 1803, mentioned Harrison, although both desperately wanted examples of colonial artists. The reason, of course, was Harrison's Toryism, which had caused him to be dropped from the national consciousness in spite of the beauty of his buildings, many of which are extant today.[69]

If one adds to the loss of part of the colonial aristocracy and of certain talented individuals the loss of printing presses, libraries, picture collections, and *objets d'art*, it can certainly be argued that the treatment of the Loyalists "altered the course of American cultural development." [70]

On the other hand, some Loyalists, not exiled, contributed much to the republic. Samuel Seabury became the first Episcopal bishop in America. Joshua Chandler of Worcester, Massachusetts, went into exile, but his daughter remained, married a Unitarian clergyman, Aaron Bancroft, and gave birth to George Bancroft, ironically the historian who did as much as anyone to keep the Loyalist record buried.

It is impossible to be dogmatic about the effect of the British defeat on talented Loyalists. Some who remained in America simply faded away, a good example being Rivington, the pre-eminent Loyalist printer, who sank into debt and obscurity.

Many talented exiles returned, including Henry Cruger, the leading American Member of Parliament; Samuel Curwen, the diarist; Nicholas Boylston, founder of the Boylston Medical Library; James Humphreys, printer; Jacob Duché and Samuel Peters, Anglican clerics; Francis Green, philanthropist; Dr. John Jeffries, anatomist and pioneer crosser of the English Channel by balloon in 1785; and Dr. James Lloyd, Boston's leading obstetrician. Sometimes a returned Loyalist's family became important, as in the case of John Gore of Boston, whose son Christopher was governor of Massachusetts in 1809 and 1810.[71]

The pace of readmission of Loyalists varied from state to state, but mostly it was remarkably quick (except for a few of the most hated Loyalists, some of whom could never have returned even if they should have wished to), and by 1790 anti-Loyalist legislation was largely a thing of the past everywhere.[72]

It must be stressed again that the majority of Loyalists never left America in the first place. In parts of New York there were simply too many Loyalists to be banished, and this is also true of other areas, such as Georgia. Among those who stayed are found many leading Loyalists, for instance, James Hamilton, of Pennsylvania, and Andrew Oliver of Massachusetts.[73] Many talented professional men, especially doctors, were never exiled—Samuel Danforth remained in practice and later became president of the Massachusetts Medical Society.[74]

The severing of the British connection did not always harm American culture, and may have had a partially beneficial effect. A recent survey of the arts in colonial America states that the Revolution did not impair the quality of silverwork, furniture (fields in which America excelled), or painting. No permanent setback is found in architecture—the late Georgian buildings of the early republic are described as the "ultimate form" of that style. Generally it is concluded that the break with Britain led to healthy, cosmopolitan experimentation—for example, the Greek revival movement.[75]

The colonial dependence on Britain was often stultifying, resulting in tame imitation. The Revolution increased the desire to find an "American" way, and the exile of many Loyalists may have added an element of guilt to the desire to outdo and be different from the British. However, it must also be recognized that even with the Loyalist loss, American dependence upon Britain, especially on the part of the upper classes and the more educated, has always been a feature of American life.[76]

America gained as well as lost talent. Mass gains include numbers of German soldiers and a few from other European countries and Britain. Individual gains include several military commanders; Frederick V. Melsheimer, a German entomologist; various Frenchmen, including Du Pont de Nemours and Pierre L'Enfant, the partial planner of Washington, D.C.; and several Britons, including Thomas Cooper, the geologist, and the great Joseph Priestley.[77] Also some losses were not complete. Thus, when Count Rumford died in 1814, Harvard, where he had set up a professorship, was his chief beneficiary.[78] It is impossible to draw up a cultural balance sheet of profit and loss caused by the upheaval of the Revolutionary period.

Another point to remember is that in spite of much Whiggishness, some articulate Loyalists did reveal a collective mentality that America did well to escape. The Revolution was seen as the result of a conspiracy of dissatisfied "Presbyterians," "Republicans," mainly New Englanders, and rapacious upstarts and "horse thieves" who were following the footsteps of the Cromwellian regicides.[79] (Strangely enough, this erroneous idea of conspiracy and the Cromwellian parallel was matched by an equally erroneous Whig belief in a conspiracy between the British Government and certain local aristocrats to enslave the colonies.[80]) An independent America, a "Monster without a head," as the Loyalists envisioned the rebel republic, could only expect "Anarchy and poverty." [81]

Loyalist aristocratic hauteur is well exemplified by the life and writings of Peter Oliver [82] and by a correspondent of Rivington's *Gazette,* who, in listing sixty members of the Congress, awarded only two of them the label "gentlemen," the rest being, for example, Samuel Adams, "Maltser"; Stephen Hopkins, "Blacksmith"; Roger Sherman, "Ditcher and Shoemaker—" in short, "the very scum of the people." [83] Some Loyalists even viewed the horrors of the Revolutionary War as God's punishment for the neglect of the Anglican Church, as the Reverend Thomas B. Chandler, with the splendid egotism of his calling, argued.[84]

The prospect of the Loyalists triumphant is not a pretty one. They would probably have instituted some kind of federal union, but the general idea was "to new-model" the

colonial governments, as Jonathan Boucher put it [85]—at best
to lessen the powers of the lower houses and increase those
of the governors, and at worst to introduce a genuine aritso-
cratic regime. Trumbull had every right to have Squire
M'Fingal look forward to "setts/ Of home-made earls in
Massachusetts." [86] The new regime would have included the
full establishment of the Church of England and strict control of American colleges, those "grand nurseries of the late
Rebellion." [87]

A Loyalist victory would have meant revenge—how violent
it is impossible to say. But in 1779 Isaac Ogden wrote to
Joseph Galloway that he was looking forward to peace, when
"every Rebbel [would] receive his deserts," [88] and in 1783 an
American newspaper published a list of punishments various
Tories had in store for the defeated Whigs:

Governor Robertson,	to Crop them.
Edward Leight,	to Curry them.
Ram Rappaljea,	to Rail them.
Linus King,	to Bully them.
Henry Law,	to Club them.
Reylanders,	to make Indians of them.
Capt. Tollemie,	to Dirk them.
Capt. Waldrin Blaw,	to FIGHT them.
Joseph Allecock,	to Negrofy them.
Oliver Templeton,	to Dispose of them.
Hugh Wallis,	to Enslave them.
Watson and M'Adam,	to Vendue them.
James Rivington,	to Devil & Press them.
Isaac Low,	to Deceive them.
David Mathews,	to Poison & Murder them.
Edmond Seamon,	to Register them.

And then Cunningham was to Hang them.[89]

Add the Loyalists' revenge to British desires to extirpate
rebellion and it is no exaggeration to suggest that "America
would have become an enormous Ireland." [90]

The British (including the opposition politicians) regarded the maintenance of the Empire as essential to the country's power and whole future. Arguments followed what has become known today as "the domino theory"—if America fell, the rest of Britain's possessions and the all-important trade that went with them would follow. As a British newspaper had remarked, applying Cato to rebellious America, "Delenda est Carthago." [91] With the failure to destroy "Carthage," the questions posed to Britain by the American Revolution in general were of paramount importance: Could Britain, shorn of the thirteen colonies, remain a great power? In the remaining Empire, how should local rights and imperial control be reconciled? What should be the political and economic relationship between Britain and the new United States?

The specific effects of the Loyalists on British history do not merit the attention devoted to those relating to American history. The Loyalists and British war policy before 1783 have already been discussed in an earlier chapter, as has the question of the peace treaty and compensation. Afterward the Tories were too few in number to affect British history much, but several individuals rose to some prominence, for example, George Chalmers, who became First Clerk of the Board of Trade. One of the Coffin brothers of Nantucket became an admiral and a friend of Nelson; the other became a British general. More important, the Loyalists provided many leading officials for the remaining British Empire, such as William Smith, confidant of Lord Dorchester, and Chief Justice William Smith. Some Loyalists produced distinguished children: Copley's son became lord chancellor; Isaac Hunt of Philadelphia was the father of Leigh Hunt, the famous Victorian poet and critic; and John Howe, who fled New England and founded the Halifax (Nova Scotia) *Journal* in 1781, was the father of Joseph Howe, a great journalist and reforming statesman in nineteenth-century Canada.

As for colonial policy, the British tried to avoid the mistakes of the American Revolution and in general sought to strengthen the powers of governors and check the self-governing tendencies of assemblies. The partial autonomy of Ireland was soon ended; representative government declined in the West Indies; and Canadian politics remained unsettled.

An immediate lesson the British had learned was never to trust loyalists again anywhere. Thus, in dealing with the French Revolution and Napoleon, Great Britain did not court "internal enemies" as she might have, and in 1799, when Grenville put some hope in the Dutch opponents of France, Dundas replied: "I cannot forget the American War, where we were so miserably disappointed in the promised and expected cooperation." [92]

The enslaved Irish found some inspiration in the American Revolution, and even most Englishmen came to accept it, partly because it could (and can) be rationalized as having worked out for the best, although there are always periodic regrets that the English-speaking world is split. At the time of the Revolution, a Frenchman forecast that America would "form the greatest Empire in the world." "Yes Sir," replied his English companion, "and they will *all* speak English; every one of 'em." [93]

The Loyalists were losers in the United States and in Great Britain. But they had some success in the Bahamas and other islands of the West Indies, whose development, in all areas except race relations, they bettered. (However, on the subject of race relations it should be stressed that the loss of America, and in particular the loss of the South, facilitated the ending of slavery throughout the British Empire in 1833, while, ironically, the country dedicated to the principles of the Declaration of Independence required a civil war to accomplish the same ends.) More important than the Caribbean was

Canada, where the Loyalists brought new life, built themselves new homes, added a non-French element to Canadian nationalism (the creation of English Canada was an essential complement to Wolfe's capture of Quebec in 1759), and generally contributed to Canadian stability. Without Loyalist strength, Canada might well have fallen to the United States during the War of 1812. And as we have mentioned, even today parts of Canada, particularly the Maritimes, retain a distinct Loyalist character.

In Canadian-American relations one does find some of that bitterness characteristic, say, of returned *émigré* loyalists in France in the first half of the nineteenth century. One United Empire Loyalist almost gloated over the American Civil War as retributive justice for the original sin of revolution.[94] Apart from the idea of justice, he had a point. The logic of the American Revolution did lead to the Civil War.

The frontispiece of a Tory pamphlet of 1775 depicted two pitchers, representing Britain and America, floating in water, with the caption, "If we Strike We Break." [95] Actually the opposite was true. Both sides were, in the long run, probably the stronger for collision and separation.

Americans and Canadians both should be grateful concerning the Loyalists: Americans grateful that they were not better utilized by the British, that the Revolution was not a worse civil war, that the loss of talent—because some Loyalists returned and the majority, in fact, were never exiled, due partly to the comparative leniency of many states—was not as serious as it might have been; Canadians grateful for the essential strengthening their country received from the Loyalists, and for their fine Loyalist heritage, both true and mythical. And Englishmen can take some refuge in the generally honorable way in which their government compensated the victims of British incompetence. Of the long-dead Loyalists themselves it must be recorded that they were a sad portent of things to come, the "displaced persons" and war refugees of their time, that they were generally an honorable, and sometimes courageous, group, that they opposed the Revolution more keenly than the British themselves, and that, in spite of all, "their Loyalty they kept. . . ."

Notes

ABBREVIATIONS USED IN NOTES

A.H.R.	*American Historical Review*
AO	Audit Office Papers, Public Record Office, London
B.M.	British Museum
CO	Colonial Office Papers, Public Record Office, London
FO	Foreign Office Papers, Public Record Office, London
K.F.	Wallace Brown, *The King's Friends: The Composition and Motives of the American Loyalist Claimants*, Providence, 1966
L.T.	American Loyalists: Transcripts of the Manuscripts, Books, and Papers of the Commission of Enquiry into the Losses and Services of the American Loyalists, 60 vols., New York Public Library
W.M.Q.	*William and Mary Quarterly*

Notes for Chapter I

1. *The Diary and Selected Papers of Chief Justice William Smith, 1784-1793*, ed. L.F.S. Upton (Toronto, 1965), II, p. 120.

2. Wesley F. Craven, *The Legend of the Founding Fathers* (Ithaca, 1965), pp. 37-38; William S. Russell, *Guide to Plymouth, and Recollections of the Pilgrims* (Boston, 1846), p. 179; Massachusetts Historical Society, *Proceedings*, 2d ser., III (1887), pp. 441n, 442n.

3. Quoted in Oscar Zeichner, *Connecticut's Years of Controversy, 1750-1776* (Chapel Hill, 1949), p. 235.

4. From their settlement in the early seventeenth century until the Revolutionary era of the second half of the eighteenth century.

5. *The Writings of Thomas Paine,* ed. Moncure D. Conway (4 vols., New York, 1894-1896), I, p. 203.

6. For the history of the five cities see Carl Bridenbaugh, *Cities in Revolt* (New York, 1955), *passim.*

7. *Ibid.,* p. vii.

8. For examples of American architects, see Louis B. Wright, George B. Tatum, John W. McCoubrey, Robert C. Smith, *The Arts in America: The Colonial Period* (New York, 1966), pp. 89, 125, 131, 136.

9. See Carl Bridenbaugh, *The Colonial Craftsmen* (New York, 1950), *passim.*

10. New England and New York were somewhat adversely affected.

11. See Brooke Hindle, *The Pursuit of Science in Revolutionary America, 1735-1789* (Chapel Hill, 1956), *passim.*

12. See Carl and Jessica Bridenbaugh, *Rebels and Gentlemen* (New York, 1942), *passim.*

13. Allan I. Ludwig, *Graven Images: New England Stonecarving and Its Symbols, 1650-1815* (Middeltown, Connecticut, 1966).

14. Bernard Bailyn and John Clive, "England's Cultural Provinces: Scotland and America," *W.M.Q.,* 3d ser., XI (1954), pp. 200-213.

15. *Democracy in America* (New York, 1964), p. 23.

16. Mary P. Clarke, *Parliamentary Privilege in the American Colonies* (New Haven, 1943), *passim.* The gentle, gradual growth and maturation of the colonial assemblies, partly in imitation of the House of Commons, has recently been very well described for four Southern colonies by Jack P. Greene in *The Quest For Power: The Lower House of Assembly in the Southern Royal Colonies, 1689-1776* (Chapel Hill, 1964). Lower houses even had some powers much beyond those of the House of Commons (see p. 222 of Greene's book). Greene well shows that the Revolution was partially a confrontation between two sovereign bodies—the thirteen colonial legislatures versus the king in Parliament.

17. Quoted in C. Haight, *Before the Coming of the Loyalists* (Toronto, 1897), pp. 7-8.

18. Mellen Chamberlain, *John Adams* (Boston and New York, 1898), p. 248. Should this story be apocryphal, it nevertheless rings true.

19. Horace Walpole, October 21, 1759. Quoted in T. Charles-Edwards and B. Richardson, *They Saw it Happen* (Oxford, 1958), p. 74.

20. For evidence of American provincialism and irresponsibility, see Jack M. Sosin, *Whitehall and the Wilderness* (Lincoln, 1961), pp. 251-252 and *passim.*

21. *The Colonial Background to the American Revolution* (New Haven, 1924), Ch. IV.

22. See Edward Eggleston, *The Transit of Civilization from England to America in the Seventeenth Century* (New York, 1901), Ch. II.

23. See Caroline Robbins, *The Eighteenth-Century Commonwealth-*

man (Cambridge, Mass., 1959); and *Pamphlets of the American Revolution, 1750-1776,* ed. Bernard Bailyn (Cambridge, Mass., 1965), I.

24. Alice M. Baldwin, *The New England Clergy and the American Revolution* (Durham, 1928), *passim;* and Baldwin, "Sowers of Sedition. The Political Theories of Some New Light Presbyterian Clergy of Virginia and North Carolina," *W.M.Q.,* 3d ser., V (1948), pp. 52-76. The Great Awakening, though partly divisive, contributed on the whole to a growing unity and certainly aided the process of Americanization and, in the long run, perhaps of revolution. Alan Heimart's *Religion and the American Mind from the Great Awakening to the Revolution* (Cambridge, Mass., 1966) may be consulted with caution.

25. Despite the optimism of the Enlightenment, the colonists' experience engendered a fundamentally pessimistic view of human nature and politics, both of which were believed to be highly prone to corruption. Miraculously a degree of liberty and virtue had developed in America, but the price was eternal vigilance, and already the danger signals were evident. This helps to explain the seemingly exaggerated American reaction to the rather mild British reforms. See Bailyn, *Pamphlets of the American Revolution;* H. Trevor Colbourn, *The Lamp of Experience* (Chapel Hill, 1965); Edmund S. Morgan, "The Puritan Ethic and the American Revolution," *W.M.Q.,* 3d ser., XXIV (1967), pp. 3-43.

Notes for Chapter II

1. Quoted in Max Farrand, *The Framing of the Constitution of the United States* (New Haven, 1913), p. 209.

2. Oliver M. Dickerson, *The Navigation Acts and the American Revolution* (Philadelphia, 1951), *passim.*

3. John C. Miller, *Sam Adams: Pioneer in Propaganda* (Boston, 1936), *passim.*

4. See Benjamin W. Labaree, *The Boston Tea Party* (New York, 1964), pp. 76-77 and *passim.*

5. *Annual Register,* 1779, p. 179.

6. *Virginia Gazette* (Rind), September 8, 1774; *Boston Gazettte,* June 30, 1777.

7. See Zeichner, *Connecticut's Years of Controversy, 1750-1776,* p. 195.

8. Thomas Hutchinson, *The History of the Colony and Province of Massachusetts-Bay,* ed. Lawrence S. Mayo (Cambridge, Mass., 1936), III, p. 75. By 1770 Daniel Leonard reported that in Massachusetts "there were two parties of pretty long-standing, known by the names of Whig and Tory" (Rivington's *Gazette,* December 29, 1774). The term "Loyalist" as distinct from "Tory" seems to have been popularized, but not introduced, by the Associated Loyalists, who were active in New York,

1780-1781 (Esther Clark Wright, *The Loyalists of New Brunswick* [Fredericton, 1955], p. 23).

9. Samuel Curwen, *Journal and Letters, 1775-1784*, ed. G. A. Ward (New York, 1842), p. 409.

10. Bruce I. Granger, *Political Satire in the American Revolution, 1763-1783* (Ithaca, 1960), p. 272.

11. L.T., XLI, p. 523; XIII, pp. 201, 320.

12. *Ibid.*, XLI, p. 523; William H. Nelson, *The American Tory* (Oxford, 1962), pp. 6-7.

13. For the Stamp Act crisis in general, see Edmund S. Morgan, *The Stamp Act Crisis*, rev. ed. (New York, 1963), especially pp. 366-367, and for the Loyalists, pp. 371-376.

14. L.T., XXXIX, p. 439.

15. One is reminded of the events leading to the English civil war in the seventeenth century. Many future royalists, like Edward Hyde, later Lord Clarendon, and even Strafford, opposed the early tyranny of Charles I but could not resist the king past a certain point. Perhaps the narrowly passed Grand Remonstrance of 1641 is akin to the narrowly defeated Galloway Plan of 1774.

16. L.T., XLIII, pp. 184-185.

17. Frequent mention is made in the text of "the claims commissioners" and "claimants." This refers to the British commission set up to hear the claims for compensation from Loyalists, that is, "claimants," who had lost property and office by the Revolution. The surviving records of the commission are a prime source of information about the Loyalists, especially the rank and file.

18. L.T., LIII, p. 388.

19. Claude H. Van Tyne, *The Loyalists in the American Revolution* (New York, 1902), p. 76.

20. Printed in *Virginia Gazette* (Purdie), April 12, 1776.

21. *Ibid.*, September 27, 1776.

22. *Dictionary of American Biography*, eds. Allen Johnson and Dumas Malone (20 vols., New York, 1928-1936), XX, p. 61.

23. L.T., XXXVI, pp. 169-170.

24. *Ibid.*, V, p. 615.

25. *Annual Register*, 1777, p. 13. The *Annual Register* was an English compilation of the year's events from a Whig point of view.

26. L.T., XXXIV, p. 505.

27. Quoted in Adrian C. Leiby, *The Revolutionary War in the Hackensack Valley, The Jersey Dutch and the Neutral Ground, 1775-1783* (New Brunswick, 1962), p. 123.

28. L.T., I, p. 11.

29. *The Royal Commission on the Losses and Services of American Loyalists,* ed. Hugh E. Egerton (Oxford, 1915), p. 340.

30. L.T., XIII, p. 151.

31. *The Works of John Adams,* ed. Charles Francis Adams (Boston, 1856), X, p. 192.

32. Van Tyne, *Loyalists,* p. 27.

33. "Salem Loyalists—Unpublished Letters," ed. John J. Latting, *New England Historical and Genealogical Register,* XXVI (1872), p. 431.

34. L.T., LVIII, p. 119.

Notes for Chapter III

1. From a sermon, "The Christian Soldiers Duty briefly Dilineated," preached by the Reverend Charles Inglis, September, 1777 (L.T., XLII, p. 555).

2. *The Public Records of the State of Connecticut,* ed. Charles J. Hoadly (Hartford, 1895), II, p. 279.

3. *K.F.,* pp. 68, 40. During the English civil war between king and Parliament in the seventeenth century Sir Edmund Verney, although he did not particularly like Charles I's policies (any more than many American Loyalists liked George III's), remained loyal, saying, in anticipation of Loring, "I have eaten his bread and served him near thirty years, and will not do so base a thing as to forsake him." Quoted in Roger Lockyer, *Tudor and Stuart Britain 1471-1714* (London, 1964), p. 278.

4. *K.F.,* pp. 37, 202-204,, 225-226.

5. See Samuel E. Morison, *The Oxford History of the American People* (New York, 1965), p. 236.

6. Cf., *K.F.,* p. 226.

7. *Ibid.,* pp. 206-207.

8. Petition of George Campbell to Lord Germain, 1776, CO5-116.

9. *K.F.,* pp. 281, 29, 122, 282.

10. *Boston Gazette,* December 23, 1776; Nelson, *The American Tory,* p. 103n.

11. J. Hector St. John Crèvecoeur, *Sketches of Eighteenth Century America,* ed. H. L. Bourdin *et al.* (New Haven, 1925), p. 310; L.T., I, pp. 85-87.

12. *Ibid.,* LIII, p. 259.

13. *Ibid.,* V, pp. 194-195.

14. See Wallace Brown, "Negroes and the American Revolution," *History Today,* XIV (1964), pp. 556-563.

15. Nelson, *The American Tory,* pp. 8, 87-88.

16. Lorezno Sabine, *Biographical Sketches of Loyalists of the American Revolution* (Boston, 1864), I, pp. 59-60.

17. *Works of John Adams,* ed. Adams, X, pp. 192-193.

18. *K.F.,* pp. 150, 174, 208, 226.

19. Dickerson, *Navigation Acts*, p. 51.

20. Virginia D. Harrington, *The New York Merchants on the Eve of the Revolution* (New York, 1935), pp. 349-351.

21. *K.F.*, pp. 180-181.

22. *Ibid.*, p. 226.

23. John Shy, *Toward Lexington: The Role of the British Army in the Coming of the American Revolution* (Princeton, 1965), pp. 341-342, 394.

24. *Pennsylvania Gazette*, July 9, 1777; *K.F.*, p. 126.

25. Rivington's *Gazette*, October 14, 1778.

26. *K.F.*, p. 149.

27. *Ibid.*, pp. 51, 69, 149, 186-187, 209, 226-227.

28. John Bakeless, *Turncoats, Traitors and Heroes* (Philadelphia and New York, 1959), pp. 24-26.

29. William Jarvis's Petition, September 7, 1784, AO13-41.

30. Rivington's *Gazette*, June 3, 1780.

31. *K.F.*, pp. 279-280.

32. AO13-42.

33. *K.F.*, pp. 279-280.

34. *Ibid.*, pp. 101-102.

35. *Ibid.*, pp. 101-106.

36. Cf. L.T., IV, p. 548. Some clergy did so rather in the manner of the civil clergy of the French Revolution.

37. *Ibid.*, LIV, p. 85.

38. Cf. *Ibid.*, p. 79.

39. *K.F.*, pp. 27, 67.

40. William Barton, *Memoirs of the Life of David Rittenhouse* (Philadelphia, 1813), p. 280n.

41. See William W. Sweet, "The Role of the Anglicans in the American Revolution," *Huntington Library Quarterly*, XI (1947), pp. 51-70; and Edgar L. Pennington, "The Anglican Clergy of Pennsylvania and the American Revolution," *Pennsylvania Magazine of History and Biography*, LXIII (1939), pp. 401-431.

42. *K.F.*, p. 150.

43. *Ibid.*, p. 89.

44. *Boston Gazette*, August 28, 1775.

45. *Virginia Gazette* (Purdie), April 4, 1777.

46. L.T., VII, p. 95; *K.F.*, p. 150.

47. *Ibid.*

48. Martha B. Amory, *The Domestic and Artistic Life of John Singleton Copley, R.A.* (Boston, 1882), p. 58.

49. Wright, *Loyalists of New Brunswick*, pp. 157-158.

50. *K.F.*, p. 88.

51. *The Writings of George Washington,* ed: Jared Sparks (Boston, 1834), III, p. 8n.

52. *Annual Register,* 1779, p. 180.

53. *K.F.,* p. 242.

54. *Pennsylvania Gazette,* January 10, 1777.

55. *Writings of Paine,* ed. Conway, I, p. 171.

56. *Annual Register,* 1776, p. 158.

57. *K.F.,* p. 137.

58. *L.T.,* XLIII, p. 14.

59. Curwen, *Journal,* pp. 283-284.

60. *K.F.,* p. 251.

61. *Ibid.,* pp. 175, 270.

62. *Ibid.,* pp. 269, 280.

63. Jules D. Prown, *John Singleton Copley: In America 1738-1774* (Cambridge, 1966), I, p. 91.

64. A. M. Schlesinger, *New Viewpoints in American History* (New York, 1922), pp. 76-77; *K.F.,* pp. 233, 269.

65. *Virginia Gazette* (Dixon and Hunter), April 11, 1777.

66. Rivington's *Gazette,* June 3, 1780.

67. Crèvecoeur, *Sketches,* pp. 251-252.

68. *K.F.,* p. 269.

69. *Writings of Paine,* ed. Conway, I, p. 174; *Connecticut Courant,* March 9, 1779.

70. *K.F.,* p. 273.

71. *Ibid.,* p. 280.

72. E.g., the issues of June 3 and August 19, 1780.

73. *K.F.,* p. 224.

74. "List of Harvard Graduates," *American Quarterly Register* (1841), XIII, pp. 405, 405n.

75. See *K.F.,* pp. 223-224; *Charleston Gazette,* January 11, 1780.

76. *K.F.,* p. 281.

77. *Ibid.*

78. *Ibid.,* p. 225.

79. *New Jersey Archives,* ser. i, X, p. 540; Catherine Fennelly, "William Franklin of New Jersey," *W.M.Q.,* 2d ser., VI, (1949), pp. 361-382.

80. *K.F.,* p. 270.

81. *The Loyalists of New Jersey, Their Memorials, Petitions, Claims, etc., from English Records,* ed., E.A. Jones (Newark, 1927), p. 103; *L.T.,* XLII, p. 555.

82. *K.F.,* pp. 277-278; Wallace Brown, "Viewpoints of a Pennsylvania Loyalist," *Pennsylvania Magazine of History and Biography,* XCI (1967), pp. 419-435.

83. *K.F.,* p. 151. However, not all Loyalists were so impressed with George III. A good example is Samuel Curwen.

84. See Chapter II, above.

85. L.T., XLII, p. 557.

86. *K.F.*, p. 48.

87. *Ibid.*, Ch. III.

88. *Ibid.*, p. 94.

89. *Ibid.*, p. 95.

90. *Ibid.*, pp. 95-96.

91. *Ibid.*, p. 14.

92. *Ibid.*, p. 223.

93. *Ibid.*, p. 94.

94. Oliver Bunce, *Love in '76* (New York, 1857), p. 3.

95. *K.F.*, p. 279; Lewis Einstein, *Divided Loyalties: Americans in England during the War of Independence* (Boston, 1933), p. 208.

96. *K.F.*, pp. 39-40, 94, 125, 245-246, 280.

97. James R. Gilmore, "Nathaniel Emmons and Mather Byles," *New England Magazine* (1897), p. 735; Arthur W. H. Eaton, *The Famous Mather Byles* (Boston, 1914), pp. 145-147.

98. *K.F.*, p. 41.

99. L.T., XLIX, p. 244.

100. *K.F.*, p. 144.

101. L.T., III, p. 436.

102. *Royal Commission,* ed. Egerton, p. 199.

103. Except where indicated all the quotations are from Pennington, "The Anglican Clergy of Pennsylvania," pp. 422-426.

104. *K.F.*, pp. 92-93.

105. *Ibid.*, p. 92.

106. *The Diary of William Smith,* ed. Upton, I, xxii, and Upton's Introduction, *passim*. See also Robert M. Calhoon, "William Smith Jr.s Alternative to the American Revolution," *W.M.Q.*, 3d ser., XXII (1965), pp. 105-118.

107. *K.F.*, p. 210; David Fanning, *The Narrative of Colonel David Fanning* (New York, 1865).

108. *K.F.*, p. 40.

109. See *Dictionary of American Biography,* XVI.

110. D. Brunton and D. H. Pennington, *Members of the Long Parliament* (Cambridge, 1954), p. xvii.

111. *K.F.*, p. 282.

112. Jonathan Boucher, *Reminiscences of an American Loyalist, 1783-1789,* ed. Jonathan Bouchier (Boston, 1925), p. 95.

113. L.T., LII, p. 5; *The Loyalists of Massachusetts,* ed. E. A. Jones (London, 1930), pp. 205-206.

114. Nelson, *The American Tory,* p. 19.

Notes for Chapter IV

1. *Writings of Paine,* ed. Conway, I, p. 174.
2. Cf. Rivington's *Gazette,* June 5, 1779.
3. Van Tyne, *Loyalists,* pp. 149, 152, 157, 161, 162.
4. L.T., XXII, p. 355; XX, p. 197; XXI, pp. 319-324.
5. See Bakeless, *Turncoats, passim.*
6. *Ibid.,* pp. 43, 24ff., 252ff., 99ff.; *Pennsylvania Gazette,* November 17, 1779.
7. James Moody, *Narrative of the Exertions and Sufferings of Lieut. James Moody, in the Cause of Government since the Year 1776* (New York, 1865), pp. 10-11, 13-14; L.T., XXXVIII, pp. 119-130; IV, pp. 4-7.
8. *Ibid.,* XV, p. 5. For some account of Loyalist spying in England, see Chapter VI of this volume.
9. Kenneth Scott, *Counterfeiting in Colonial America* (New York, 1957), p. 253.
10. Quoted in Kenneth Scott, "New Hampshire Tory Counterfeiters Operating from New York City," New York History Society *Quarterly,* XXXIV (1950), p. 37.
11. L.T., XXVII, p. 265.
12. *Pennsylvania Gazette,* July 9, 1777.
13. *Ibid.,* July 23, 1777.
14. Bakeless, *Turncoats,* pp. 96-97.
15. *Loyalists of Massachusetts,* ed. Jones, p. 93; L.T., VIII, p. 372.
16. See Scott, "New Hampshire Counterfeiters."
17. Jonathan Smith, "Toryism in Worcester during the War for Independence," Massachusetts Historical Society, *Proceedings,* XLVIII (1914), p. 26.
18. Quoted in Scott, *Counterfeiting,* p. 254; see also *Pennsylvania Gazette,* May 14, 1777.
19. Thomas Anburey, *Travels Through the Interior Parts of America, 1776-1781* (Boston, 1923), II, p. 231.
20. Quoted in Scott, "New Hampshire Counterfeiters," p. 32.
21. *Annual Register,* 1779, p. 180.
22. Rivington's *Gazette,* January 6, 1779; *Boston Gazette,* January 10, 1774; *K.F.,* pp. 30-31.
23. *Writings of Paine,* ed. Conway, I, pp. 215-216.
24. *K.F.,* p. 30.
25. *Virginia Gazette* (Dixon and Nicholson). March 12, 1779.
26. L.T., V, p. 687.
27. *Pennsylvania Gazette,* February 21, 1778.
28. For newspapers in general, see Frank L. Mott, *American Journalism* (New York, 1950); Clarence S. Brigham, *History and Bibliography*

of American Newspapers, 1690-1820 (Worcester, 1947); A. M. Schlesinger, *Prelude to Independence* (New York, 1958).

29. *Plain Truth* was not written by the Reverend William Smith of Philadelphia, as is often asserted.

30. Catherine S. Crary, "The Tory and the Spy: The Double Life of James Rivington," *W.M.Q.*, 3d ser., XVI (1959), pp. 61-72.

31. David Ramsay, *The History of the American Revolution* (Philadelphia, 1789), II, p. 319.

32. Oral communication was certainly more important than written for the majority of Americans, but probably not for the leaders. Even today with wider literacy, half the population never read a book.

33. In general, see Miller, *Sam Adams: Pioneer in Propaganda;* Philip Davidson, *Propaganda and the American Revolution, 1763-1783* (Chapel Hill, 1941); Moses C. Tyler, *The Literary History of the American Revolution* (New York and London, 1897); Granger, *Political Satire in the American Revolution.*

34. John R. Alden, *The American Revolution, 1775-1783* (New York, 1954), pp. 86-87; Evarts B. Greene, *The Revolutionary Generation, 1763-1790* (New York, 1943), p. 228. Alden thinks 8,000 is too high an estimate.

35. Paul H. Smith, *Loyalists and Redcoats: A Study in Revolutionary Policy* (Chapel Hill, 1964), pp. 60-61, 77.

36. *Ibid.,* p. 60.

37. Sabine, *Biographical Sketches,* II, p. 511; Robert O. Demond, in *The Loyalists of North Carolina during the Revolution* (Durham, 1940), pp. 52-53, claims great things for Hamilton, but with little evidence to back them up; it seems that Hamilton should be more fully investigated.

38. *Loyalist Narratives from Upper Canada,* ed. J. J. Talman (Toronto, 1946), p. xxxvi; see George F. Stanley, "The Six Nations and the American Revolution," *Ontario History,* LVI (1964), pp. 217-232.

39. Sabine, *Biographical Sketches,* I, p. 260.

40. L.T., XXVII, pp. 160, 164, 167.

41. Howard H. Peckham, *The War for Independence* (Chicago, 1958), p. 136.

42. Sydney G. Fisher, *The Struggle for American Independence* (Philadelphia, 1908), I, p. 257.

43. Van Tyne, *Loyalists,* p. 161.

44. L.T., XLI, p. 485.

45. Rivington's *Gazette,* July 7, 1779.

46. *Ibid.,* June 22, 1782; *Annual Register,* 1779, p. 6.

47. On King's Mountain, see Peckham, *War for Independence,* pp. 136-138, 147-149; John R. Alden, *The South in the Revolution, 1763-1789* (Baton Rouge, 1957), pp. 249-250; Edward McGrady, *The History of South Carolina in the Revolution, 1775-1780* (New York, 1901), pp.

776-805; Lyman C. Draper, *King's Mountain and Its Heroes* (Cincinnati, 1881), *passim;* Christopher Ward, *The War of the Revolution* (New York, 1952), II, pp. 737-747; Hugh F. Rankin, *The American Revolution* (New York, 1964), pp. 256-264.

48. Rivington's *Gazette,* June 5, 1779.

49. *Virginia Gazette* (Dixon and Nicholson), February 26, 1779.

50. Van Tyne, *Loyalists,* p. 262.

51. Rivington's *Gazette,* March 11, 1780.

52. *Loyalists of New Jersey,* ed. Jones, pp. 76-77.

53. *Annual Register,* 1781, p. 14.

54. Gerald O. Haffner, "Captain Charles Asgill, An Anglo-American Incident, 1782," *History Today,* VII (1957), pp. 329-334; Carl Van Doren, *Secret History of the American Revolution* (New York, 1942), p. 430; James Thacher, *A Military Journal during the American War* (Boston, 1827), p. 303; Katherine Mayo, *General Washington's Dilemma* (New York, 1938), pp. 71, 79, 83, and *passim.*

55. L.T., XL, p. 381.

56. A London source quoted in *Pennsylvania Gazette,* January 24, 1778.

57. Parallels with recent troubles in Ireland, Algeria, Viet Nam, and so on suggest themselves here.

58. Mackesy, *War for America, 1775-1783* (London, 1964), *passim.*

59. November 25, 1778, Balch Papers, New York Public Library.

60. Mackesy, *War for America,* pp. 435-436.

61. Smith, *Loyalists and Redcoats,* p. 57.

62. Mackesy, *War for America,* pp. 134-135, 59.

63. Quoted *ibid.,* pp. 252, 88.

64. Piers Mackesy, "British Strategy in the War of American Independence," *Yale Review,* LII (1963), pp. 550-551.

65. Mackesy, *War for America,* pp. 253-254. The strength and weakness of the plan for using the putative majority of Loyalists was seen in miniature when the British took Savannah in December, 1778. Colonel Archibald Campbell's occupation of Georgia proved popular, and his sympathy for the Georgians and desire to restore civil government was well received. The success was short-lived, however, because the Swiss General Prevost, the commander in East Florida, who was ordered to reinforce Campbell, lacked the Colonel's understanding, and "his advance across Georgia was more like a plundering expedition" than a step in a plan of reconciliation (*ibid.,* p. 267).

66. *Ibid.,* p. 159.

67. *Diary of Frederick Mackenzie* (Cambridge, Mass., 1930), II, p. 447.

68. Mackesy, *War for America,* pp. 341-345.

69. *Diary of Frederick Mackenzie,* II, p. 525.

70. Smith, *Loyalists and Redcoats,* pp. ix-x.

71. Peckham, *War for Independence,* p. 198.

72. E.g., Isaac Ogden to Joseph Galloway, November 22, 1778, Balch Papers, New York Public Library.

73. Hugh E. Egerton, *The Causes and Character of the American Revolution* (Oxford, 1923), p. 161.

74. See Chapter VI of this volume.

75. L.T., XLIV, p. 139.

76. "Letters of Jonathan Sewall," Massachusetts Historical Society, *Proceedings,* 2d ser., X (1896), p. 420.

77. *Pennsylvania Gazette,* January 10, 1777.

78. Mackesy, *War for America,* pp. 257, 269.

79. See William B. Willcox and Frederick Wyatt, "Sir Henry Clinton: A Psychological Exploration in History," *W.M.Q.,* 3d ser., XVI (1959), pp. 3-26.

80. Rivington's *Gazette,* February 28, 1781.

81. See Alden, *South in Revolution,* p. 293; William B. Willcox, "The British Road to Yorktown: A Study in Divided Command," *A.H.R.,* LII (1946), pp. 1-35. Willcox (p. 34) places the primary blame on Cornwallis.

82. L.T., XL, p. 281.

83. *Ibid.,* LVIII, p. 204.

84. *Ibid.,* L, pp. 263-264.

85. *Ibid.,* XXXVIII, p. 390.

86. "Letters of Rev. Jonathan Boucher," *Maryland History Magazine,* VIII (1913), p. 254.

87. Labaree, *Boston Tea Party,* p. 225.

88. L.T., L, pp. 412-413.

89. Oscar T. Barck, Jr., *New York City during the War for Independence* (New York, 1931), p. 62.

90. Van Tyne, *Loyalists,* p. 147; Smith, *Loyalists and Redcoats,* pp. 33, 33n, 35, 36, 37, 48n, 50, 53, 54, 64, 66, 73, 74.

91. *Annual Register,* 1776, p. 157.

92. *Virginia Gazette* (Dixon and Hunter), November 29, 1776.

93. "Colonel Robert Gray's Observations on the War in Carolina," *South Carolina Historical and Genealogical Magazine,* XI (1910), p. 144.

94. E.g., L.T., V, pp. 411, 491.

95. *Pennsylvania Gazette,* April 23, 1777.

96. E.g., Charles M. Andrews, *Guide to the Materials for American History to 1783, in the Public Record Office of Great Britain* (2 vols., Washington, 1912, 1914), II, p. 335.

97. *Boston Gazette,* January 16, 1775.

98. Rivington's *Gazette,* April 14, 1779.

99. L.T., II, pp. 294-302.

100. *Ibid.*, L, p. 537; I, pp. 80-81.

101. Cf. Anburey, *Travels*, II, p. 159.

102. Rivington's *Gazette,* February 21, 1778.

103. L.T., XXXVIII, pp. 296-297.

104. Egerton, *American Revolution*, p. 169.

105. Isaac Ogden to Joseph Galloway, November 22, 1778, Balch Papers, New York Public Library; W. O. Raymond, "Loyalists in Arms," New Brunswick Historical Society *Collections,* (St. John, N.B., 1904), No. 5, p. 189.

106. L.T., V. pp. 409-415.

107. *Annual Register*, 1777, p. 156.

108. "Journal of Rev. Joshua Wingate Weeks, Loyalist Rector of St. Michaels Church, Marblehead, 1778-1779," Essex Institute of Salem, *Historical Collections,* LII (1916), p. 163.

109. Isaac Ogden to Joseph Galloway, November 22, 1778, Balch Papers, New York Public Library.

110. Rivington's *Gazette,* August 25, 1779.

111. Many uprisings went unsupported, outstanding examples being found in Delaware, Georgia, and also in Maryland, North Carolina, New Jersey, and Virginia (Van Tyne, *Loyalists,* p. 167).

112. Quoted in Willard M. Wallace, *Appeal to Arms* (New York, 1951), p. 271.

113. *Diary of Frederick Mackenzie,* II, p. 525.

114. Anna Rawle, "A Loyalist's Account of Certain Occurrences in Philadelphia after Cornwallis' Surrender in Yorktown," *Pennsylvania Magazine of History and Biography,* XVI (1892), p. 104.

115. L.T., XL, p. 382.

116. Historical Manuscript Commission, *Report on the Manuscripts of Mrs. Stopford-Sackville* (London, 1910), II, pp. 216-218.

117. Quoted in Egerton, *American Revolution,* p. 164.

118. Weeks, "Journal," p. 10.

119. No one knows how close the British secretary of state for America, Lord George Germain, came to gaining a heroic reputation comparable to Chatham's, instead of the, at best, mediocre one that most historians have assigned him. Mackesy, in his *War for America,* p. 516 and *passim,* somewhat rehabilitates Germain. I am most indebted to Mackesy's brilliant work. For a general discussion of the historiography of the war, see Don Higgenbotham, "American Historians and the Military History of the American Revolution," *A.H.R.,* LXX (1964), pp. 18-34.

Notes for Chapter V

1. Anonymous, Loyalist Rhapsodies, Library of Congress, Manuscripts Division.

2. See Chapter II of this volume.

3. A summary of the the laws may be found in Van Tyne, *Loyalists*, Appendixes B and C.

4. *Ibid.*, pp. 140-141.

5. *Ibid.*, pp. 274, 276.

6. Quoted in Robert A. East, *Business Enterprise in the American Revolution* (New York, 1938), p. 111.

7. L.T., I, p. 172.

8. *Loyalists of New Jersey*, ed. Jones, p. 186; L.T., I, p. 172.

9. E.g., *Ibid.*, XLVIII, pp. 138, 263; XXXIV, p. 46. Legislation was passed against this sort of thing.

10. William L. Sachse, *The Colonial Americans in Britain* (Madison, 1956), p. 200.

11. L.T., VI, p. 298.

12. Claude H. Van Tyne, *The American Revolution, 1776-1783* (New York, 1905), map facing p. 250.

13. *Ibid.*, p. 255.

14. L.T., LVIII, p. 84.

15. Andrew F. Davis, *The Confiscation of John Chandler's Estate* (Boston, 1903), pp. 1-24 and *passim*.

16. E.g., William Byrd and Lord Fairfax in Virginia (Nelson, *The American Tory*, p. 145).

17. Van Tyne, *Loyalists*, p. 201.

18. Peter Force, ed. *American Archives*, (6 vols., Washington, 1837-1846), 4th ser., V, p. 405.

19. *K.F.*, pp. 64, 85.

20. Crèvecoeur, *Sketches*, p. 264.

21. L.T., I, p. 17.

22. George M. Wrong, *Canada and the American Revolution* (New York, 1935), p. 378.

23. *Boston Gazette*, September 9, 1776.

24. *K.F.*, pp. 136, 63-64; Rivington's *Gazette*, September 8, 1774; Arthur M. Schlesinger, *The Colonial Merchants and the American Revolution, 1763-1776* (New York, 1918), p. 476.

25. L.T., V, pp. 409-413.

26. *Ibid.*, XVII, p. 52.

27. *K.F.*, p. 216; L.T., XLVIII, p. 140; Carl Bridenbaugh, *Peter Harrison, First American Architect* (Chapel Hill, 1949), p. 156; *K.F.*, p. 116; L.T., XXVII, p. 551; *K.F.*, p. 215; L.T., XLVIII, pp. 701, 704; *K.F.*, p. 65; *New Hampshire Spy*, November 21, 1786.

28. *Boston Gazette,* August 19, 1776.

29. Rivington's *Gazette,* May 29, 1779.

30. L.T., XLV, p. 497; *K.F.,* p. 116. Also on the subject of Tories and feathers, the use of the tail feathers of a Tory's rooster to decorate a drink served to some patriot officers is sometimes given as the origin of the word "cocktail."

31. For good accounts of Malcolm, with long quotations from the sources, see Frank W. C. Hersey, "Tar and Feathers: The Adventures of Captain John Malcolm," *Publications* of the Colonial Society of Massachusetts, XXXIV (1941), pp. 429-473; *Peter Oliver's Origin and Progress of the American Revolution, A Tory View,* ed. Douglas Adair and John A. Schutz (San Marino, Calif., 1961), p. 94; L.T., III, pp. 276-277; *Loyalists of Massachusetts,* ed. Jones, pp. 208-209; Ann Hulton, *Letters of a Loyalist Lady* (Cambridge, 1927), p. 70; George G. Wolkins, "The Seizure of John Hancock's Sloop *Liberty,*" Massachusetts Historical Society, *Proceedings,* LV (1923), pp. 239-284; Daniel Malcolm and the Writs of Assistance," *ibid.,* LVIII (1925), pp. 5-84; and *K.F.,* pp. 34, 203. For an excellent description by a victim of tarring and feathering, see L.T., LIII, pp. 99-100.

32. *K.F.,* p. 78.

33. L.T., XII, p. 193.

34. Fisher, *Struggle for American Independence,* I, p. 264; *K.F.,* pp. 35, 64; Royal Institution Transcripts (New York Public Library, Manuscripts Division), I, p. 369.

35. L.T., XLIX, pp. 420-423; Sabine, *Biographical Sketches,* I, p. 597; Frank Moore, *Diary of the American Revolution* (New York, 1860), I, p. 148.

36. Force, ed., *American Archives,* 4th ser., IV, p. 203.

37. See *Oxford English Dictionary.*

38. George M. Wrong, in "Background of Loyalist Movement, 1763-1783," Ontario Historical Society, *Papers and Records,* XXX (1934), p. 176, puts the number at "hundreds."

39. L.T., XLV, p. 536.

40. *Ibid.,* IV, p. 174; *Virginia Gazette* (Dixon and Hunter), June 20, 1777; *K.F.,* pp. 7, 65, 134.

41. Sabine, *Biographical Sketches,* II, p. 219.

42. *Ibid.;* L.T., L, pp. 227-241; *K.F.,* pp. 134-135.

43. Epaphroditus Peck, *The Loyalists of Connecticut* (New Haven, 1934), p. 23.

44. Royal Institution Transcripts, I, p. 488.

45. *Ibid.,* V, pp. 49-50.

46. AO13-41.

47. L.T., XVIII, p. 179.

48. Anburey, *Travels,* II, p. 303; L.T., XXI, p. 54; Richard H. Phelps,

Newgate of Connecticut (Hartford, 1892), *passim;* "Letters to Joseph Galloway, from leading Tories in America," *The Historical Magazine,* V (1861), pp. 271, 301.

49. Moore, *Diary,* II, pp. 434-436.

50. AO13-41.

51. *K.F.,* p. 65.

52. *Ibid.,* p. 10.

53. *The Diary of Thomas Vernon,* Rhode Island Historical Tracts, No. 13 (Providence, 1881), p. 42 and *passim.*

54. Greene, *Revolutionary Generation,* p. 205.

55. Quoted in Haight, *Before the Coming of the Loyalists,* p. 12.

56. Rivington's *Gazette,* May 29, 1779; Hulton, *Letters,* p. 18.

57. E.g., L.T., LIX, p. 289.

58. Peter Force, ed., *American Archives* (9 vols., Washington, D.C., 1848-1853), 5th ser., III, p. 1488.

59. Crèvecoeur, *Sketches,* pp. 289-290, 270.

60. Alden, *South in Revolution,* p. 328.

61. George Rudé, *The Crowd in History, 1730-1848* (London, 1964), pp. 229-230.

62. Frank R. Diffenderffer, "The Loyalists in the Revolution," Lancaster County Historical Society, *Historical Papers and Addresses,* XXIII (1919), p. 119.

63. *Documents Relating to the Colonial History of New York,* ed. E. B. O'Callaghan (Albany, 1857), VIII, p. 801.

64. Fisher, *Struggle for American Independence,* I, p. 272.

65. There were also Whig prison ships (e.g., L.T., LII, p. 73).

66. Leiby, *Revolutionary War in the Hackensack Valley,* p. 120.

67. Force, ed., *American Archives,* 4th ser., II, pp. 94-95; see also Edwin T. Bowden, *The Satiric Poems of John Trumbull* (Austin, 1962), p. 220.

68. *Virginia Gazette* (Dixon and Nicholson), June 5, 1779.

Notes for Chapter VI

1. The Earl of Macclesfield, letter to an unknown correspondent, 1784, Library of Congress, Manuscripts Division.

2. "Letters of Rev. Jonathan Boucher," p. 344.

3. Sachse, *Colonial Americans,* pp. 192, 194-195.

4. AO13-41.

5. FO4-1.

6. Einstein, *Divided Loyalties,* p. 230.

7. L.T., I, p. 87.

8. New Hampshire Loyalists: Transcripts from the Records of the Commission for Enquiring into the Losses and Services of American

Loyalists, 1783-1790, preserved in the Public Record Office, London, England (5 vols. in the New Hampshire State Library, Concord), II, p. 694.

9. L.T., III, p. 240.

10. *Loyalists of Massachusetts*, ed. Jones, p. 54.

11. Quoted in Lawrence S. Mayo, "The Massachusetts Loyalists," *Commonwealth History of Massachusetts*, ed. A. B. Hart (New York, 1929), III, p. 273.

12. Curwen, *Journal*, p. 237.

13. L.T., XLVI, p. 403.

14. *Ibid.*, IV, p. 70.

15. FO4-1.

16. E.g., New Hampshire Loyalist Transcripts, II, p. 690.

17. Cf. L.T., IV, p. 481; VII, pp. 289-291.

18. Cf. *ibid.*, VIII, p. 425; XLV, p. 389.

19. *Ibid.*, XLVIII, pp. 361-370.

20. Cf. Petition of James Molloy, June 2, 1784, FO4-1.

21. Cf. L.T., LVI, p. 102.

22. E.g., *ibid.*, VI, pp. 718-721.

23. FO4-1.

24. New Hampshire Loyalist Transcripts, I, pp. 377-378.

25. AO13-41.

26. "Sufferings and Losses of Jolley Allen," *Proceedings* of the Massachusetts Historical Society, XVI (1878), pp. 69-99.

27. *Loyalists of Massachusetts*, ed. Jones, p. 123.

28. E.g., *K.F.*, p. 235.

29. Einstein, *Divided Loyalties*, pp. x-xi, pp. 4-20, 37, 40, 51-55.

30. Sachse, *Colonial Americans*, pp. 197, 273.

31. L.T., XXXV, p. 89.

32. *Ibid.*, XLVIII, p. 165.

33. *Ibid.*, XLV, pp. 331-332.

34. *Ibid.*, IV, p. 252, V, pp. 213, 260, 318. Several loyal Negroes in London were fleeced by the landlords of the boardinghouse in which they stayed.

35. *Loyalists of New Jersey*, ed. Jones, p. 159.

36. Weeks, "Journal," p. 346.

37. *Loyalists of New Jersey*, ed. Jones, p. 159.

38. Cf. Rivington's *Gazette*, March 11, 1780.

39. *Boston Gazette*, July 8, 1776.

40. Quoted in G. E. Mingay, *English Landed Society in the Eighteenth Century* (London, 1963), p. 261.

41. *The Morning Chronicle and London Advertizer*, December 30, 1777. For another example of English fund raising, see Jay B. Botsford,

English Society in the Eighteenth Century (New York, 1924), pp. 315-316.

42. Whitfield, J. Bell, Jr., "Scottish Emigration to America: A Letter of Dr. Charles Nisbet to Dr. John Witherspoon, 1784," *W.M.Q.*, 3d ser., (1954), XI, pp. 276-289.

43. FO4-1; Rivington's *Gazette*, November 3, 1775.

44. "Letters of Robert Proud," *Pennsylvania Magazine of History and Biography*, XXXIV (1910), 65; Einstein, *Divided Loyalties*, p. 188; Curwen, *Journal*, p. 74; L.T., VI, p. 16; *The Diary of William Smith*, ed. Upton, I, pp. lii, 53, 53n.

45. *Boswell: The Ominous Years, 1774-1776*, ed. Frederick A. Pottle and Charles Ryskamp (New York, 1963), pp. 160, 160n, 170n.

46. Charles R. Ritcheson, "The London Press and the First Decade of American Independence," *Journal of British Studies*, II, (1963), pp. 99, 105-106.

47. *Boston Gazette*, July 9, 1775.

48. Einstein, *Divided Loyalties*, pp. x, xiii; Lewis Namier and John Brooke, *The House of Commons, 1754-1790* (London, 1964), I, pp. 159-161.

49. Curwen, *Journal*, p. 90.

50. FO4-1; "Letters of Jonathan Sewall," Massachusetts Historical Society, *Proceedings*, 2d ser., X (January, 1896), p. 423; quoted in Justin Winsor, *Narrative and Critical History of America* (Boston, 1888), VII, p. 208n.

51. L.T., III, p. 358.

52. Royal Institution Transcripts, IV, 201; See also Aubrey C. Land, *The Dulanys of Maryland* (Baltimore, 1955), p. 330.

53. "Letters of Jonathan Sewall," p. 423.

54. Weeks, "Journal," p. 203.

55. *The Diary of William Smith*, ed. Upton, I, pp. 24, 82, 83, 176.

56. *Ibid.*, I, p. liv; II, p. 15; I, pp. 83, 84; II, p. 80.

57. "Extracts from the Journal of Edward Oxnard," *New England Historical and Genealogical Register*, XXVI (1872), p. 119.

58. *The Diary of William Smith*, ed. Upton, I, p. 52.

59. Curwen, *Journal*, p. 45.

60. *The Diary of William Smith*, ed. Upton, I, p. 110.

61. John L. Watson, "The Marston Family of Salem, Massachusetts," *New England Historical and Genealogical Register*, XXVII (1873), p. 400.

62. *K.F.*, p. 271.

63. Weeks, "Journal," p. 205.

64. Chandler to Samuel Thorne, August 6, 1783, "Loyalists" box, New York Public Library, Manuscripts Division.

65. Nelson, *The American Tory*, p. 161.

66. Quoted in Einstein, *Divided Loyalties*, p. 204.

67. *Ibid.*, p. 338.

68. Sachse, *Colonial Americans*, pp. 195-196.

69. Einstein, *Divided Loyalties*, pp. 308-309.

70. R. B. Mowat, *Americans in England* (Boston, 1935), p. 43.

71. Wallace Brown, "The Loyalists and the American Revolution," *History Today*, XII (March, 1962), p.155; Curwen, *Journal*, pp. 30, 45, 348; Van Tyne, *Loyalists*, p. 256n; Einstein, *Divided Loyalties*, p. 229.

72. "Letters to Joseph Galloway, from leading Tories in America," p. 363.

73. R. P. Baker, "Poetry of Jacob Bailey, Loyalist," *New England Quarterly*, II (January, 1929), pp. 71-72.

74. *The Diary of William Smith*, ed. Upton, I, pp. lv, 2.

75. The issues of Rivington's *Gazette, passim;* Van Tyne, *Loyalists*, pp. 245, 249, 251-252, 264ff.; Barck, *New York City, passim.*

76. Corey Ford, *A Peculiar Service* (Boston, 1965), p. 296.

77. Van Tyne, *Loyalists*, pp. 255, 260-262.

78. L.T., XIII, p. 219.

79. FO4-1.

80. Curwen, *Journal*, p. 92.

81. FO4-1.

82. AO13-41.

83. Cf. Memorial of James Moody, May 30, 1783, FO4-1.

84. L.T., VII, p. 333. There is some disagreement here: Alden, in *American Revolution*, p. 225, names £70,0000 as the total of annual payments, and so does Edward Channing, *A History of the United States* (6 vols. New York, 1905-1925), III, p. 361; see Lorenzo Sabine, *A Historical Essay on the Loyalists of the American Revolution* (Springfield, 1957), pp. 70-71.

85. Demond, *Loyalists of North Carolina*, p. 202; Catherine S. Crary, "The Humble Immigrants and the American Dream: Some Case Histories, 1774-1776," *Mississippi Valley Historical Review*, XLVI (June, 1959), p. 53.

86. L.T., VI, p. 527.

87. Boucher, *Reminiscences*, p. 144.

88. FO4-1.

89. Curwen, *Journal*, p. 412.

90. See Chapter V of this volume.

91. Hersey, "Tar and Feathers: The Adventures of Captain John Malcolm," pp. 429-473.

92. Additional Manuscripts, 36591, British Museum.

93. Einstein, *Divided Loyalties*, p. 238.

94. The articles are reproduced in Sabine, *Historical Essay*, p. 99n.

95. Cf. L.T., I, pp. 322-348.

96. *Gentleman's Magazine*, LIII (1783), Pt. I, p. 470; Einstein, *Divided Loyalties*, p. 233.

97. Quoted in Sabine, *Historical Essay*, p. 101.

98. Quoted in E. A. Benians, "The Beginnings of the New Empire 1783-1793," *Cambridge History of the British Empire*, eds., J. Holland Rose, A. P. Newton, and E. A. Benians (Cambridge, 1940), II, p. 9. On the peace treaty, two very different books may be consulted: Richard W. Van Alstyne, *Empire and Independence: The International History of the American Revolution* (New York, 1965); Richard B. Morris, *The Peacemakers: The Great Powers and American Independence* (New York, 1965).

99. Egerton, *Royal Commission*, p. xxxi.

100. Historical Manuscript Commission, *Stopford-Sackville*, II, p. 252.

101. *Gentleman's Magazine*, LIII (1783), Pt. 1, p. 174; Curwen, *Journal*, p. 373.

102. *Ibid.*

103. Merrill Jensen, *New Nation* (New York, 1950), p. 266.

104. *K.F.*, p. 272.

105. L.T., IX, 85; *Correspondence of Thomas Barclay*, ed. George L. Rives (New York, 1814), p. 32.

106. Jensen, *New Nation*, p. 267.

107. The precise number of those who returned awaits further research, but will never be accurately known.

108. *The Complete Works of Benjamin Franklin*, ed. John Bigelow, (New York and London, 1888), IX, p. 131.

109. L.T., I, p. 348.

110. E. Alfred Jones, ed., "Letter of David Colden, Loyalist, 1783," *A.H.R.*, XXV (1919), p. 83.

111. Egerton, *American Revolution*, p. 175.

112. *Boston Gazette*, July 7, 1783.

113. L.T., I, p. 259.

114. *K.F.*, p. 214.

115. *Boston Gazette*, August 25, 1783.

116. *K.F.*, pp. 116-117.

117. *Boston Gazette*, November 10, 1783.

118. L.T., V, p. 23.

119. *Boston Gazette*, May 5, 1783.

120. Ward Chipman, "Diary," ed. J. B. Berry, Essex Institute of Salem, *Historical Collections*, LXXXVII (1951), p. 216.

121. Quoted in Sabine, *Biographical Sketches*, I, p. 89.

122. Jensen, *New Nation*, p. 267.

123. *K.F.*, p. 80.

124. *Ibid.*, p. 66.

125. Oscar Zeichner, "The Rehabilitation of the Loyalists in Connec-

ticut," *New England Quarterly,* XI (1938), p. 324; Greene, *Revolutionary Generation,* p. 307.

126. L. H. Gipson, *Jared Ingersoll, A Study in American Loyalism in Relation to British Colonial Government* (New Haven, 1920), pp. 372-374.

127. *K.F.,* p. 117.

128. *Ibid.,* p. 197.

129. Chipman, "Diary," p. 231.

130. Curwen, *Journal,* p. 393.

131. Alden, *South in Revolution,* p. 328.

132. *K.F.,* p. 214.

133. *Ibid.,* p. 272.

134. *Ibid.,* pp. 136, 160, 168, 80.

135. *Ibid.,* pp. 7, 35, 48, 66, 80, 116, 136, 160, 168, 183, 197, 214.

136. *Ibid.,* pp. 116-117.

137. CO5-116.

138. Liverpool Papers, Additional Manuscripts, 38284, fols. 234-237, B.M.

139. L.T., I, pp. 221-243.

140. Chatham Papers, AO30-8, p. 220.

141. 23 Geo. III, Ch. 80.

142. Curwen. *Journal,* pp. 331, 365-367.

143. On this last point, see *A Brief State of the Case of the American Loyalists,* Hartley Russell Papers, Berkshire County Council, Reading.

144. See Van Tyne, *Loyalists,* p. 302; John Eardley Wilmot, *Historical View of the Commission for Enquiry into . . . the American Loyalists* (London, 1815), *passim.*

145. L.T., I, p. 92.

146. *The Diary . . . of . . . William Smith,* ed., 35n.

147. *The Winslow Papers,* ed. W. O. Raymond (St. John, N.B., 1901), p. 198.

148. *Loyalists of Massachusetts,* ed. Jones, p. 114.

149. L.T., I, pp. 355-359.

150. *Ibid.,* I, p. 112.

151. Tobias Smollett, *Humphrey Clinker,* Modern Library edition (New York, 1929), p. 392.

152. *Correspondence of Thomas Barclay,* ed. Rives, p. 37.

153. FO4-1.

154. *The Diary of William Smith,* ed. Upton, I, p. l.

155. *Ibid.,* I, p. 35.

156. William Kingsford, *The History of Canada* (Toronto, 1894), VII, p. 217.

157. Egerton, *Royal Commission,* p. xliii.

158. L.T., II, p. 394.

159. *Ibid.*, IV, pp. 144-145.

160. *Ibid.*, XXVI, p. 545.

161. *Ibid.*, V, pp. 329, 327.

162. *Ibid.*, V, pp. 482-485.

163. *Ibid.*, V, p. 499. Some Negroes did get small pensions, and almost none wished to return to the United States.

164. For more on Negroes see Brown, "Negroes and the American Revolution," pp. 556-563.

165. Van Tyne, *Loyalists*, p. 303.

166. Sabine, *Historical Essay*, pp. 105-112; Alexander C. Flick, *Loyalism in New York during the American Revolution* (New York, 1901), p. 211; Desmond, *Loyalists of North Carolina*, p. 210; Egerton, *Royal Commission*, p. xl; Alexander Fraser, ed., *Second Report of the Bureau of Archives for the Province of Ontario, 1904* (Toronto, 1905), p. 20; Nelson, *The American Tory*, p. 168; Van Tyne, *Loyalists*, pp. 302-303; Wilmot, *Historical View, passim;* Arthur G. Bradley, *Colonial Americans in Exile* (New York, 1932), p. 139.

167. L.T., XLII, 473; William S. Wallace, *The United Empire Loyalists* (Toronto, 1920), p. 118.

168. *The Diary of William Smith,* ed. Upton, I, p. lii; L.T., II, p. 350; VIII, p. 385; V, p. 637.

169. On this last point, see Sabine, *Historical Essay,* p. 112.

170. *Winslow Papers,* ed. Raymond, p. 198.

171. *The Diary of William Smith,* ed. Upton, II, p. 139.

172. Adolphus E. Ryerson, *Loyalists of America and their Times* (Toronto, 1880), I, pp. 181-182; Einstein, *Divided Loyalists,* p. 241.

173. E.g., Claudius Charles to Evan Nepean, October 24, 1792, FO4-1; Additional Manuscripts, 38363, fol. 200, B.M.

Notes for Chapter VII

1. *Boston Gazette,* August 14, 1775.

2. Douglas Brymner, *Report on Canadian Archives, 1894* (Ottawa, 1895), p. 413; the claims commissioners reported from Halifax, March 11, 1786, that almost 30,000 were "entered on the Rolls for receiving the King's Bounty" (L.T., XXXIII, p. 363); some estimates go as high as 37,000 (see J. J. Talman, "Loyalty, Nationalism and the American Revolution—Nova Scotia and Quebec," Williamsburg Seminar Typescript, p. 17).

3. Wright, *Loyalists of New Brunswick,* p. 167.

4. W. S. MacNutt, in *New Brunswick, A History, 1784-1767* (Toronto, 1963), p. 465, thinks not.

5. Wallace, *United Empire Loyalists,* pp. 79-83.

6. See John Davidson, "The Loyalist Tradition in Canada," *Mac-*

millan's Magazine (1904), pp. 390-400, reprinted in an excellent collection edited by L.S.F. Upton, *The United Empire Loyalists: Men and Myths* (Toronto, 1967), pp. 162-172.

7. W. S. MacNutt, *The Making of the Maritime Provinces, 1713-1784,* Canadian Historical Association Booklet, No. 4 (Ottawa, 1962), *passim;* and MacNutt, *New Brunswick, passim.*

8. See Wallace, *United Empire Loyalists,* pp. 91-93; Gerald M. Craig, *Upper Canada: The Formative Years, 1784-1841* (Toronto, 1963), p. 3.

9. Wallace, *United Empire Loyalists,* p. 95.

10. Vincent T. Harlow, *The Founding of the Second British Empire, 1763-1793* (London, 1964), II, p. 773.

11. Wallace, *United Empire Loyalists,* pp. 122-126; *Loyalist Narratives,* ed. Talman, p. xvii.

12. Chester Martin, *Foundations of Canadian Nationhood* (Toronto, 1955), p. 62.

13. The "Loyalist cult" did not develop until the mid-nineteenth century (Craig, *Upper Canada,* p. 7; *Loyalist Narratives,* ed. Talman, p. lxi). Many American emigrants were loyal to Canada in 1812 (see Talman, p. lxi), and Talman argues that (p. lxii ff.) certainly after 1812 the Loyalists cannot be distinguished as a distinct element in Canadian history.

14. Martin, *Foundations,* p. 62.

15. See a thought-provoking essay by Kenneth D. McRae, "The Structure of Canadian History," in *The Founding of New Societies: Studies in the History of the United States, Latin America, South Africa, Canada and Australia,* ed. Louis Hartz (New York, 1964), pp. 239-244.

16. *Pennsylvania Gazette,* February 12, 1777.

17. *Loyalists of Massachusetts,* ed. Jones, p. 292.

18. Hanbury Davies, "The American Loyalists and Australia: Matra's Proposal," *United Empire,* XXV, (1934), pp. 470-471. Australia did indeed become a British substitute for America for the dumping of convicts and other undesirables.

19. Franklin to Shelburne, FO95-511.

20. L.T., I, p. 259.

21. Harlow, *Founding of Second British Empire,* I, p. 291.

22. Morris, *Peacemakers,* p. 533.

23. L.T., IV, pp. 144-145.

24. For the transference of the Loyalists to Canada, see Wright, *Loyalists of New Brunswick,* pp. 29-79.

25. Wallace, *United Empire Loyalists,* p. 57.

26. Wright, *Loyalists of New Brunswick,* p. 61.

27. L.T., XXVII, p. 483.

28. E.g., Rivington's *Gazette,* November 8, 1783.

29. Smyth to Blagden, September 1, 1783, Blagden Collection, The Royal Society, London.

30. Van Tyne, *Loyalists,* p. 292.

31. Wallace, *United Empire Loyalists,* p. 117.

32. Kingsford, *History of Canada,* VII, pp. 217-218.

33. Loyalist Petition to Lord North, June 26, 1783, FO4-1.

34. FO4-1.

35. FO4-1.

36. Wright, *Loyalists of New Brunswick,* pp. 164-165. Also, see the paper marked "Daniel Parent," Saunders Papers, Box 1, University of New Brunswick.

37. Van Tyne, *Loyalists,* pp. 300, 303.

38. *Gentleman's Magazine,* LIII (1783), Pt. II, p. 969.

39. *Boston Gazette,* February 10, 1783.

40. MacNutt, *Making of the Maritime Provinces,* p. 17.

41. See Hazel C. Mathews, *The Mark of Honour* (Toronto, 1965), Ch. VIII, for the rise and fall of Shelburne.

42. Wrong, *Canada and the American Revolution,* p. 426.

43. Mathews, *Mark of Honour,* pp. 105, 111-112.

44. FO4-1, pp. 419-423.

45. Christopher Fyfe, *A History of Sierra Leone* (London, 1962), pp. 35, 42, and *passim.*

46. Quoted in Van Tyne, *Loyalists,* pp. 293-294.

47. "Salem Loyalists—Unpublished Letters," ed. Latting, p. 247.

48. FO4-1.

49. L.T., XII, p. 595.

50. *Ibid.,* XV, p. 298.

51. *Correspondence of Thomas Barclay,* ed. Rives, pp. 36, 33.

52. Sabine, *Historical Essay,* p. 63.

53. "Salem Loyalists—Unpublished Letters," ed. Latting, p. 247; L.T., XIX, 489.

54. *Ibid.,* VI, pp. 14, 18, 96.

55. AO13-41.

56. Wallace, *United Empire Loyalists,* pp. 58-59, 74-77, 86-90.

57. *Ibid.,* p. 58.

58. Emily Weaver, "Nova Scotia and New England during the Revolution," *A.H.R.,* X (1904), pp. 66-67.

59. *Winslow Papers,* ed. Raymond, p. 337.

60. *Ibid.,* pp. 251, 338.

61. Wallace, *United Empire Loyalists,* pp. 98-104; Jean N. McIlwraith, *Sir Frederick Haldimand* (Toronto, 1909), pp. 266, 270.

62. *Winslow Papers,* ed. Raymond, p. 150.

63. *Ibid.,* p. 337.

64. MacNutt, *Making of the Maritime Provinces,* p. 17.

65. *Winslow Papers*, ed. Raymond, p. 469.

66. Wallace, *United Empire Loyalists*, pp. 105-106.

67. Wrong, *Canada and the American Revolution*, pp. 451-455.

68. *Loyalist Narratives*, ed. Talman, p. 318.

69. Craig, *Upper Canada*, p. 8; Wright, *Loyalists of New Brunswick, passim; K.F.*, Appendix; Alfred L. Burt, *The Old Province of Quebec* (Toronto, 1933), p. 361.

70. Talman, "Loyalty," pp. 25-27.

71. William Dunlop, *Recollections of the American War, 1812-1814* (Toronto, 1905), pp. 70-71.

72. *Loyalist Narratives*, ed. Talman, p. 320.

73. Kingsford, *History of Canada*, VII, p. 224. The strength of United Empire Loyalist feeling in Ontario in 1897 may be seen by perusing Haight, *Before the Coming of the Loyalists*, especially p. 19.

74. Cecil Johnson, *British West Florida, 1763-1783* (New Haven, 1943), pp. 144-149.

75. W. H. Siebert, *The Legacy of the American Revolution to the British West Indies and Bahamas* (Columbus, 1913), pp. 11-14.

76. L.T., V, pp. 98-99.

77. *Ibid.*, III, p. 265.

78. Charles L. Mowat, *East Florida as a British Province, 1763-1784* (Berkeley and Los Angeles, 1943), pp. 125-126; Siebert, *The Legacy*, pp. 6-8.

79. L.T., LX, pp. 143-144, 339, 369-370.

80. *Ibid.*, LX, pp. 472, 552; XVIII, p. 587.

81. CO23-26.

82. CO71-2.

83. Mowat, *East Florida*, p. 147.

84. Siebert, *The Legacy*, pp. 45-50.

85. CO23-28.

86. Siebert, *The Legacy*, pp. 15-16, 34-43.

87. *Ibid.*, pp. 22-23; Michael Craton, *A History of the Bahamas* (London, 1962), pp. 162, 164.

88. Siebert, *The Legacy*, pp. 17, 21; L.T., LVII, pp. 32-47; VI, pp. 514-517.

89. Craton, *History of Bahamas*, pp. 160-161.

90. FO4-1.

91. Siebert, *The Legacy*, p. 21.

92. CO23-26.

93. Craton, *History of the Bahamas*, pp. 163-164.

94. E.g., Petition to Lord Sydney, May 12, 1786, CO23-26.

95. "Miscellaneous Papers," CO23-26.

96. Craton, *History of the Bahamas*, pp. 166-170, 173; Siebert, *The*

Legacy, pp. 25-31; Alan Burns, *History of the West Indies* (London, 1954), pp. 536, 550, 601; G. Barry to ?, June 30, 1786, CO23-26.

97. Craton, *History of Bahamas,* p. 294; L.T., VII, pp. 351-366, 534-556.

98. Craton, *History of Bahamas,* pp. 256-257.

Notes for Chapter VIII

1. Curwen, *Journal,* p. 307.
2. See Chapter IV of this volume.
3. *Virginia Gazette* (Purdie), February 2, 1776.
4. Nelson, *The American Tory,* pp. 19, 47, 55, 56, 63, 115.
5. Rivington's *Gazette,* August 19, 1780.
6. L.T., XL, pp. 541-605.
7. *Virginia Gazette* (Purdie), February 2, 1776.
8. Rivington's *Gazette,* December 29, 1774.
9. *The Works of John Adams,* ed. Adams, X, p. 196; "List of Harvard Graduates," p. 412; Forrest McDonald, *E Pluribus Unum: The Formation of the American Republic, 1776-1790* (Boston, 1965), pp. 214, 219.
10. See Sydney G. Fisher, "The Legendary and Myth-Making Process in Histories of the American Revolution," American Philosophical Society, *Proceedings* LI (1912), pp. 53-75.
11. American history is literally too short for the luxury of forgetting the Loyalists.
12. *Gentleman's Magazine,* LIII (1783), Pt. I, p. 475.
13. *K.F.,* p. 252.
14. *Ibid.,* Ch. XIV.
15. *Ibid.,* p. 249.
16. America's population was two and a half million; Cuba's, six and a half. See Theodore Draper, "Cubans and Americans," *Encounter,* XVII (July, 1961), p. 60.
17. Arthur Johnston, *Myths and Facts of the American Revolution* (Toronto, 1908), p. 226.
18. L.T., I, p. 186; XXVII, pp. 294, 305.
19. On figures relating to the number of Loyalists, see *K.F.,* pp. 249-258.
20. Elsewhere Maine was generally Whig, partly because of the British attempt to reserve the pine trees for the Crown.
21. *K.F.,* p. 32.
22. *Ibid.,* p. 33.
23. Charles W. Rutschky, Jr., "Thomas Barton's Collection of Minerals," *Pennsylvania History,* VIII (1941), pp. 148-150.
24. L.T., VI, p. 319.
25. *Royal Commission,* ed. Egerton, p. 126.

26. L.T., XLVII, p. 218.

27. *Ibid.*, XIII, pp. 343-355; *Loyalists of Massachusetts*, ed. Jones, p. 290.

28. L.T., XXIV, pp. 640-642.

29. *Ibid.*, XIII, pp. 385-392.

30. *Boston Gazette*, August 19, 1776.

31. The following paragraphs are based on *K.F.*, Ch. XIV and *passim*.

32. *Ibid.*, p. 260.

33. E.g., Dr. Marshall Spring of Watertown, Massachusetts ("List of Harvard Graduates," p. 412).

34. *K.F.*, p. 26.

35. *Ibid.*, p. 100. It is possible that King's College was more loyal than Harvard—no one has yet tracked down all the alumni.

36. Leonard W. Labaree, "Nature of American Loyalism," *Proceedings* of the American Antiquarian Society, LIV (1944), p. 19n.

37. *K.F.*, p. 276.

38. L.T., VII, pp. 140-141.

39. See Henry P. Thompson, *Into All Lands* (London, 1951); and Sweet, "Role of Anglicans."

40. *Ibid.*, p. 54.

41. *K.F.*, p. 121.

42. Rivington's *Gazette*, July 3, 1782.

43. Chamberlain and Flynt, *Historic Deerfield*, p. 15.

44. Sweet, "Role of Anglicans," pp. 64, 67.

45. *Boston Gazette*, October 20, 1777.

46. *K.F.*, p. 268.

47. *Ibid.*, p. 105.

48. *Ibid.*, pp. 54, 239.

49. Nineteenth-century Loyalist partisans gleefully contrasted United States lynchings with Canadian law and order. See *United Empire Loyalists*, ed. Upton, pp. 138, 142.

50. For this suggestion, see William H. Nelson, "The Revolutionary Character of the American Revolution," *A.H.R.*, LXX (1965), p. 1009.

51. *Boston Gazette*, May 5, 1783.

52. Lee Benson, *The Concept of Jacksonian Democracy: New York as a Test Case* (Princeton, 1961), p. 302.

53. Richard B. Morris, "Class Struggle and the American Revolution," *W.M.Q.*, 3d ser., XIX (1962), p. 3; Clement Eaton, *Henry Clay and the Art of American Politics* (Boston, 1957), p. 133; Charles Sellers, *James K. Polk: Continentalist, 1843-1846* (Princeton, 1966), pp. 138, 188.

54. Lloyd Wendt and Herman Kogan, *Big Bill of Chicago* (Indianapolis and New York, 1953), p. 248.

55. J. Franklin Jameson, *The American Revolution Considered As a Social Movement* (Boston, 1956), pp. 35-36.

56. James Truslow Adams, *The Epic of America* (Boston, 1932), p. 93.

57. See Robert S. Lambert, "The Confiscation of Loyalist Property in Georgia, 1782-1786," *W.M.Q.*, 3d ser., XX (1963), pp. 80-94, Catherine S. Crary, "Forfeited Lands in the Western District of New York—Albany and Tryon Counties," *New York History*, XXV (1954), pp. 239-258; Morris, "Class Struggle and the American Revolution," pp. 3-29; and Beatrice G. Reubens, "Pre-Emptive Rights in the Disposition of a Confiscated Estate: Philipsburgh Manor, New York," *W.M.Q.*, 3d ser., XXII (1965), pp. 433-456. Reubens does find democratization in her area of study.

58. Mayo, "Massachusetts Loyalists," p. 252.

59. Although no final answers are possible, we may well ponder whether, with a more organic base, the extreme American Right, exemplified by such groups as the Antimasons, the Know-Nothings, and the followers of Coughlin and Welch, might have proved itself more mature. Cf. McRae, "The Structure of Canadian History," pp. 219-274. Some Loyalist intellectuals, such as Jonathan Boucher and Jonathan Sewall, certainly exhibit a somewhat Burkean turn of mind. See Nelson, *The American Tory*, pp. 187-188.

60. *K.F.*, pp. 41-42; Jessica Hill [Bridenbaugh], "Catherine and Mary Byles" (1931), pp. 62, 14, and *passim* (typescript in the possession of Carl Bridenbaugh).

61. *K.F.*, p. 67.

62. Wrong, *Canada and the American Revolution*, pp. 423-424.

63. James H. Stark, *The Loyalists of Massachusetts* (Boston, 1910), p. 381.

64. Cf. Heimart, *Religion and the American Mind from the Great Awakening to the Revolution.*

65. *K.F.*, p. 93.

66. Watson, "Marston Family," pp. 399-400.

67. *Annual Register*, 1776, p. 147.

68. Wrong, *Canada and the American Revolution*, pp. 378-379.

69. Bridenbaugh, *Peter Harrison*, p. vii.

70. Howard M. Jones, *O Strange New World: American Culture, the Formative Years* (New York, 1964), p. 319.

71. Brooke Hindle, "American Culture and the Migrations of the Revolutionary Era" in *"John and Mary's College," The Boyd Lee Spahr Lectures in Americana* (Carlisle, 1956), pp. 113-115; Loyalists of Massachusetts, ed. Jones, p. 112.

72. See Chapter VI of this volume. Details may be found in Jensen, *New Nation, passim; K.F., passim.*

73. See Hindle, "American Culture," p. 115n.

74. *Loyalists of Massachusetts,* ed. Jones, p. 112.

75. Wright *et al., The Arts in America: The Colonial Period,* pp. 36, 145, and *passim.*

76. Dixon Wecter, in *The Saga of American Society* (New York, 1937), p. 68, quotes amusingly from the preface by Porter Sargent of Boston to his annual *Private Schools: 1936:* "The aristocrats of Boston all left with Lord Howe. The old Boston families of today are for the most part derived from the rabble of smugglers and privateersmen—men who poured in as the Tories left with the British fleet."

77. Hindle, "American Culture," pp. 116-126.

78. W. J. Sparrow, *Knight of the White Eagle* (London, 1964), p. 257.

79. Anthony Allaire, "Diary," in Draper, *King's Mountain and Its Heroes,* p. 512; L.T., XLII, p. 545.

80. See *Pamphlets,* ed. Bailyn, I, pp. 86-89.

81. L.T., LVI, p. 12.

82. See his *Origin and Progress of the American Revolution, A Tory View.*

83. March 8, 1780; March 11, 1780.

84. *K.F.,* p. 121.

85. "Letters of Rev. Jonathan Boucher," p. 247.

86. *M'Fingal,* II, pp. 613-614.

87. *Loyalists of New Jersey,* ed. Jones, p. 159.

88. Letter of February 6, 1779, Balch Papers, New York Public Library.

89. *Boston Gazette,* May 5, 1783.

90. Fisher, *Struggle for American Independence,* II, p. 553.

91. *The Gazeteer and New Daily Advertiser,* December 24, 1777.

92. Mackesy, *War for America,* p. 518.

93. Additional Manuscripts, 36596, B.M.

94. Haight, *Before the Coming of the Loyalists,* p. 21.

95. Isaac Hunt, *The Political Family* (Philadelphia, 1775).

INDEX

A Note About the Author

WALLACE BROWN was born in 1933 in Edmonton, Alberta, Canada. He has received a B.A. and an M.A. from Oxford, an M.A. from the University of Nebraska, and a Ph.D. from the University of California, Berkeley. Among the colleges at which Wallace Brown has taught are the University of Alberta, Brown University, and the University of New Brunswick in Fredericton, New Brunswick, where he now teaches and lives with his wife. Wallace Brown's previous book, *The King's Friends: The Composition and Motives of the American Loyalist Claimants,* was published in 1966.